9th December 1993

WILLOW PATTERNS

By the same author

Richie Benaud's Way of Cricket

A Tale of Two Tests

Spin me a Spinner

The New Champions

WILLOW PATTERNS

by

RICHIE BENAUD

HODDER AND STOUGHTON
LONDON AND SYDNEY

First published May 1969
Second Impression June 1969
SBN 340 04276 1

Printed in Great Britain for Hodder and Stoughton Limited, London and Sydney, by Cox & Wyman Limited, London, Fakenham and Reading.

Contents

		Page
	Introduction	9
1	England	13
2	Australia	51
3	West Indies	102
4	The Names	124
5	South Africa	139
6	India	155
7	Pakistan	164
8	New Zealand	169
9	Leg Spin Bowling	173
10	The Greats	191
11	The Changing Face of Cricket	203
12	The Captain	214

Illustrations

Full descriptive captions appear on the text page facing each group of illustrations.

	Following page
England	24
Australia	56
Australia	88
West Indies	104
South Africa	136
India	136
New Zealand	136
The Captains	136
The Greats	200

Picture Acknowledgements

Following page 24

Bailey: Associated Press Ltd; May: *Sydney Morning Herald*; Barrington: Central Press Photos Ltd; Statham: Central Press Photos Ltd; Tyson: Associated Newspapers Ltd; Trueman: Central Press Photos Ltd.

Following page 56

Benaud (batting right): Sport & General Press Agency Ltd.

Following page 88

Bradman (batting): Radio Times Hulton Picture Library; Bradman (on crutches): Central Press Photos Ltd.

Following page 104

Kanhai: Central Press Photos Ltd; Butcher: Central Press Photos Ltd; Hall: Central Press Photos Ltd; Gibbs: Central Press Photos Ltd; Ramadhin: Sport & General Press Agency Ltd; Weekes: Central Press Photos Ltd.

Following page 136

McLean: Associated Press Ltd; Adcock: Central Press Photos Ltd; Sutcliffe: Central Press Photos Ltd; The Captains: *The Daily Mail.*

Following page 200

Hutton: Topix Thomson Newspapers Ltd; Harvey: Sport & General Press Agency Ltd; Miller: Associated Press Ltd; Lindwall: Radio Times Hulton Picture Library; Laker: Central Press Photos Ltd; Grout: Sport & General Press Agency Ltd.

Introduction

Last year I went home to Jugiong. Even thirty years after the last time I had seen it there wasn't a great deal of change. The Billy Sheahan Drive provided an attractive entrance but the big hill that had seemed so terrifying when I was seven years of age and a passenger in a 1930 Chevrolet lost its terrors as I swept down to the roofs nestling below. The hotel was still on the corner and so was Vicq's all-purpose store, and the small town was now more sprawling than I remembered it.

It was here that I learnt my cricket and I realised, driving through the town towards the schoolhouse, that I had always wanted to go back just to see what had happened to the place where I first was taught to pick up a bat and let go a ball.

Memories are always exaggerated and the place itself seemed smaller and less romantic than I remembered as I parked the car below the school with the residence attached; it was no problem to remember many of the things that had happened back in 1937.

My father was a good cricketer, not just by country standards but by Sydney Grade cricket standards, and he used to take me to all the pleasant little country matches when the Jugiong side went to Harden, Cootamundra, Gundagi, and the other towns blessed with what to a 7-year-old were extremely exciting names.

In the residence of the schoolhouse there was a store-room with concrete walls, trowelled smooth and painted cream, with, on the left-hand side, a window outside which the leaves of a peach tree would blow gently whilst I happily played cricket for much of the day. It was a tiny school and there was no one else for me to play with, but, with my father's gentle urging, I used to bowl a tennis ball against the wall of this room and hit it on the rebound trying, even at the age of seven, to place it between what I had ensured was a tightly set field around the other three walls.

The school itself was one of those one-teacher schools that abound in Australia—my father had already served some time at

One Tree Farm and Koorawatha, and Jugiong was to be his final country stint before moving to Parramatta where he has lived for the past twenty-nine years. Peppercorn trees were the feature of the landscaping when I was a boy in Jugiong and I remember my father carrying a five-foot-long brown snake past one of these on the back of a spade as I peered terrified from the window. I remember too the paddocks that stretched away from the residence : but most of all I remember that store-room where I started to play cricket.

It was nice to go back though I didn't go inside to have a look at it. Sometimes it is more pleasant to remember things as you knew them rather than see the way they have aged.

It is a long way from Jugiong to Lord's and when I first saw the historic home of cricket it was as a 22-year-old on my first tour away from Australia. I had been told that the ground had great atmosphere and others had told me that it wasn't level—I had seen pictures of it and I expected to be thoroughly overawed when the great moment came to gaze on this hallowed turf. I found it a distinct disappointment—it was April 1953 and the seats weren't painted, the ground was empty and it certainly wasn't level. Like most young fellows on their first sight of the ground, I made that comment, but some of the older players were able to tell me that the only time to judge Lord's was on playing there. They were absolutely right, for the ground has an atmosphere all of its own; nothing like the Melbourne Cricket Ground, nor Sydney, nor even the pretty little ground at Newlands in Cape Town.

There aren't very many Frenchmen who have played cricket for Australia. Jim de Courcy was one and I was another whose antecedents had come from just across the water from Dover. My forebears came from a little place called La Rochelle and a few years ago I made a sort of pilgrimage back there. It is a tiny fishing village with a pretty harbour and a most helpful librarian who managed to trace the Benauds back to just before 1800 when one of the lineage came to Australia with the crew of a French sailing vessel. He settled on the north coast of New South Wales in the Coraki area.

My father was born in 1906 and seemed to gravitate towards cricket, and by the time the family had moved to Penrith, where I myself was later born, he was a very useful bowler. In the 1920s, when just out of High School, he took 20 wickets in a match in the Penrith District and, as far as I know, this is the only time it has ever been done in any class higher than school cricket.

Being a teacher, whose life was controlled by the Education Department, he was then sent to One Tree Farm, Koorawatha and Jugiong but the latter is the only place I remember and, sitting in the car below what had been my home from 1930 to 1937, I was able to muse on the odds against any 7-year-old kid throwing a ball against this schoolhouse wall eventually finishing up bowling the last over of a Test Match at Lord's. They must be astronomical for in the history of Australian Test cricket only a few hundred have been chosen and many less than that have played at Lord's. To have been given the chance and to have played for Australia is something for which I am extremely grateful—to have been allowed to play cricket I am even more so.

1

England

It was mid-April 1961 when I stood by the rail of the ship with Neil Harvey as we approached the dock where, inside an hour, we would be berthed. "Have a good look at it", I said to him, "because neither of us might ever see it again." "You're right," he replied, "so we'd better make this a good one."

It was the last tour I ever made to England as a player and so far Harvey has not been back, either as a player or writer, though after the tour was over we both continued playing for a few years in Australia. For me it was the third tour to England and it was Neil's fourth, in the course of which he had established himself as one of the greatest cricketers of all time. We both shared a great regard for English cricket and a delight in playing in England where the game first began, and we had been good friends ever since my first trip to England in 1953.

There is nothing like a tour of England to bring on any young cricketer though I do believe there is too much cricket played in the country these days—for a youngster from overseas who is normally a Saturday afternoon cricketer, the business of playing six days a week cannot fail but to improve him. If, however, he were to do this every season it would certainly jade him. Nowadays my cricket in England is confined to village matches or the occasional club match, but such is the hold of the game that I sometimes believe I get as much enjoyment out of these matches as some of the higher class cricket I originally played.

The history of cricket is set out in detail in many publications with names like Fuller Pilch and Alfred Mynn taking much of the space before the great W. G. Grace came on the scene. England is a lucky country to have so much tradition, in both civil life and cricket, for by comparison a country like Australia is a fledgeling, with only a hundred years of important cricket as a background.

So it was that in 1953, arriving in England on the *Orcades*, I was much in awe of everything that was English and very concerned as to how I would manage in opposition to cricketers such as Hutton, Bailey, Graveney, Simpson and Compton, against whom I had played only the one match in Australia. On this tour Australia had what nowadays would be termed one of its strongest sides without Bradman, players like Hassett, Lindwall, Miller, Johnston, Morris and Harvey, together with Davidson, Ron Archer and myself, Tallon and Langley, McDonald and Hole.

English cricket was just on the way back after the Second World War, having won the last Test match of the 1950–1 series in Australia which gave them the first victory of a Test side over Australia in twenty-seven Tests. It was in this game in Melbourne that Reg Simpson made a brilliant 156 not out, finally to allow Hutton and Compton to be together when the Yorkshireman made the winning hit. That was in 1951 but the momentary faltering of the Australian side was halted the next year when the West Indies were beaten in Australia, but then again missed a beat or two when South Africa drew the series in 1952–3.

The team to tour England was announced at the conclusion of that final Test match in Melbourne, when McLean had batted so magnificently to win the match for South Africa, and it was a very exciting thing to hear my name called out for the first time in a touring side. It happened that the 1953 series began what seemed an interminable line of defeats for Australian sides, broken only by a win against the West Indies in 1955 on their home pitches. There were various reasons for Australia being beaten in 1953, 1954–5 and 1956 by England, and the main and most important one was that England had the better side.

Lindsay Hassett, leading Australia overseas for the second time, had a very good first XI at his disposal, providing everyone stayed fit, and a useful number of young players who would be of some benefit to Australian cricket in the years to come. Harvey, to begin with, was in magnificent touch and in the end scored over 2,000 runs on the tour. It was an extremely close-fought rubber in 1953, weather intervening in four of the matches and producing draws, and only the final Test at the Oval being decided, this one in England's favour. The series marked the first occasion of Sir Leonard Hutton leading England against Australia in what was to be a ten Test match span with only one match lost, when he sent Australia in to bat in the first Test in Brisbane in 1954–5.

I first met Sir Leonard in 1950 on Freddie Brown's tour but I can't remember saying anything more to him than "how do you do", to which I presume he replied in kind. Many considered him a dour personality and I have no doubt they were right from what I could see, but in the early days we were rarely in conversation so I can guarantee nothing first hand. The first time we spoke at any length to one another was in the Festival match at Scarborough that year when Australia had been set 320 to make in the fourth innings of a match that had been played in friendly fashion, in the sense that everyone was allowed one to get off the mark—then, without ever getting into Test match rivalry, the game was played solidly, with little given away and an aim to entertain the crowd. Len needed 120 to become the leading run-getter of that season and he made them, and also topped the averages of all county players, before throwing his innings away.

Lindsay Hassett had called for volunteers to open with Arthur Morris in this game and I had jumped at the chance and been dismissed for 29 in the first innings. When Arthur Morris and I went in in the second with 320 needed in 220 minutes he said to me, "Have a look at it for a while, then I'll give you the word and we'll push it along." After three-quarters of an hour we had made 45 against Bedser and Bailey and I walked down the pitch to meet Arthur and to hear him say that he thought now was the time to give it a go as the pace bowlers were just about to come off.

Before I got to him Len walked past and said, "What's the matter with thee, lad—playing for average?" I was still swearing when I arrived where Arthur was tapping the pitch just past halfway, and he said, "What the hell's the matter?" I told him and he just raised his eyebrows and shook his head, saying, "Well, I think it's about time we really got stuck into it." It served a purpose for we added some quick runs and eventually the side won the game, with a contributing 135 from me.

That, I suppose, was the longest Benaud–Hutton conversation in 1953, and in 1954–5 he was never desperately keen either to allow his players to mix too much with the opposition or to do so himself. But to consider him dour and unimaginative because of this would be to do him a great injustice, for he was in my time a great cricketer but one who preferred to play the game without recourse to friendly, after-the-match drinking sessions, or any general *bonhomie* that might lead competitors to believe that something other than a Test match was in progress. Who could blame him for that?

He was a fine judge of a cricketer and his labelling of me after Scarborough as a "Festival cricketer" might have been a trifle sharp for a 22-year-old but, at that stage, it was fairly accurate.

He was one of the greatest batsmen I have ever seen, let alone bowled to, and although I have heard it said that he was not great against spin because he played slow bowling from the crease, I can't say that I ever noticed this as a disability against either myself or any other slow bowler.

Like many of his era, he lost six of his best years through the war, and how many runs he would have made but for that, as a bowler I shudder to think. It is true, too, that the same applies to Bradman and to Hammond and Compton, but for Hutton to conclude his Test match pre-war career against Australia with a score of 364, and then not play again against them until 1946 in Australia, makes one realise just what a tremendous run-getter he could have been. I would think that had he not missed those years he must have been very close to becoming the greatest run-maker of all time—as it was, only ten made more runs than he and only Wally Hammond has a better average of those who made over 30,000 runs.

In 1946, when I first saw him, I expected a dour player who would grind out the runs with scant regard for the feelings of either spectators or bowlers. But, in fact, he was a delightful strokeplayer—not in the vein of his 37 in that Sydney Test match when Miller bowled at his fastest and Hutton hit his wicket in attempting to hook just before lunch, but in the sense that when a ball slightly off line or length came along he was superbly equipped to play the right stroke at it. This above mentioned was a short innings, never to be forgotten, and many of his later innings were just as memorable to me, despite the fact that he was on the other side and, in addition, was the finest batsman on the other side.

It is a great tribute to his skill that he made as many runs as he did after the Second World War for his left arm was shorter and weaker than his right, following an accident in a gymnasium whilst in the Army.

With this disability he had to face Lindwall and Miller at their fastest and, believe me, there was nothing faster in the world until Tyson and Hall came on the scene.

In an era that encompassed the latter two fast bowlers, I sometimes wondered between matches how some of the batsmen of the world felt facing Miller and Lindwall when they were bowling short—a length they managed to use quite often. It would not be going too far to say that they troubled Hutton, as they did many other batsmen, and, whilst this did not become a phobia with him, it certainly left a mark in his latter day conversation. I was talking to him at Nottingham one day when two medium pacers had just concluded their opening spells in a Test match and, in typical humour, he commented on the fact that it seemed a different sort of game these days. "The bowlers seem a little different," he said, with a wry smile, "not quite as quick as the new ball bowlers used to be a few years ago."

In that 1953 series he played a magnificent innings of 145 at Lord's in the Test match that was drawn, batted well on one or two other occasions, and was always the one man that we had to dismiss to have a chance of winning the game. But his greatest contribution to English cricket, though not to the spectators, was in 1954–5 when he took the M.C.C. side to Australia. He had just captained England twice against Pakistan and there was some thought that David Sheppard, who led England in the other two Tests of that series, would lead the touring team.

But England chose the right man in Hutton and they gave him, I suspect at his own urging, one of the best bowling attacks ever to leave England. Tyson, Statham, Bailey, Bedser, Loader and Appleyard provided a versatile and always hostile attack which, when allied to the time it took the bowlers to get through their overs, kept run getting to a minimum. Hutton marshalled his forces for this Test series with the sole aim of going back with the Ashes, still held from the 1953 series, and he made most runs himself on the tour as a sideline. It was the bowlers though who won the matches, Tyson bursting from obscurity and carefully nursed by Hutton, as was his partner Statham, with Bailey at times bowling as well, though not as fast, as either of them.

Australia won the First Test match of that 1954–5 series, after Hutton had won the toss and put us in to bat, only to see his side go down to a crushing innings and 154 run defeat. But the most interesting aspect of this game was Hutton's use of Tyson and Statham, both of whom were able to make the ball bounce from just short of a length, despite the fact that this was a beautiful batting pitch. England dropped 11 chances in that game, at least six of them off the luckless Bedser, during Australia's score of just over 600. It is worth noting that it took until lunch-time on the third day for the 600 to accumulate. It must have been an unnerving match for Hutton, leading a Test team in Australia for the first time, and having made a decision that went part of the way towards losing the game.

The Second Test match of that series saw the real breakthrough in Hutton's tactics and from that moment he never looked back, though for some, myself included, the business of waiting for what seemed like hours for every delivery, slowed the game down in an astonishing and, at times, boring manner. In one five-hour day England bowled only 54 eight-ball overs, which works out at 86 balls an hour, and I shudder to think of a public relations officer in 1968 trying to explain that away. Hutton was one of the most efficient captains I have seen, even taking into account my dislike of this particular tactic, and he thoroughly deserved the honour of being the only English captain in over thirty years to win the Ashes in his own country and then hold on to them in Australia.

He took part in Australia in one of the most astonishing Test matches of all time when the Melbourne pitch, after cracking and threatening to break up on the Saturday of the match, then had a 100-degree sun beating down on it on the Sunday and came up on Monday as though it had never been played on. As often happens, no Australian player had been near the pitch on the Monday morning before play started but had been practising over on the right near the outer stand and scoreboard. When we did get there, with the batsmen following close behind, we found that the half-inch cracks had mysteriously joined up, despite the parching, northerly wind that had blown all day the day before.

Australia, with a lead of 40 but condemned to bat last, looked at this rejuvenated strip with narrowed eyes, and looked even harder when May, not out overnight, made a grand 91 on this improved surface. Some said that an underground spring at the ground had, in some manner, opened up and pulled the edges of the cracks together, but Percy Beames, one of the most respected cricket writers in the world, alleged that the pitch had been watered on the Sunday. Otherwise it would have been unplayable for the edges of the cracks had turned up and widened to a ridiculous degree in the blazing sun and hot wind. Officials denied this—I believe it—and there were plenty of other journalists who wished they had been as conscientious as Beames to be at the ground at the right moment to observe the watering.

Unfortunately for Australia, but fortunately for England and Hutton, the alleged underground spring dried up on Monday night, at a time when I was not out with Harvey. The next morning Tyson and Statham began the bowling, Tyson having Harvey caught behind to a brilliant catch by Evans, and then I stood at the other end whilst Keith Miller faced his first two balls from

Statham. I had never seen anything like the surface of this pitch and at these first two balls Miller, as he often did, played straight down the line off the front foot. Both deliveries were on a good length and the first one ran straight along the ground underneath his bat, just missing the off stump. The second, landing within six inches of the same spot, went over the top of his head as he played forward.

Australia were all out for 111 and then beaten conclusively in Adelaide when they were dismissed again for 111 in the second innings to give Hutton a rare triumph that he rubbed in by forcing Australia to follow on in the Fifth Test. Hutton retired from Test cricket after this, and what a way to retire—very few captains in the history of the game had ever had a better record than he, being unbeaten in complete series against Pakistan, Australia and the West Indies.

One of the most memorable matches I remember playing in against Hutton was on my first tour at Leeds, where Lindsay Hassett took the daring step of sending England in to bat—the first time an Australian captain had done this since Noble won both the toss and the match from MacLaren at Lord's in 1909. To this moment the first three Tests had been drawn and Hassett's judgement was vindicated when England could make only 167 in the first innings when both Hutton and Compton were dismissed without scoring. An Australian lead of 99 gave us a good chance of winning the match and although Hutton hadn't closed his innings, the side being dismissed for 275, he obviously had thoughts of winning the match himself, and opened the bowling with Bedser at one end and Lock at the other. Perhaps it was significant that Bailey was kept behind, as it were, for a back to the wall fight, for this is just the tactics he and Hutton used later in the game to slow down the chase for victory.

Ninety-two an hour were required at over five runs an over and Morris, Harvey and Hole took the score to 111 in the first seventy-one minutes, thrashing the bowling in a manner certain to give nightmares to any Test skipper. A reasonable 66 in the last three-quarters of an hour were needed when Hutton played his trump card in the match-saving stakes, bringing on Bailey to bowl well outside the leg stump for six of the next twelve overs. One of Trevor's overs took seven minutes and such is the fervour for attractive cricket in 1968 that I don't believe any captain these days could get away with such tactics.

This was a grim introduction to Test cricket against England for a 22-year-old and I was rather amused recently to read that Bailey thought I was a tough captain who never gave anything away. I came up in a tough school! There was a delicious moment at Manchester in 1956 when, with the sun shining, Ian Johnson appealed against the sawdust. The umpires, straightfaced, refused the appeal and Bailey was said to be the only one on the field not smiling—it was claimed he was muttering to himself, "Why didn't I think of that?" Close, I suppose, can only ruminate on the problems of the modern age.

In many ways English cricket suffers from a case of chronic hypochondria, in that most of those on the cricket scene in England are often seeking illnesses in the game, whether real or imagined. This is a comparatively recent thing and I put it down not to the fact that there is anything wrong with cricket in England but mainly to the fact that, from 1956 onwards, England's cricketers have not been winning matches or series. They have beaten the West Indies in the Caribbean and they have beaten South Africa in 1960, and India and Pakistan. But they have not beaten Australia in twelve years, nor the West Indies at home since 1957, and South Africa beat them in a short series in 1965.

Whilst this is one explanation it doesn't really explain the seemingly desperate urge on the part of everyone connected with cricket in England to write down and take down the game in which they are interested. On every hand administrators and players for the past two or three years have been complaining about the manner in which the game is played and seeking different points-scoring systems and different types of competition to pull people back to the grounds. But it happens that cricket is one of the few mid-week sports played regularly and very few people I know in England, or any other country for that matter, have the time to do anything mid-week but work. Public opinion polls show that in England at the moment cricket interest is just as high, or higher if you take into account the increase in population, than at any other stage of its being, but I am quite certain that large crowds at county matches Monday to Friday are a thing of the past. Even the Australians and the West Indians can't drag people from their work desks for ordinary mid-week games, though they still draw them at week-ends and for Test matches.

I disagree wholeheartedly with the general theme that English cricket is down and out but I do think that there are various ways in which the game could be assisted by both players and administrators. It is only seven years since I brought to England what was generally considered to be one of the weakest teams ever to leave Australia. Certainly at the end of the tour critics were saying that it was the weakest bowling attack ever to represent Australia in England, although we won the Ashes that season.

We pulled in excellent crowds simply because the series was close and exciting, and the West Indians pulled them in again in 1963 and 1966, whilst the Australians did the same in 1964.

Not all cricket of importance is played at Test level and some of the most delightful incidents happen on the village green where one day a friend was cavorting in the sun, plagued only by the voice of the skipper. This enthusiast apparently believed in the old adage that a catch missed is a game lost and he continually informed his nearest team mate that a chance would be coming their way at any moment. Sure enough, the batsman, in playing a lofted shot, merely got a thick edge and the ball went high in the air behind the enthusiast's head. He, moving with pace attuned to a hefty girth, circled around it noisily until in the end he cried out, "It's no good, I've lost it in the sun." "No wonder", was the dry remark, "Mid-on has caught it and the umpires have taken off the bails for lunch."

I was interested in the results of the players' poll conducted a couple of years ago by M.C.C. when county players were asked their opinions on the game and whether or not they thought there was too much cricket played in England. I believe that in 1968 the answer to that is yes, and I believe that English cricket would be better served, from every point of view, if the season were to be reduced. I don't know that county players would like this so much, for playing county cricket is a pleasant occupation and one that I wouldn't mind myself as a youngster and I can imagine nothing better than playing cricket in good weather for a living. But most of the corrective legislation in England comes to naught when one takes into account the weather. It is impossible to legislate for a rain-marred summer and only last year, when the Indian touring side were here, they made a start to their tour in May that produced as little cricket as I can remember.

I find it the more astonishing then that many of the grounds in England operating for first-class cricket do not possess adequate covers for the pitch and the square, and that they have thrown out the idea of complete covering for first-class matches other than Tests. Some counties adhere to covering the pitch all the way through but the excuse for not doing it as a general thing, as in Australia, is that when they tried it a few years ago it allowed the seam bowlers to operate perpetually on a pitch freshened by overnight sweating.

One of the things with which I am in full agreement is the direction that first-class pitches in England should be as hard and true as possible. This is the only way to produce strokeplaying batsmen and attacking bowlers where the players have to work hard for their success on a sound surface. For some years before this direction came out in 1967, bowlers, many of them mediocre, had had a field day on pitches that made batting too hazardous a business to be fair.

When I first came to England in 1953 and 1956, some of the pitches were prepared to obtain a result, and there were certainly plenty of results about, particularly for teams possessed of the right type of attack. If, for instance, Surrey journeyed from the Oval to another county ground where the pitch had been under-prepared but with some green grass left on top, then they were superbly equipped with Bedser and Loader to bowl out the opposition in the early part of the game. When, however, the pitch began to turn, as it invariably did, late on the first afternoon, they were just as well equipped to take advantage of these conditions for they had Eric Bedser, Lock and Laker to make up their attack. If a third seam bowler were needed then Stuart Surridge would do the job, in addition to leading the team in spirited fashion, as he did for so long.

I thought the pitches in 1956 in England were deteriorating even further and the ones provided for the Test matches at Leeds, Old Trafford and Nottingham bore little relation to cricket pitches that were fair to both sides. By contrast, the one at Lord's that year produced an excellent game of cricket, with the batsmen able to play their shots and bowlers, both fast and slow, given a chance to take wickets. I am not one who believes that all this denigrating of cricket by administrators, players and critics will serve any purpose. The game is played no slower now statistically than it was in the era known as the Golden Age—run-getting rates are much the same per hundred balls—but one point that should be continually hammered home to the players is that over rates should be kept at a maximum. It is not necessary for players to run between overs but there is nothing more annoying than seeing lethargic changeovers and fast bowlers dawdling back to their marks.

But, in England, the overriding feature must always remain the weather, for if players cannot get on to the field then they can't provide any sort of fare, whether it be good or bad. One of the great English summers of all time was in 1947 when Compton and Edrich had their vintage year, and they were able to do this only because of the continual stretch of cloudless days that brought out the best in all cricketers that year. Edrich, who was a wonderful fighting cricketer for England and Middlesex, scored 3,539 runs in this year where his county won the Championship, but the cavalier Compton surpassed even that in making 3,816.

I had just left school when Compton had this great year and wasn't even approaching first-class cricket, being more intent on holding my place in the First Grade side with my own Cumberland Club. But having seen Compton in later years, and played against him, I can only say that I wish I'd been there! I first saw him in 1950–1 when he came with Freddie Brown's side to Australia and then he had a shocking series averaging less than 10 in the Tests. But in 1946–7 he had been in such good form, prior to his English record-breaking season, that he made two centuries in the one Test in Adelaide in the midst of a fine tour. He, like the other English players, was never quite able to fathom Iverson in 1950–1 and he was at this stage beginning to show some lack of movement from knee problems sustained on the football field. This didn't stop him coming back in 1953 to be at the crease when England regained the Ashes for the first time since 1932–3. He was in the side that came to Australia in 1954–5 and then played against us at the Oval in 1956, in a year where the England selectors successfully brought back Washbrook, Sheppard and himself.

In modern days, where quite often to be an unorthodox player is frowned on, the image of Compton is a refreshing one. I suppose I never really saw him at his best, a time that must have coincided with the end of the Second World War and the period just after. His knee troubles were already with him in 1950 but before that his deeds stand comparison with those of any of the true greats in the game. Sir Donald Bradman classes him as one of the greatest batsmen he has ever seen and a wonderful improviser, and I am quite certain that, in the five post-war years, there must have been a touch of genius about his batting.

He was born at Hendon on May 23 1918, and by the time the Australians were in England in 1938 was a cricketing prodigy who represented his country at the tender age of 20. He had already made something of a name for himself, not by making nought in his first county match for Middlesex, but by arriving at

ENGLAND

A fine action series of Denis Compton playing an off drive in Sydney in 1950—a series well worth study by any young cricketer anxious to play the stroke correctly. In (1) Compton is just moving to drive the slow bowler, beautifully side on in position and his left foot just coming down to the ground as his bat starts its downswing. (2) All the weight is being transferred to the front foot to bring about the perfect position in (3) where the bat has met the ball, head in line with the ball, hands slightly ahead of the blade and the left leg just starting to straighten. In (4) there is the start of the follow through with the left leg completely straightening and the weight transferring a little bit to the back foot and (5) the perfect end to a perfect shot—or is it? They say in the text books that the hands must always be together on the bat and there is certainly a big gap between Compton's hands in this series of five shots. But then Compton was such an individual that he could get away with just about anything.

They didn't come any tougher than Trevor Bailey on the cricket field and it was with a wry smile that I read last year that Brian Close had lost the England captaincy because of time wasting in a county match at Edgbaston. Trevor, pictured above, cutting Ron Archer, once took seven minutes to bowl an over at Leeds and was regarded as a hero when Australia hadn't enough time to win the match. He was always a stern competitor and was immensely valuable to England in an era where runs were measured in terms of victory rather than spectator appeal. Time and again he held the side together when all others had failed and his brilliant fielding close to the wicket and very useful seam bowling made him one of the best and, at the same time, most underrated cricketers in my time in the game.

Some are lucky, some are not—Peter May is well short of his crease here as Barry Jarman breaks the stumps and the visible bail is lifted from its socket. It just goes to show how difficult an umpire's task can be when only a matter of inches makes the difference between being run out or going on to make a hundred.

The enigma that is Ken Barrington. He possesses a fine defence and has a range of attacking strokes as good as anyone in the game. But far too often he concentrates on defence to the complete exclusion of attack, as indicated by the picture (*left*) which could be captioned "Ken Barrington playing a typical stroke during his innings against New Zealand in the First Test at Edgbaston in 1965" He made a hundred in this game and then was dropped for having made it so slowly. But what a difference in the picture (*right*) where he suddenly launched an attack on Veivers and hit him into the stand. Five times Barrington has brought up a Test match hundred with a six—can anything be more enigmatic than that?

Statham *(top left)*, Tyson and Trueman *(lower)* were as good a trio of fast bowlers ever possessed by any country. Statham didn't swing the ball a great deal but cut it a lot off the pitch—Trueman, pictured here magnificently side on in delivery, relied more on swing when the ball was new and had plenty of pace as well, whilst Tyson concentrated almost exclusively on sheer speed. Tyson came to Australia in 1954/55, partnered by Statham, and the three of them came in the 1958/59 team that lost the Ashes. Tyson didn't last long but the other pair played for many years for England, Statham taking over 250 wickets and Trueman establishing himself as the greatest wicket-taker the world has known.

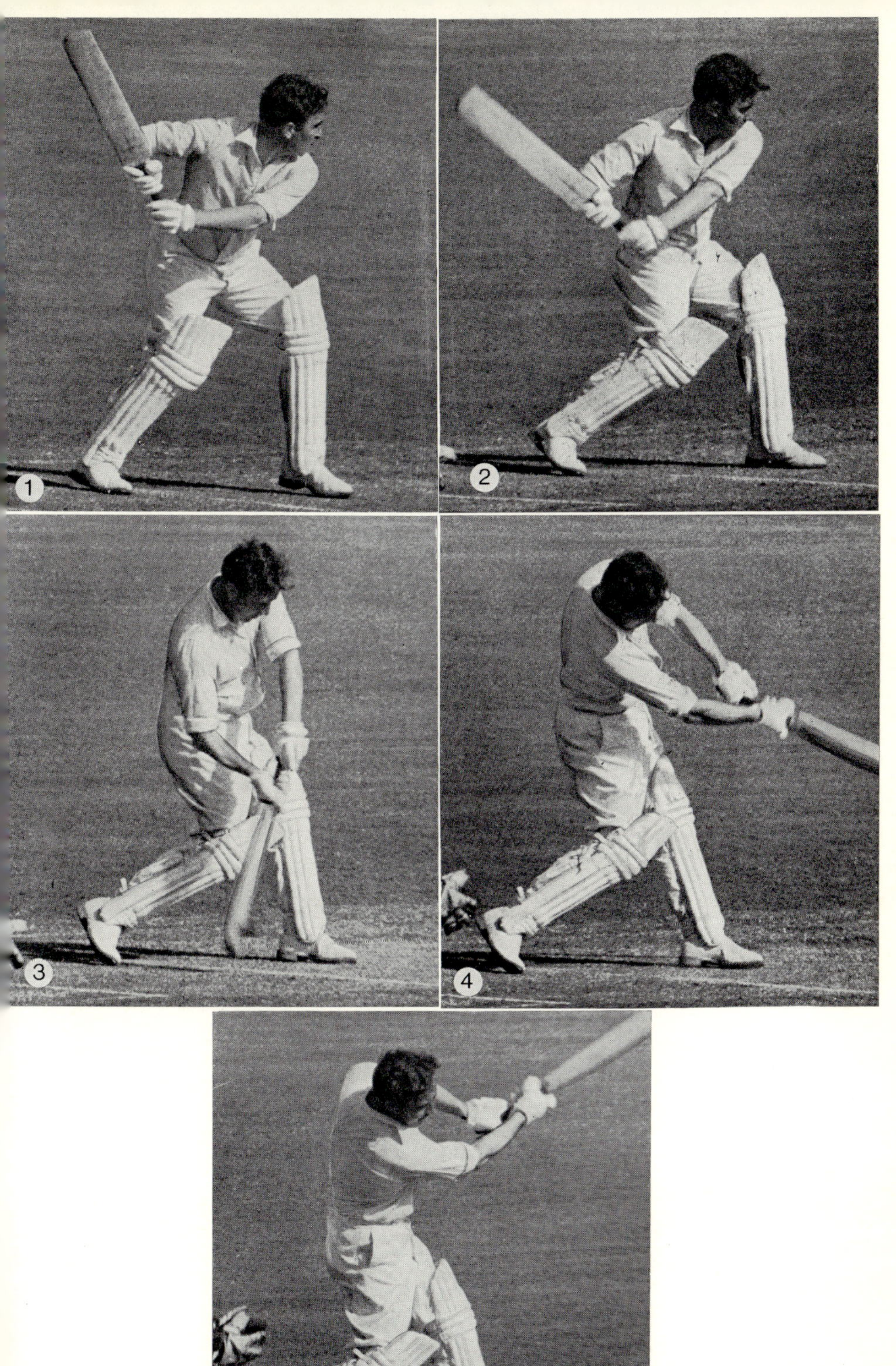
1
2
3
4
5

the ground without any gear—a typical happening that was the beginning of a chain of similar events over the years. He was not the most punctual of men but was a great public figure—and still is—captivating cricket watchers and followers with the very daring and lack of care of his batting. He would dance yards down the pitch as the bowler brought his arm over or else decide to sweep or cut, irrespective of the length or direction of the ball.

Running between the wickets was far from his strongest point, and I well remember in 1956 bowling to him in the Middlesex match and, sensing that he was moving down the pitch before I bowled, I threw it faster and wider outside the off stump. It made no difference for he was across to it, driving it between cover and mid off, and continuing to run, calling his partner for a single at the same time. Unfortunately he hit it just wide of Harvey's right hand and the ball was gathered in a flash, in time to change Compton's cultured "yes" to an almost traditional "oh hell, sorry". On this occasion Harvey's throw broke the stumps at the bowler's end, with Denis still ambling down the pitch, but by now laughing at his own mistake.

Not so lucky were team members in the Middlesex side—his brother Leslie was a victim in his own benefit match—and John Warr sums up the situation perfectly when he says "he was the only player to call his partner for a single and wish him good luck at the same time—the crowd was kept in delicious suspense throughout".

I suppose over the years he must have angered a number of people by not turning up on time for different functions but he is not really the sort of person who can anger anyone. Delightfully vague, a watch and a calendar are two of the last things he looks at in life, and I particularly like the story of him not being able to turn up to a golf match. Sitting working at his home, he suddenly remembered that in ten minutes' time he was due on the first tee at a Golf Club twenty miles away—and had no chance of getting there to face the anger of a particularly acid organiser. Nothing loth, he picked up the telephone, rang the Club and explained that Mr. Compton had asked him to pass on a message that he was unable to be present at the great occasion. The voice at the other end was suitably gruff and unsympathetic in replying, "Well, you give Mr. Compton a message from me—he's just as unreliable as ever and the golf match is next Sunday, not today. . . ."

I bowled to Compton a number of times in recent years in

minor matches in England and though his genius is understandably dimmed he is, for a 50-year-old man, still quite remarkable in his ability.

I can't imagine any batsman to whom figures meant less, for if he had cared for averages and statistics he could never have batted as he did, always carrying the attack to the bowler and always defying him to bowl accurately enough to tie him down. He spends his time nowadays in business and in writing and televising cricket, and in this he is the very reverse of his own batting and cricket life. He is a sound commentator with good ideas on the game and a yearning once again to see England back on top, as I believe they might well be by the time the 1968 Australian tour is over. I doubt if there has ever been a more popular English cricketer, perhaps with the exception of Patsy Hendren who, oddly enough, also came from Middlesex.

Traditionally England and Australia are great rivals and there always seems to be something extra in a match between these two countries that doesn't exist when others are playing. Unfortunately this is not always good and some of the cricket played by the two countries in recent years has not been as good as that produced by other countries, such as West Indies and South Africa. Some of the Test series have been exciting, though never as exciting as the tied Test series between Australia and the West Indies, nor I doubt as some of the matches in 1963 between England and the West Indies. England's success against Australia since the war has been as widely diverging as possible, being based, in the first instance, on the magnificent medium pace bowling of Bedser and then, in turn, on the fiery speed of Tyson and Statham and the spin of Laker and Lock.

Bedser in 1953 stood head and shoulders above any other medium pacer I have ever seen. He played for Surrey as far back as 1939 but it wasn't until 1946 that I first knew of him, listening on the short-wave radio to a Test match between England and India, in which the England bowling was opened by Gover and Bedser. I know it is not possible for a cricket ball to move faster off the pitch than on the way from the bowler's hand to the pitch, but Bedser seemed to get it off the pitch surface quicker than most. He had a model action, left arm high and left shoulder pointing to the batsman with his eyes looking over it. He wasn't one of these inswingers who point the ball from behind their left ear but his follow through completed one of the loveliest sights in cricket. Very rarely did he bowl an outswinger, though I did see him one day in Sydney from the other end bowl me three in succession. Whether or not they were deliberate I have never bothered to find out, and he himself used to say that he concentrated only on the inswinger and leg cutter. Though possessed of a nice, dry sense of humour, there was nothing funny about his cricket which, like his bowling, was based on hard work and maximum effort, and he was at his best when the going was tough for his side. He took five wickets in an innings fifteen times for England and was a magnificent bowler for Surrey, at a time when their county Championship victories kept every other side in a lower place in the table.

He came to Australia first in 1946 where he was just about the only bowler in the side, and in 1948 in England he was the best bowler in England. Again in Australia in 1950–1 he carried the attack, reaching his peak in 1953 where he used the conditions better than any other bowler on either side. Sadly, in 1954–5, he suffered an attack of shingles that kept him out of the early games, and Hutton's dependence on the express bowling of Tyson and Statham kept him out of all Tests except the first. In that one he was extremely unlucky and, had he been playing in Sydney in the Second Test, the Australians had no doubt that England's margin would have been even greater on a well-grassed pitch that cried out for Bedser, even in a supporting role. He was discarded in much the same way as was Tate in the Bodyline tour and, as it turned out, England won both series by relying almost entirely on speed.

I don't think I have ever seen a greater hearted bowler and I have certainly never met anyone in any class of cricket anywhere who was a better team man. He had the biggest hands of any cricketer of my time and the ball sometimes looked like an apple as he came moving towards you at the other end, his feet pounding, and in the last three strides his magnificent action beginning to take shape.

The bowlers who took over from him, Tyson and Statham, were possessed of none of his ability to move the ball in the air but of plenty of other qualities that made them important to English cricket. Tyson was like lightning! He rarely swung the ball, and when he did it was only away from the right-hander, whilst I can't ever recall Statham worrying anyone with swing.

Perhaps Tyson owes his start in Test cricket to the fact that Neil Harvey took a century from him in a match at Northampton in 1953—perhaps I do him an injustice and he would have come on the scene anyway. At Northampton this day Hole and McDonald fell before two of the fastest and most unpredictable overs I have ever seen from this unknown bowler who ran from somewhere back near the sightscreen at the county ground. He was inaccurate, wild in fact, but he was fast. Harvey then came in and made a hundred before lunch but when he came off he said "that fellow mightn't be much to look at but he's the quickest in the world today". Those few overs splashed Tyson's name all over England and, although I have no doubt the selectors had him in mind, it was probably the fact that only Harvey was able to combat him that helped him that day.

He kept his ultra-long run at the start of the 1954–5 tour, having secured his place with a fiery performance in the Middlesex–Northants match the year before, sending Edrich to hospital after that courageous batsman had tried to hook a bumper off his eyebrows—and failed. On the bone-hard Australian grounds his long run was a liability rather than an asset, and even early in the tour there were those who said he would be better if he cut fifteen yards from it. He did this after the First Test, played in body-drooping humidity in Brisbane where he was forced to bowl for much of the time while Australia made over 600.

Sydney and Melbourne pitches in that series were unpredictable, Sydney being covered with a thick mat of grass and Melbourne requiring watering on the Sunday in an unavailing bid to keep the pieces together. And Tyson made the most of this. That is not to detract from his performance, for even on the best of Australian pitches in that season he was so fast as to produce hesitancy in the batting and, with Statham at the other end, England had one of their finest attacks of all time. They should really be spoken of together for they were the perfect pair, though Tyson dropped out of cricket quickly and allowed Statham to continue with Trueman as a new partner.

Statham, with his slim build and pale face, had been a late addition to Freddie Brown's 1950–1 touring side and even then had looked a useful bowler. "The Greyhound" they called him, partly because of his leanness and partly because of his slick work around the boundary edge, even on the hottest of days and no matter how much he bowled. I was never quite able to work out why he couldn't swing the ball, for his action was side on and his arm high, and, if it had been too high to bowl an outswinger, then surely he should have bowled late inswingers. That in theory is right but I believe, having watched him closely over the years, that, either accidentally or deliberately, he sacrificed swing for cut and was quite prepared to forgo movement in the air to worry the batsmen in playing him off the pitch. There is no doubt in my mind that he was the best fast bowler England had in the period from 1946 to 1960 and to see him until recently, at the age of 37, still wheeling away in county cricket, was a treat for the eyes of any purist.

He was the catalyst with Tyson and Trueman and was the one most feared by opposition batsmen for many years. There have been slightly faster bowlers over the years, and obviously many who moved the ball more, but none have been more honest in their work than this Lancashire-born quickie. He took in all 252 Test wickets in seventy Test matches and I can't recall ever seeing the slightest touch of histrionics from him, no matter what the provocation. One of the great memories of my cricketing time is of Statham, at the end of a day having bowled thirty overs, sitting with a beer in his hand and saying to his feet—"Sorry about that, but you've a day's rest tomorrow".

It is a measure of Freddie Trueman's ability as a bowler that he was able to play in the same era as Tyson and Statham and yet, in his own right, be regarded as a great fast bowler. In the last Test match of the 1964 series against the Australians Colin Cowdrey caught Neil Hawke at slip to give Trueman his 300th wicket in Test cricket, a feat that at the moment is likely only to be equalled by Australia's young fast bowler, Graham McKenzie. Trueman, commenting on the possibility of anyone breaking his record, was reported to have said "someone might do it, but whoever it is will be bloody tired". . . . Something of an indication of the forthright manner and Yorkshire humour he brought to the game between 1949 and the present time.

Trueman was a great character—and still is, for that matter—and but for his own volatile temperament would certainly have played far more for England in the early days of his career. In 1952 he demoralised the Indians with fast bowling that inevitably chased them towards the leg side, and he was never averse to testing them with the short pitched delivery. Even at this stage his colourful language and forthright manners were bringing him something of a reputation and before we arrived in England in 1953 we knew of him as a promising, young fast bowler who could be on the Test scene for many years to come.

His first year against India found him with Alec Bedser at the other end and saw the introduction of many famous Trueman stories that were to be embellished over the years. He is reported, in the Manchester Test of that series, to have told the great Bedser to keep them quiet at his end whilst he removed them at the other. Many of the stories credited to him over the years were not entirely his but they seemed to sound better when applied to Trueman's bluntness with opposition batsmen, whom he made it quite plain he detested—on the field. He had little time for the true blue elder in the game unless he was, in addition to a university graduate, also a competent cricketer able to hold his own in the hurly-burly of Test cricket.

When I first saw him he was a raw young National Service trainee, selected to meet the Australians in the Fifth Test Match at the Oval. He bowled in this match on the first day on a pitch green with orange undertones, good for fast bowling in the humid atmosphere of the opening day and obviously destined to be useful for spin later on. He took wickets in that match and bowled well, but with less pace than we had presumed from his reputation build up. But there was nothing at all fluky about his wicket taking and, assuming a normal rate of progress, it was clear that he would become a useful bowler for England, possibly better out of the country on harder pitches than inside it on the slow strips that were at that time being prepared. That was an early judgement of Trueman and one that later was to be proved incorrect for he became a master of his craft in any conditions and a hard-working fast bowler on even the deadest surface imaginable.

He gained much, I believe, from playing in the same era as Lindwall and Miller and set out to emulate Lindwall in many aspects of his bowling. The main one of these, and the one that brought him greatest success, was in the perfection of the outswinger to the right-hand batsman and, in a period where so much emphasis has been placed on the inswinger, his was a welcome deviation. There was much to like about his action but it was a rough action, sometimes labouring in the run up, and too much emphasis placed on the first few yards rather than on the final stride, and too often he was off balance in the instant of delivery.

This though, I hasten to add, was very early in his career, and it needed only a year or two, under the watchful eyes of the hard-headed Yorkshiremen, to smooth him out and to produce in him one of the best actions in post-war cricket. Like most fast bowlers of this time he had quite a drag in his final stride and when the Front Foot Law was introduced a few years ago he was one who suffered but, as befits a great bowler, he suffered less than most.

I didn't see him again until 1956 after that 1953 tour, for he had spent the winter of 1953 and early 1954 in the West Indies under Len Hutton's captaincy, and this was a tour that gained him a reputation in keeping with his nickname "Fiery Fred". He was fast enough on that tour to worry even the best batsmen and already his great talent was making him one of the most promising fast bowlers England had produced, but even this was not enough to gain him selection in the '54/55 side to Australia. Loader went in his place on that tour, after bursting on to the scene with Surrey in 1953, and it was he who did a lot of the work with Bailey, when Tyson and Statham were not operating.

By 1956 though, he was a fully established fast bowler but only in the Second Test of that series at Lord's did the conditions allow full rein to good fast bowling. For the rest of the time the surfaces on which we played resembled rolled orange powder more than the cricket pitches we had been brought up to expect in England. It wasn't until 1958–9 in Australia that he first became a real force in Anglo-Australian cricket and from that moment on until he took his 300th Test wicket he was one of the greats of the game, constantly probing at the batsmen—a hard-trying fast bowler, with most variations in pace and movement, a useful hard-hitting batsman late in the order and a brilliant fieldsman in any position.

It is an interesting feature of his career that although he took 300 wickets in Test matches he has only 79 in Tests against Australia, but then he only played the one Test in 1953 and missed all five in 1954–5. But he stands comparison with any of the great bowlers, averaging a wicket every eight overs against Australia. Only one English bowler in the post-war period, Alec Bedser, has taken a hundred wickets in Anglo-Australian Tests and he got his at approximately one every ten overs—but there it must be taken into account of course that in his early days Bedser was quite often virtually a one-man bowling attack.

Reticence was never one of Freddie's strong points and he was always prepared, and still is I have no doubt, to explain concisely exactly how he took a wicket at any stage of a day or match in any year gone past. These were never ordinary deliveries and there was generally something of a plan about them—perhaps he had tested a batsman with a couple of outswingers and then fizzed one back between bat and pad, or perhaps it had been the reverse. But he was always engaging company, whether on the field or off, and is a great lover of cricket of any kind.

I find it astonishing that in his career he never visited South Africa with an M.C.C. side, even in 1956–7 when he was obviously becoming a fine bowler, and in all he played sixty-seven Test matches for his country in his thirteen years in Test cricket. His best period in the game was from 1958 to 1962 and it was in this time that he played three series against Australia, having a great deal to do with England's bowling success in each one. I remember him vividly in Melbourne in 1962 bowling magnificently for Dexter, and at Leeds in 1961 making the most of his versatility to slow down and bowl off cutters on the extraordinarily prepared pitch of that match.

Then too, in 1961 at Manchester, he turned in a wonderful performance, not completely reflected by figures, but was dropped for the Oval Test of that series because it was alleged he ran down the line of the leg stump, thus making the furrows that eventually led to England's defeat. I personally have a very real interest in that game for it was these furrows that I went out to look at on the second last night of the match to see whether or not it was feasible to bowl leg spinners around the wicket. The pitch itself for this game was unscarred, except from the bowlers' footmarks, and it was popularly supposed that Trueman was the offender in this. Well, just as Brian Close was badly done by by the critics when England batted a second time, so too was Trueman for his part in making these footholes. Freddie did run down the line of the stumps on occasions in this game but far more persistent offenders were Jack Flavell and Ted Dexter when they were operating from the railway end.

Which one of the trio made the most marks I haven't the faintest idea, but I do know that it was six feet rather than two that scarred the pitch and made possible the remarkable last day's play. It was Trueman though who was left out of the Oval Test and Flavell and Dexter, who played in that match, took great care to keep their feet, in the follow-through, as far away from the line of the leg stump as possible.

Towards the end of his career, Freddie laboured on unsympathetic surfaces from the belief that he was still a fast bowler when, in fact, although he was in the past a great bowler, he had lost a yard or two in pace. I saw him in 1965 against New Zealand on a dead pitch, sacrificing accuracy for attempted speed, where the great Lindwall would have slowed his pace and concentrated more on movement in the air and off the pitch. This was around the time when Trueman was having a lot of trouble with the Front Foot Law that decreed that his left foot must land behind the batting crease in delivery. The year after he left Test cricket the law was changed to allow the front foot to land on the batting crease—a change that came a year too late for the Yorkshireman.

He did more in the air than Statham or Tyson but, at their peak, he was never quite as quick as either, despite what he might tell you himself! But he was one of the best bowlers I ever encountered, or watched for that matter, and the game of cricket was much enriched by his presence in the years I played. Freddie had a sharp and penetrating wit both on and off the field and stories about him and about his remarks are legendary. He was a quick wit as well. I clipped Statham off my toes in Melbourne in 1962 straight to David Sheppard behind square leg and the catch was put down almost at the same instant as Freddie cried in anguish, "Ah, come on Rev., you've had enough practice at putting your hands together."

One of the most endearing things about cricket is the amount of fluctuation that occurs in different eras in every country. They talk about the Golden Age in cricket and yet, in a sense, every age is a golden age with players whose records assume more important stature as time goes on. From 1951, when Freddie Brown led England to the first post-war victory over Australia, to 1957, England didn't lose a Test series against any country, and if this is not a golden age I don't know what is. Brown himself was a great leader of men, in charge of a good but not great side, strong in batting but up against Lindwall, Miller and Johnston, and weak in bowling with the exception of the great Bedser. I suppose he could have been a legendary captain had he possessed an attack of Tyson, Statham, Trueman, Laker and Lock, plus Bedser—and then, of course, there is always Bailey.

The careers of Bailey, Laker and Lock coincided for much of their time in English cricket.

Bailey began bowling for England in 1949 and he was in the team until 1959 when probably it was Ted Dexter who forced him out of the line up. He was a great servant of English cricket, making over 2,000 runs and taking 100 wickets, and, to me, his finest year was in 1954–5 in Australia when he was only a second string bowler. His defensive batting is well noted in the record books where he is listed five times as one of the slowest scorers of all time.

But he was a fine team man and a very good bowler, given conditions in the least conducive to movement of the ball, and on that 1954–5 tour he took ten wickets in the series, most of them at vital times, and in his own way, albeit an often defensive way, he was a controversial figure. In Brisbane in 1958–9 his dark, wavy hair glinted in the sun for seven hours and thirty-eight minutes in making 68—this was ridiculous but there were many other occasions, as at Lord's in 1953, when his rearguard-actioned batting served England well.

As Bailey came on the English scene so too did Lock and Laker, and although Laker suffered the indignity of being in the losing side at Leeds in 1948 he was, by the time the Australians came to England in 1956, a wonderfully good off spinner. One of my fondest memories of him is to have fielded at leg slip at Cranbrook School, Surrey, when he was aged 44, and gave an immaculate bowling performance against a strong South African Combined XI. Laker went to the West Indies in 1953–4, having already been there on an earlier tour in 1947–8. Between these two tours he turned in at least one astonishing performance in taking eight for 2 in 1950 in a Test trial and he played three Test matches against Australia in 1953, taking nine wickets at an average of 23 apiece. But in 1954 it was Appleyard who appeared in Australia instead of Laker and the latter had to wait until 1956 really to make his name in cricket.

Make his name! He absolutely annihilated us, if annihilate is the term to use for a bowler of his relatively gentle pace and guile. I bought a newspaper in Piccadilly in 1956 and read that Laker had taken ten for 88 that day playing for Surrey against my side. I was not playing in the game, having played the two previous matches, and this was astonishing—was there no other spin bowler in the side? In fact, also in the Surrey team, was Laker's sparring partner Tony Lock, a left-arm bowler of some distinction, who had failed to take a wicket at the other end, a happening that was to be repeated on other occasions during the tour.

That 1956 season was Laker's greatest, against a team that was unable to play good off-spin bowling on turning pitches, but he was far from being a one season bowler. In many ways he was a perfect model for any slow bowler, whether a finger spinner or an over the wrist bowler, for his accuracy and looping flight made him outstanding in these particular spheres.

It seems that in 1948 Miller and Harvey—particularly the former—punished him at Leeds enough to cause Yardley to use Compton and Hutton rather than the number one spinner in the side. This match stayed with him for a long time and, though he went to the West Indies in 1953–4, and though in 1950 he took over 150 wickets, he was not able to command a regular place in the England side until 1956. He took forty-six wickets against us in that series, and deserved every one of them, for he was simply too good on the pitches of that year for any Australian batsman.

Lock, at the other end, had a relatively mediocre series for the simple reason that his stock ball, whether delivered from over or around the wicket, was spinning away from the right-handers and, on many occasions, allowed them to let the ball pass to Evans. For much of the time in that series batsmen existed and needed time as much as runs, and it was Laker's off-spin, landing on or just outside the off stump, that caused by far the most trouble. I know from personal experience that year that I was much happier facing Lock, good bowler though he was, than Laker.

That was the first time I had encountered two such great bowlers of this type in these conditions and it was most necessary to adjust one's technique to combat the pair bowling together. For Laker I used to bat often well outside the leg stump and even went to the extent of changing my grip of the bat so that the back of the left hand in a defensive stroke would be facing gully rather than mid off, as proposed by the text-books.

In this way I found that it was much easier to keep the handle of the bat in front of the blade and, therefore, to keep the ball out of the grasping hands of four short legs. Laker made you play every delivery whereas Lock, although he endeavoured to do the same thing, was denied the pleasure because on a turning pitch the ball would, on perhaps 50 per cent of occasions, spin away from the bat, past the edge, towards the waiting slips. As the pitches were quite slow, even if the ball found the edge the batsman had only to play it with a completely dead bat to make sure that it fell well short of the slips.

There were many annoyed Australians after the 1956 series—not annoyed with Laker and Lock because they had done so well, but because of the pitches that had been provided for them—pitches that, although they eventually finished up damp and turning because of the rain, had started off by being red and crumbling. It was this particular year and these circumstances that produced a strong determination in a number of Australian players, myself and Harvey included, that the Ashes should be returned to Australia in 1958–9. Laker and Lock were both on that trip, Lock taking five wickets at 75 and being dropped from the Fifth Test match in Melbourne, and Laker taking fifteen wickets in the series, compared to his forty-six in 1956.

On paper, this might seem to reduce them both to human proportions, particularly Laker, but in fact Australia's batsmen, after 1958–9, had an even greater respect for Laker for he proved himself in that series to be the best spin bowler in the world. Hardly ever did he have a pitch that suited him and yet his command of length, spin and flight left no doubt in our minds that this man was a great bowler.

Lock found it tougher going but proved himself in later years also to be a fine bowler for he came back to settle in Australia and set about changing his style for the conditions. So well did he do it, as Western Australia's leading spin bowler, that he regularly took forty-fifty wickets each season on pitches that in 1958–9 caused him untold trouble. He did this by altering his action and bowling slower, concentrating more on flight, though he still commanded the same perfect length that had made him so difficult to play in the years before. Laker retired in 1959 but Lock was still going eight years later, playing for Western Australia in the Australian summer and captaining Leicestershire with enthusiasm in 1967.

Luck often comes into bowling, as I know only too well, but one of the main requirements, apart from good fortune, is for a bowler to have a good wicket-keeper to assist him. I don't think it is Australian prejudice to say that we have been better served in this than England in the years I have been in the game, having Tallon, Langley and Grout in our line-ups in the post-war period. But England had Evans who, although he started in 1946 as a second string to Paul Gibb, soon took over and held his position until 1959 on returning from Australia. He was an outstanding 'keeper, very popular with the public and often unorthodox, as well as spectacular, on the field.

I put him slightly below both Tallon and Grout in my list, probably because I saw him miss more chances than they did over the years, but this was probably for the reason that he stood over the stumps far more than did any other 'keeper. My interpretation of a wicket-keeper is that he should take the catches and make the stumpings, as Evans certainly did, but I think it is fair to say that, brilliant as he was, by standing over the stumps as much as he did he missed more chances than did those standing back.

He certainly brought the game alive more by doing so and he was a wonderful and pleasant competitor in any opposition team and a great mixer on any tour. I can't remember one day in the time we played against one another when Evans was not the happiest of souls, no matter how the game had gone on the field, and he must have been a wonderful tourist to have in the side. His wicket-keeping to Bedser was always of the very highest class because the big England bowler was always better than medium pace and, though very accurate, his variations of movement in the air and off the pitch would have provided a testing time for even a wicket-keeper standing back.

A measure of Evans's great ability and the dependence of English cricket on him came on his retirement. From that moment on England's selectors, unable to find another of his ability, concentrated on choosing batsmen-wicket-keepers rather than those who were primarily 'keepers and, secondly, batsmen. It wasn't until England's lack of success against the West Indies in 1966 brought John Murray back into the side that the position was redressed. Fortunately he made a century in that game and thus made sure of his place in the side for a time but, even better from England's point of view, it brought the number one 'keeper in the country at that moment back into the team. There have been a number of things over the years that Australians have been unable to fathom in English cricket and Murray's omission from the side was one.

In 1961 he had a wonderful series behind the stumps but then in 1962–3, when Dexter's side went to Australia, he was left out in favour of Alan Smith of Warwickshire. Smith is a pleasant cricketer, and I found him on that tour to be a fine team man, but, much as I like him, he is not in the same street as Murray as a wicket-keeper or, for that matter, as a batsman. Again, when Mike Smith's side went to Australia in 1965–6, Murray was passed over for Jim Parks, a decision that could only have been taken because of Parks's batting. There is no comparing their ability as wicket-keepers!

I sat in the Press Box at Melbourne in the Second Test match of that tour when Barber drew Burge down the pitch to drive and Parks missed what was a relatively simple stumping chance. The game was eventually drawn but Burge moved from 34 to 120 after that chance and my notes of that game tell me that at the time I marked it as the crucial miss of the match. There is no telling that Murray would have made the stumping but, as far as I was concerned, it merely underlined the fact that wicket-keepers should always be played for their wicket-keeping and for no other reason.

There is no question that Parks is one of the best batsmen in England and would challenge any of the present line-up for a place in the side, a fact that he emphasised during the 1965–6 tour by finishing third in the batting averages with 771 runs at an average of 64, fourth in the Test match batting with 290 runs at 48, and then topped the batting figures against New Zealand.

Not the least of England's problems since the war has come in the fact that they have had sixteen Test match captains in a time where the leadership of other countries has been relatively stable. The post-war period seems to have got off to an unhappy start with Hammond's tour in Australia, and then Norman Yardley led the side in steady fashion until Freddie Brown took the team to Australia in 1950–1. Gubby Allen, Ken Cranston, Nigel Howard, Donald Carr, George Mann and David Sheppard all captained England in the late forties and early fifties and then in 1952 against India Len Hutton took over. This was to be one of the most successful periods in English cricket, with series won against India, Australia twice, and a drawn series against the West Indies in their own country. Peter May acted as understudy to Hutton in 1954–5 and then took the team to South Africa and Australia in 1956–7 and 1958–9, as well as to the West Indies in 1959–60. But, following his retirement, Colin Cowdrey, Ted Dexter, Mike Smith and Brian Close have provided four different styles of captaincy in five years. In addition Tom Graveney led the side when Colin Cowdrey was unfit at Headingly in 1968.

To my mind, no single happening in English cricket since the game resumed after the Second World War has had more influence on the country's lack of recent success than Peter May's premature retirement after the 1961 series against Australia. May was at Cambridge University until 1952 and first played for Surrey in 1950 before becoming a regular member of the side on leaving the University. He came up in a hard captaincy school, having Stuart Surridge as his leader at Surrey, and serving his apprenticeship in Test cricket under, first of all, Freddie Brown and then Len Hutton.

He played his first Test at the age of 21, a remarkable feat in post-war England, hit a century against South Africa and, even at that early stage, was earmarked for the England captaincy in later years. He was a sensitive cricketer, and a hard and very good one, at his best when his side was in trouble. That this was a regular feature of England's batting in the time in which he played made some of his performances even better than they appeared on paper, and Australians in general, and I in particular, held him in very high regard.

There were two things that seemed to bring about his premature retirement—illness in the West Indies in 1960 and increasing criticism in the publicity mediums where he was singled out when blame was being apportioned for England's downfall. I first saw him play at the Oval in 1953 when Lindwall bowled him an over that has gone down in cricket history as one of the great six consecutive deliveries of all time. This was the time of the umbrella field, with grasping slip fieldsmen awaiting the benefits of a regularly taken new ball, and the Australians, under Hassett, were trying to make sure that the youngster's confidence would be at anything but an all time high when the Tests came along. Lindwall in that over repeatedly beat him with a wonderful variety of swing and movement off the pitch, and then Archer bowled him with a full toss from the other end—but the wicket will, in my mind, always be credited to Lindwall.

May made only two appearances against Australia that year but this was to be the last time there was ever any doubt about his selection in an England side. When he brought the M.C.C. side to Australia in 1958–9 it was considered by critics to be almost invincible, despite the fact that Australia had just beaten South Africa three–nil. It was one of the strongest teams ever produced on Australian soil for, in addition to May, there was a bowling attack of Trueman, Statham, Loader, Tyson and Bailey, together with Laker and Lock with Mortimore flown out later as an additional player.

There was nothing wrong with the bowling on this tour of Australia, with six of the team taking over twenty wickets, but it was the batting that let the side down. May, Cowdrey and Graveney were the only three to stand out, all scoring over 900 runs, with May the only one to make a thousand. But of the remainder, only three could top the 500 mark, Milton, Richardson and Bailey, and Milton and Richardson were far from successful in the Tests. They failed against both pace and spin and found Davidson a particular problem, bowling, as he was at that stage, at the peak of his career. The failure of the openers put tremendous pressure on May in particular, and the fact that he had his then fiancée in Australia at the same time was seized on by the critics as a reason for failure. There were some bitter reports cabled back to England and I have no doubt that the business of blasting and blaming others for M.C.C.'s shortcomings on the field left an acrid taste.

As the series went along in 1958 so did Australia's supremacy become more evident, but those on the spot, looking on the games objectively, would know that fortune did not always smile on May in that series. He won the toss in Brisbane and was later blamed for not putting Australia in to bat—I suppose as Hutton had done four years earlier to be beaten by an innings! The plain fact was that, had I won the toss that day, I too would have batted, as May did, though I would have hoped that my batsmen played better than did England's. Certainly I'd have wanted them to bat better than the touring side did in the second innings where some of the slowest Test cricket on record was produced.

In retrospect, it is quite obvious that May was captaining a side not as good as it used to be, whereas Australia was on the way up again—in the same way that Test cricket has fluctuated throughout every era. I thought May a fine captain, probably the best of all the English leaders, but not as lucky as a captain has to be to win consistently.

He led England again in 1961 in the Third, Fourth and Fifth Test matches for a win, loss and draw, but the loss at Old Trafford cost England the rubber though May himself turned in once again fine performances in the series. I thought he only did one thing wrong in that Old Trafford match and that was in taking off David Allen when Davidson had just hit 20 in one over from the off spinner. I am probably—almost certainly—in a minority in thinking that Allen should have been kept on but, at that stage of the game, Australia was desperate to get rid of the bowler who had just taken three quick wickets and was threatening to remove McKenzie, the last man, just as quickly. Davidson determined on the only course he knew—to hit Allen out of the attack—and he launched such a blistering array of strokes at him that the plan succeeded. They were all great shots but I doubt if it could have happened in the next over and sooner or later Allen must have got a go at McKenzie with disastrous consequences for Australia.

McKenzie was on his first tour overseas and the basis of his batting was that he was able safely to play down the line to the medium pacers, and this he proceeded to do from the moment they returned to the attack. Hindsight is not difficult but there was no hindsight about the relief felt in the Australian dressing-room at Manchester that day when Allen disappeared from the attack.

May played only one more Test for England after this match and from that moment on England has had no really stable leadership.

At different times Cowdrey, Dexter and Smith have led the national team and Close, after serving an apprenticeship with Yorkshire, was called in to captain the side in the final Test against the West Indies in 1966. I have no doubt though that had May continued to lead England, success would have come her way more often in the past three or four years for he was a good, sound captain, quite outstanding in the post-war period.

Ted Dexter took over from May at the end of 1961, taking the M.C.C. side to Pakistan and India with indifferent success, winning the one decided match in Pakistan and then going on to India where the first three games were drawn and India won the last two. Dexter was a brilliantly gifted cricketer though it was arguable whether or not he was able to transpose these gifts into terms of captaincy and holding together a team. From my contact with him, I thought him a good captain though probably a very stubborn one once he got an idea into his mind—I thought the choice of three off-spinners for the 1962–3 side, and their use, a particular case in point, as well as the use of Alan Smith ahead of John Murray as wicket-keeper on the same tour. These, of course, were decisions taken by a selection committee as well as by the captain but Ted himself made it quite plain in conversation that they were his ideas as well.

There is no argument though about Dexter's place in modern day batting and I would mark him down as not only one of the best batsmen I have ever seen but also one of the most exciting, and in 1968 this is one of the most valuable things in cricket. Sadly, he is now not playing much cricket, having had to decide whether business or cricket came first, a decision that has bothered a lot of us in recent years.

In 1957, just before the M.C.C. side went to Australia, Dexter hit the headlines in London by taking five for 8 for the Gentlemen against the Players and becoming a real threat to the selection prospects the following year of some of the more established players. As it turned out, he was left out and then sent on later when the side was handicapped by injury to Arthur Milton—he got the message that he was to fly to the Southern Hemisphere when he was on the Continent in a near freezing climate. He played in the Third and Fifth Test matches of that series, being l.b.w. to Slater in Sydney without offering a stroke and brilliantly caught by Lindwall at slip in the Fifth Test from Meckiff's bowling. His Test debut against New Zealand earlier that year had been more auspicious for he made 52 in good time against a useful attack but he seemed, understandably, to be somewhat at sea when called to Australia as the replacement.

Dexter was a more than useful medium-pace bowler and a brilliant field, though later in his short career he was often handicapped by knee injuries that denied him full movement in his specialist cover position. But, despite these other two attributes, it is with his attacking batting that he imprints himself on the memory. No one has ever batted better than Dexter at Old Trafford in 1961 when he made 76 in England's bid for victory, nor can I believe that anyone has carried the fight to the bowlers in better fashion than he in 1963 at Lord's when he made a glorious 70 against Hall and Griffith at their fastest.

It is interesting that he went to Old Trafford in 1961 facing the possibility of being dropped from the England side, although earlier in that tour at Birmingham he had made a magnificent 180 to deny Australia victory after England had been forced to bat again 321 behind Australia's first innings 516 for nine declared. These are merely statistics that cannot convey the complete majesty of his driving when in full flight, nor the difficulty bowlers found in keeping him quiet when he was on the attack. In 1958–9 he was thought overrated in Australia but later in the tour it was quite clear that this was merely because he had been pulled from an English winter to an Australian summer with no practice, and asked to join a side that was itself on the defensive. I suppose he really came of age as a batsman in the West Indies—that breeding-ground of tough cricketers—when he began to bat number three for his country against some of the fastest bowlers in the world.

He was, in many ways, an individual cricketer of magnificently individual gifts and it is for this reason perhaps that he seemed to find it difficult to communicate these gifts to his team when captain. The ideal, to my Australian mind, would have been for May to continue leading England with Dexter in the side as a number three batsman, a position that was vacant in the England team until he came on the scene.

Then, too, there was Cowdrey who, until August 1967, had often been referred to in English cricket as always being the captaincy bridesmaid without ever achieving the desired nuptial state. There are few more pleasant characters in cricket than the burly Kent and England right-hander but his cricket would have been better served, in my opinion, had there always been a captain available to lead him. He is one of the most gifted players of the post-war era but one who often has difficulty in deciding on his particular role as a batsman—and whether or not this is the day for attack or defence—and I thought this extended into his captaincy as well.

He captained England on a number of occasions from 1960 onwards, when he first led the side against South Africa, but was never able to become a commanding leader purely, I believe, because of his innate pleasant nature. There is, of course, no harm in anyone being pleasant and I much prefer a cricketer of that character to one who makes himself thoroughly unpopular by word and deed. But decisiveness is a prime requirement for any captain for an opportunity can disappear in a matter of an over and I felt that Cowdrey was too often cautious rather than decisive in his approach. He too I think would have been better served in always playing under a firm skipper rather than in occasionally leading England with, always in the distance, the promise of the permanent captaincy. In the end in 1965 it became a battle in the Press to see whether Cowdrey or Mike Smith would take the side to Australia and it was finally given to Smith with M.C.C. Secretary, Mr. S. C. Griffith, acting as manager and controller of policy.

Smith is one of the most prolific run-getters ever to play in England and he made over 30,000 runs in his time in first-class cricket, as well as over 2,000 in Test matches. It looked at one stage two or three years ago that Smith was to be the ideal player to lead England, particularly as a touring captain, for he had that priceless gift of being able to weld a team together. But I suspect that the fact that M.C.C. appointed an overseer for the Australian tour would hardly have pleased him, and certainly he didn't last long when he returned to England to lead the side against the West Indies.

This was one of the most ruthless "chops" I have seen in cricket in recent years—the fact that Smith was discarded after only one Test match of that series although he had led his side in Australia in such striking fashion that, for a lot of the tour, they provided some of the most entertaining cricket seen since the West Indies were in my country in 1960–1. He failed twice against the West Indies at Old Trafford in 1966 and then Cowdrey was given the job of skippering the next three Tests with Close coming in for the last one. It has often been said that Smith was not quite a good enough cricketer to hold his place in a Test side and certainly he wasn't as good a player as Dexter or May. But in that 1966 series against West Indies Cowdrey was left out after the Fourth Test having made 252 runs at an average of 31, so presumably he too was discarded because of batting failures.

Then England had Close who fell into something of the same category as Smith, in that he is a good county cricketer without ever doing quite enough to ensure a permanent place in a Test side. Close came in for the Fifth Test against the West Indies in 1966 and led England to a very good victory over Sobers's team. He was certain to take the side to West Indies in 1967–8 until he wasted time in a Yorkshire–Warwickshire match—M.C.C. took such a poor view of this that he was denied the captaincy of the touring team and Cowdrey was again reinstated to the top position.

I thought Close did an excellent job to get England back into the habit of winning—a habit that had escaped them for quite some time before he took over. I looked at the Close incidents as an outsider and found them, in one sense, somewhat amusing. Close, no doubt, saw little humour in the happenings but, speaking as one who has been on the receiving end of time wasting from players under the auspices of M.C.C., I can only say I thought it an ironic touch that Close should lose the captaincy for doing something for which others have merely received a pat on the back.

The whole concept of world cricket has changed in recent years for up to 1961, when Sir Frank Worrell completed his triumphant Australian tour, cricket in the Commonwealth had been dominated by England and Australia. South Africa and West Indies had produced good sides and some magnificent individual cricketers but they had never been able to emerge as the top cricket country. They won the occasional series and were obviously, on all types of pitches, more formidable combinations than India, Pakistan and New Zealand but it was always England and Australia who held the stage.

Sir Frank's Australian tour did more than just provide exciting cricket for spectators from Perth to Brisbane—it changed the face of the game. Australia's cricket machine was running down at this time and England was on the brink of a series of unsuccessful ventures against different countries. In 1963 and 1966 West Indies beat England, as did South Africa in 1965, and then South Africa beat Australia in 1966–7, to complete the turn of the wheel.

All this brought about in England a series of queries as to whether there was ever again the chance of a good Test side and continual urging of the players on the first-class scene to provide more and desperately exciting entertainment. I have seen a lot of English cricket from 1961 onwards—on the field in 1961 and from the Press and television box from that time on. I spoke earlier of the strange desire of those connected with the game in England incessantly to seek methods of improving the game as public entertainment.

England though is in a unique position in cricket in that the game began there and has always been played on a six-day week basis. In every other country the basis is that of one afternoon—probably on Saturdays and sometimes Sundays—with a certain number of first-class matches each year. English cricketers, however, begin their season at the beginning of May and go through to September when traditional Festival matches are played to close the season. As an observer I am quite convinced that this provides too much cricket for both the players and potential spectators, though I am very much at odds with those who don't consider this the reason that cricket in England has suffered from a loss of spectator interest.

I stress here that my ideas that there should be less cricket played in England are purely those of an observer and that if I myself were playing county cricket then I should want to preserve the *status quo*. I don't believe that first-class cricketers in England are on to any gold mine in the fact that they step on to a cricket field for six months of every year and then work at either another cricket job or some other employment for the remaining six months. But the life of a first-class cricketer is not at all bad for he is doing something that he (I hope) enjoys and is getting plenty of exercise, and pleasant exercise at that, for six months of the year.

The cricketers themselves, when questioned in the poll conducted by M.C.C., made it plain that they wanted to continue playing six days a week, with other different types of cricket thrown in to add variety to the season. They may be right and certainly there are valid arguments both for and against, one of the most telling of which is that although few people watch the game in England these days there are many more who are interested in seeing games on television, listening to them on the radio, or in following the scores in the Press. There is a readership of something like 80 per cent of sport followers in the summer months and this, in a sense, defeats my own argument that there should be less cricket played. I don't believe though that this interest would be any less if the six-day week cricket were reduced to week-end matches, on a similar basis to the methods used in Australia.

One of the biggest problems in England these days seems to be the weather and in May 1967 a record number of games were abandoned and hardly any worthwhile cricket could be played prior to the beginning of the Indians' First Test match at Leeds. There were many, myself amongst them, who advocated a later start to the season, as well as a later finishing date, and I was delighted in 1967 to see that the 1968 Australian tour of England had been curtailed in length from the ridiculous seven months that we took to leave and arrive back in Australia in 1961. This particular length of time was no fault of England's but mainly the fact that it took so long to sail both ways from Sydney to London. But with the agreement of M.C.C., Australia was able to reduce its playing time in England to four months for this present tour.

I don't believe there are any radical changes needed in English cricket but I would like to see (*a*) less cricket played, with an emphasis on more important matches, and (*b*) covered pitches and surrounds that will allow players to get on with the game as soon as rain ceases. I have never been able to understand why the attempt to cover pitches fully throughout the season was abandoned after only a one-season trial. They said that it was because the pitches sweated and gave too much assistance to seam bowlers but if hard, fast pitches were prepared then I can see no reason why the idea should not work, and work well. It would certainly force bowlers to earn their wickets and I can't believe that it would be impossible to get results in three days—it is not so long ago in the history of cricket that Test matches were played over four days between the cream of English and Australian cricket and there was plenty of brilliant batting and fine bowling from players on both sides in that era.

Then too pitches are always covered in Australia, though in four-day matches, and we get quite a few results out there even if many of them are first innings results rather than outright finishes. There seems though, in England in recent years, to have been something of a fetish to produce outright results and thus gain maximum points. No one was ever more keen than I on getting as many points as possible when captaining New South Wales in Australian first-class cricket but we had plenty of exciting cricket without having to manufacture results.

There were times when, for what I thought was the good of the game, I would make an unorthodox decision, such as against Western Australia in Sydney one day when they made 420 and we passed them on the second day with only one wicket down. I closed the New South Wales innings at that point although the obvious thing would have been to continue batting and then bowl them out on the last day on a turning pitch. There was much criticism of this decision but in the end it provided far better cricket for spectators, and much better publicity for the game, for we had to make runs against time on the fourth day and still won the match with eight wickets to spare—but there was something left in the game for both sides rather than only the one. It is not the sort of thing I'd do all the time but it is the sort of thing that could be done if the first-class system in England had a similar duration of play and points scoring system to ours in Australia.

So many varieties of cricket have been proffered in England in recent years that one is inclined to become lost in the maze of ideas, not to mention the maze of theory that is put up about the game. But I adhere strongly to the thought that English cricket would be well served by playing on Friday, Saturday, Sunday and Monday in the first-class Championship, with a one-day match on Wednesday to keep the interest of the members. Membership has become a big thing in English cricket and this is one of the reasons the counties are loth to change the system of playing. Not all the members are able to attend mid-week matches but they follow their county's fortunes with great interest and they pay their fees every year irrespective of whether or not they attend the games. Their views seem to be quite clear—they want to see, as do the players, the present system retained, and having canvassed these two groups and received the verdict there seems little doubt that M.C.C. and the various Committees will bow to their wishes.

My thoughts are written as one who is not bound by adherence to county tradition but one who writes as a close observer of the way the English game is played. The total covering of pitches and four-day week-end cricket might not be the answer to everyone's prayer but it is my belief that it might well be the answer for English cricket.

One of the prime requisites in cricket all over the world, but I believe particularly in England, is that both administrators and players should live with the times. There is, to my mind, more interest in cricket in both England and Australia than there has been for many years but it must be realised by both the playing and administrative fraternity that people cannot consistently see their way clear to visit three-day county games in England and follow four-day Sheffield Shield matches in Australia from anywhere but their city office, or wherever work may find them.

England at the moment have something of a compromise set-up in that one-day Gillette Cup matches provide entertainment that is concluded in a six-hour span and then televised Sunday matches, and the occasional county game played on a Sunday, add to the enjoyment of those with only week-end leisure time to spare. But, as I believe that Sunday cricket must arrive in Australia, I believe even more firmly that it will come to stay in England with great benefit to the game and to all connected with it.

M.C.C., which after all is only a governing body and does not control the many counties set up within its precincts, is well alive to the situation and in the past couple of years has endeavoured to move into the public relations field by the appointment of one or two officers to police this particular side of cricket. But having visited England for the past eight years working for my newspaper in Australia I believe the real need at the moment is to avoid, as far as possible, any further changes in the laws in English cricket.

I have mentioned earlier how the various changes since the variable taking of the second new ball have affected the game, and I would dearly like to see the laws revert to the way they were pre-war. Everyone tells me that this was the golden age of cricket but at least cricketers in those days didn't have to play under a set of rules that requires a small booklet to encompass every change made in succeeding seasons. Now there is talk of widening the wicket and bringing back the old l.b.w. law. Perhaps the latter mightn't be a bad idea, in fact I am all in favour of anything that will make the bowler work hard for his wickets, and was in favour of this even when still playing the game. But why widen the wicket? As I see it, the difficulty in recent years has been with batsmen far too concerned with the fact that their stumps are too wide and too easy for the bowlers to hit. Increase the width of the stumps and you merely produce another excuse for batsmen endeavouring to keep out the ball with studied defence rather than exciting attacking strokes.

It has been a favourite party game of cricket followers in England to blast the game as it is played in that country but, having watched it since 1953, I can find very little wrong with it and know that it would be even better with more co-operation between players and administrators—in fact, I very nearly had a go at a few seasons of English cricket myself! In 1966 I was asked by a county if I would consider taking over the captaincy for an indefinite number of years and only work commitments prevented me from accepting what I believed to be something of a challenge.

But it would have been useless had it all been a one-way effort and it would have needed great co-operation between the new captain, the committee and players to make a success of it. I say this because my task would have been to win matches and, at the same time, provide the best cricket possible for those interested in the game. The players' task is to win the matches and also hold their places in the side, and this is best done in a successful team. The committee's job is to be the committee of a successful county and I believe that it is with a clash of these three needs that part of the trouble arises in some English first-class cricket at the moment.

If, for instance, I took over a county side, I wouldn't want the committee breathing down my neck if the side weren't successful in playing the type of cricket I decreed. Nor would I want the players believing they wouldn't have the committee's support if they were beaten chasing a target when they could conceivably have played for a safe draw. And I certainly wouldn't want the players believing they had no place in first-class cricket simply because they were endeavouring to provide entertainment that is so often called for by the committees themselves.

I thought long and hard about the possibility of making a come-back to first-class cricket at the age of 36 in a new country and it would certainly have been very enjoyable, though perhaps a trifle chastening if the pattern of play I aimed for eventually had to be sacrificed because of a desire for points. I doubt that the latter would have happened for I believe it only needs somebody to give a lead in this regard, and make it quite clear that good cricket at all times is the aim, and there will then be many fewer problems associated with cricket in England.

I found in 1961 that having said the Australian side was intent on playing good cricket and that we were out to get as many results as possible in the county games, even if defeated in the process, that we were always met half-way by the counties. Three games on that tour, where the opposition was captained by Raman Subba Row and Colin Cowdrey, stand out in the mind—on each occasion the opposition batted last and kept going in their quest for runs, despite the possibility of being beaten. One ended in a draw and the other two were won by Australia but all three were very exciting affairs, simply because the captains and the players entered into the spirit of things without thought of defeat. It is not always done in county games where points are at stake and if a succession of matches are lost then I know there are cases where committees will issue a stern reminder about the position of the team in the competition table. This is why I urge more co-operation between player and administrator—and everyone would benefit.

2

Australia

Australian cricket has been based on the legend of the sunburnt country for as long as I can remember, with young cricketers gaining their early experience in conditions rougher and tougher than any experienced by comparable English players.

In addition, the legends of Trumper and Bradman have adorned the game Down Under and still these two are spoken of with a reverence not given to the lesser names. There have been other great players, of course, but from the time I grew up it was always "but you should have seen Trumper" or "Bradman was the greatest". The backers of these two individuals will argue long into the night about their respective abilities and their place in the Australian game.

Those to whom I speak about Trumper turn, eyes glinting, and explain that the cricket world will never again see his like. Bradman was a ruthless destroyer of bowling who scored over 5,000 runs in Tests against England alone and nearly 7,000 in all Tests at an average slightly under 100. By legend it was Trumper who used to give his wicket away to a deserving bowler and yet in forty-eight Test matches only six Australians have scored more runs than he.

The system of playing cricket in Australia is such that any youngster good enough can eventually play for the national side in Tests against another country. Bradman himself was a country boy and so was McCabe, and I was born and bred in the country not far from where Bradman spent his boyhood.

Plenty of others saw only cities in their early development but their chances of playing for Australia were no more or less than those of their country contemporaries. Environment has a lot to do with success in cricket in Australia and education even more, for the youngster who is encouraged at home stands a far better chance of getting on in the game than the one who receives only encouragement in the schoolyard.

I was seven years of age when my parents moved to Sydney where my father was to take up a teaching appointment under a Headmaster called "Banner" Edwards, a cricketer of some note with the Cumberland Club with whom my father, myself and my brother were later to play. My father taught at Burnside School and there were both dirt and concrete wickets where the pupils could play cricket.

There is scope in Australia for all Primary School children who learn about the game but it is not really until they start on Secondary education that their game begins to prosper. This was so in my case when I went to Parramatta High School and at the same time played cricket on matting over concrete pitches that gave full scope to both batting and bowling ability.

Most Australian cricketers have come up this way, playing on this artificial surface that allows the batsman much more confidence in his strokeplay, knowing that the bounce of the ball will always be more true than that of an inferior turf pitch. Hundreds of thousands of cricketers turn out all over Australia on Saturday afternoons to play either on the bare concrete or matting over concrete and I am certain that this is one of the reasons they generally play so well off the back foot.

I never saw an English pitch before 1953 but most of those I have seen since then require good front foot play more than sound back foot play, though the latter is of course essential if one is going to become a top batsman. But, generally speaking, in Australia the bounce of the pitch is so true and the deviation of the ball so little that forcing play off the back foot is possible and much the same applies in the West Indies where, if anything, the pitches are even faster and truer.

People tell me that before the Second World War most pitches in Australia were black and shiny with only a minute amount of spin until late in the match and so much zip off the pitch that even good quality medium pacers bowling on a length could be forced away off the back foot.

I saw my first match of any consequence in 1940 when South Australia played New South Wales at the Sydney Cricket Ground in a game that brought together many of the greats about whom I had read. Bradman captained South Australia and McCabe New South Wales and it seemed a wonderfully exciting Saturday sitting on the steps of the Sheridan stand with a record crowd present. Harold Mudge was dismissed early and then McCabe battled with Grimmett, dancing down the pitch to drive at every opportunity whilst Cohen played more circumspectly at the other end.

These things stick in the memory, even when twenty-seven years distant, as does Grimmett's six for 118 and the sight of him trapping Chipperfield with a wonderful top spinner. Late in the day Bradman came in to play out time—no nightwatchman here—and was 24 not out at the close of play after tilting with O'Reilly in the latter part of the afternoon.

I only ever again saw Bradman when he was past his best. I know this because when I watched him he was only a slightly better player than the others in the side and reason, and those who saw him at his top, tell me that when in his prime he was consistently greater than any other player on show.

I went home after this match and threw a tennis ball up against a narrow piece of brick wall for many hours, trying to be like Bradman and Grimmett combined, but I think it was this avid watching of Grimmett more than any other one thing that made me want to be a leg spinner.

I didn't see Bradman again until 1946 in the Second Test match when, on the Saturday night, Barnes was batting in poor light against Wally Hammond's English attack. Because of the number of appeals against the light on that occasion, the law was eventually changed to allow only one appeal a session, but Bradman came out on the Monday and he and Barnes both made 234. I can only vaguely remember Barnes's part in this combination though it does stick in the mind that his was an extremely steady and valuable contribution.

Bradman that day gave some little inkling of how good he must have been when right at his top for he was merciless in his strokeplay against Bedser, Edrich, Wright and Peter Smith. Most of the strokes by now are dim in the mind, with only the overall brand of excellence remaining, but never will I forget the superb arrogance with which he treated Denis Compton when the left arm googly bowler came on late in the day. Bradman swept him and then swept him again, and again and again, and the farther Compton landed outside the off stump the squarer Bradman hit him, almost as if he had made up his mind that every delivery of that over was to be swept, as a final contribution for the crowd.

I watched him in the Fifth Test of that series when Bill Edrich should have caught him off Doug Wright—a chance that could have turned the match—and then I saw him the following year make his 100th hundred against India in the Australian XI match.

He retired the next season after the tour of England and, from the playing side of things, that was the last I ever saw of him.

It was just about this time that I came into first-class cricket myself and two years later joined the State in which he started his cricket. I first played for New South Wales in the New Year match of 1949 against Queensland, performing without the slightest distinction. I made 2, took no catches but dropped none either, and fielded probably a dozen balls at fine leg.

This was the era of the forty-over new ball rule, brought in supposedly to ease the lot of the bowler, and fortunately scrapped, or rather extended gradually, until the slow bowler was brought back into the game.

When I watched cricket in Australia in 1946 and 1947 slow bowlers predominated, despite the fact that Miller and Lindwall were right at their top. Colin McCool and Ian Johnson were fine bowlers for Queensland and Victoria and all States used to play two spinners to take advantage of the 200-runs new ball rule. This, in turn, allowed the batsmen full rein to their strokes and the sight of spin bowlers bowling to quick-footed batsmen was one much appreciated by the spectators.

By the time the 1948 tour of England was over and the 1948–9 season in Australia well under way, the fast bowler had taken over. Now the crowds had the spectacle of the long run and only the one spin bowler in the side perhaps to bowl a couple of overs before the advent of the second new ball.

The first match in which I played against Queensland saw Miller, Lindwall and Alan Walker crash through the Queensland batting with Len Johnson and Aub Carrigan doing a similar job for the Queenslanders. Such was the dominance of the new ball at this particular stage that spin played little part in the game at all, though Colin McCool did bowl in the New South Wales second innings when Arthur Morris and Jim Burke shared an opening partnership of 143 to win the match by ten wickets after New South Wales had been led on the first innings.

I saw my first first-class hat trick from fine leg during the Queenslanders' second innings when Alan Walker dismissed Don Tallon as his third victim, having already removed McCool and Raymer. When he really let himself go Walker, with his rather jerky action, could be as fast as any and this day, on a pitch sporting an inch of thick grass, he was terrifying enough for me to be delighted that I was on the fence and not holding the bat. Tallon, in fact, showed little interest in proceedings, preferring I think to make sure that his valuable hands were not damaged at a stage of his career where he still hoped to represent Australia for at least another five or six years.

This was the first game where I had been a part of the forty-over rule but in the next few years it was to happen frequently and on one such occasion we even took the second new ball in Brisbane with the score at 89, Miller, Lindwall, Toshack, Walker and Davidson doing all the bowling with no spinner included in the side. I bowled one over—the 39th of the innings—as a gesture, but in those days I was regarded primarily as a batsman.

Toshak went out of big cricket but Miller, Lindwall, Davidson and Walker continued and so did the emphasis on speed and the new ball until gradually administrators came to realise that it was doing the game harm from the spectacular point of view to have nothing but nagging pace performing for the paying spectators.

In those days it was no use merely being a good player of spin bowling and one had to have ability against pace of the quicker variety as well as the stock medium variety.

It was in this era that Lindwall and Miller really came into their own as great Australian bowlers to follow on the performances of McDonald and Gregory after the First World War. Quite often fast bowlers seem to hunt in pairs though I suspect it is more true to say that some of the very good fast bowlers could have become greats if only they had had a similar type of bowler at the other end. The two who immediately come to mind in Australian cricket are McCormick and Davidson, the one playing before the Second World War and the other coming on the scene in 1949–50. Apparently McCormick was genuinely fast, certainly for his first three or four overs, though by repute he was unable to keep this up for long spells, as were Miller and Lindwall.

From the time McDonald and Gregory left the Australian scene no pair combined as did Miller and Lindwall and generally a stock medium pacer would share the new ball with his faster contemporary. McCabe did it with McCormick and Davidson had a variety of partners including Meckiff, Connolly, Hawke and Rorke, but all were supplementary to Davidson's own attack. On the other hand, Miller and Lindwall for much of their career hunted as a pair and, in addition, had the valuable support of Bill Johnston, Toshack, Alan Walker, Noblet and Loxton in South Africa, and then towards the end of their own careers, Davidson himself.

AUSTRALIA

Alan Davidson's job in the World team I name later is to carry the drinks and to replace anyone who might break down — normally twelfth men are not chosen in world teams but Davidson was such a magnificent cricketer that I feel loth to leave him out of the running when naming this side. He began his cricket career with two other Colts, Ron Archer and myself, around the 1952/53 period and we went to England in 1953 as raw youngsters of not a great deal of assistance to Lindsay Hassett. Davidson was left-handed in everything he did on the cricket field whereas Archer (*left*) and myself (*right*) batted, bowled and threw right-handed. Unfortunately Archer tore a muscle on the mat in Pakistan so badly that he never again played for Australia — what a valuable cricketer he would have been if he had played in the era from 1957 onwards alongside Davidson. The selectors in Australia showed great faith in the trio shown here for it was, in the early days, a case of potential far outweighing performance.

The beginning and the end — the first time I ever appeared on the Sydney Cricket Ground I made only two before being lbw to Queensland pace bowler Len Johnson in the match where Morris made his magnificent second innings century. In the second picture I walked from the S.C.G. at the end of the Fifth Test — never again to walk on the field as an Australian player.

When I talk in the leg spin bowling section about keeping your back foot parallel to the bowling crease and as side on as possible to the batsman, I can perhaps explain it better with the aid of this picture. This was taken bowling to Colin Cowdrey in the nets in Perth in 1965 and young cricketers will see that both feet are pretty well parallel to the batting or bowling crease, thus keeping the left shoulder to the batsman as well as the let side. The left arm has been in the air but has started to pull through at the start of the follow through as the the right arm begins to come over with the ball in the right hand.

All young spin bowlers face the problem of the tearing of the spinning fingers as the ball is flipped out and consequent discomfort whilst bowling — discomfort that has been known to prevent players taking the field. The best remedy I have found for this is the one I picked up in Timaru and here I am pictured giving it to Bob Paulsen, the young Queensland spinner, who was having a lot of trouble with his fingers at the start of last season. The player on the right is my young brother who, later in the match, became one of Paulsen's victims — not really a brotherly gesture on my part!

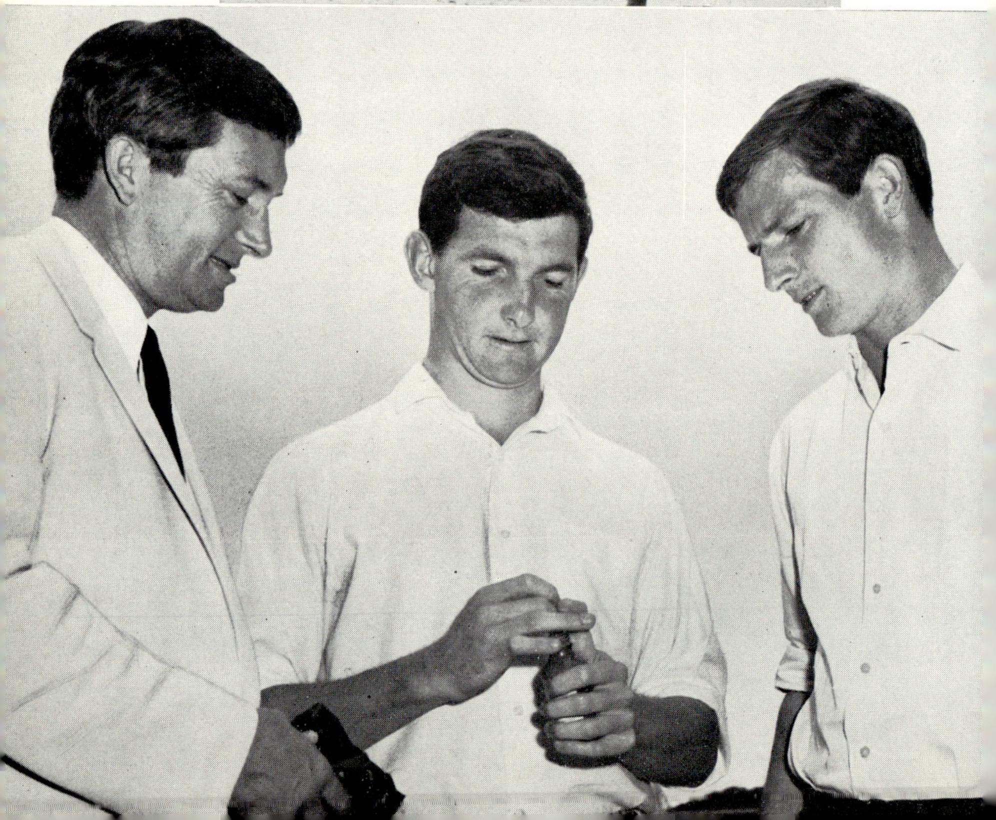

I first saw Lindwall bowl in the Services matches that preceded the resumption of Test matches in Australia after the war. Stockily built, with a magnificent pair of shoulders and a glorious run to the bowling crease, he was the very image of everything a fast bowler should be.

We had a young left-hander in the Cumberland Club at this time named Bert Alderson, a prolific run-getter, and, until Lindwall came on the scene, one who seemed destined for far higher honours. Playing for New South Wales in these matches he had to open the innings against Lindwall bowling for the Services and "Lindy" continually removed him in the opening overs. Not only Alderson was in trouble against this potentially great fast bowler but his speed and late swing, together with an ability to produce a bumper at throat height, caused many other potentially promising players' careers to be checked. The big feature of Lindwall's bowling, even at this stage of his career, was his pinpoint accuracy with every variety of delivery. Although naturally he later improved in this department, even as far back as 1944 and 1945 he was never giving the batsman anything loose, as were many of the other fast bowlers on show.

Apart from Lindwall there was not a great deal of pace about in New South Wales at this time—Victor Trumper, son of the great batsman of the same name, was decidedly quick for a few overs, as was Tom Brooks, but much of the bowling with the new ball was done by Harold Stapleton who had been a useful left-hand medium pacer for some seasons with Bill O'Reilly's St. George side. Ray Frost played one or two representative matches but he too was only medium pace and the big need at this time was obviously to find someone to partner Lindwall.

In 1945 in the Services matches in England a tall all-rounder named Miller began to make his name as a fast bowler as well as a fine strokeplayer and hitter of prodigious sixes. In the Victory Test matches he was reportedly one of the fastest bowlers seen in England since McCormick had played there in 1938 and when he returned to Australia with Hassett's side a great deal of interest was taken in his performances in the matches against the States. He had already played in India and, with the rest of the Services side, was probably jaded with continuous cricket, but not too jaded to show just how quick he could be in the match against New South Wales.

He made 105 not out during what was a Services batting débâcle but this was least important from the Australian selectors' point of view for they knew from as far back as 1939 that he was a talented batsman, having made a century against Grimmett for Victoria against South Australia. This day in Sydney he bowled very fast for a few overs having Barnes badly missed at gully by Hassett and then seeing the right-hander go on to make 102. Most of the Services wickets were taken by left-hand spinner Reg Ellis who played little first-class cricket after this year and Miller's bowling performances were in the eyes rather than in the score-book but he was always thereafter an automatic choice as Lindwall's opening partner.

Two fast bowlers could hardly be more dissimilar than Lindwall and Miller. Lindwall, around 5 feet 10 inches in height with a run up that never varied, except in the angle of delivery from the bowling crease, was everything that a fast bowler should be as a model to young cricketers. On a wet day Lindwall's footmarks could be seen from the start of his run to the position of the back foot in delivery stride—and they never varied in their positioning.

For a bowler of such speed he was remarkably precise but then he was also a great bowler in matters other than speed. I knew of no fast bowler who used his head more than this product of Bill O'Reilly's all-conquering St. George side, and quite often it was not a fast ball that got him his wickets but one of the many varieties he bowled as an adjunct to his fiery pace. At his fastest I never saw any Australian to better him for sheer pace—I suppose Miller occasionally could be as quick, coming from a higher trajectory, and, bowlers from overseas, Tyson and Hall were certainly as quick and possibly quicker. No one, though, was as clever as Lindwall in his constant variations of pace and his ability to think faster than the quickest-footed batsman.

He was known as "Wacka" to some of his team mates, a name started by Jimmy Burke, and he was known to others as "Lindy", an obvious shortening of his surname. But to the batsmen at the other end he was a frightening figure though with a beer in his hand at the end of the day it would be impossible to find a more pleasant opponent. One of the problems of being a great bowler is that people lose sight of abilities in other directions and Lindwall was a fine batsman who never really received his due place in that regard. He was a good close to the wicket field and if he had to field at cover or on the boundary would stand comparison with all but the very greats in these positions.

I once asked Sir Donald Bradman what he thought was the reason for Australia's dominance in a period of post-war cricket and one of the reasons he gave was the number of all-rounders we possessed. Players like Miller and Davidson, and he included Lindwall in this, adding that he thought Ray to have been a very fine all-rounder indeed.

Very few fast bowlers over the years have taken 150 wickets in Test cricket. Lindwall is one of these, having taken 228, and Davidson, 186, and Miller, 170, are others. All three were fine all-rounders and Miller as well scored nearly 3,000 runs and Lindwall made 1,500. Miller was the better all-rounder of the two but Lindwall deserves a very high rating in the great all-rounders of Australian cricket.

I don't think I'd have cared to be an opening batsman in the opposition in this era, for as a combination they were very dangerous to both one's tenure of innings and personal safety. At this particular time, with Miller transferring from Victoria, pitches in Sydney, their home ground, were remarkably green. One match against Victoria finished in two days, a galling experience for the Treasurer of the Association, and one that produced protests from the Victorians themselves, and not without reason. There was so much grass on the pitch that it was scarcely distinguishable from the rest of the square and the fast bowlers made the most of it.

Miller, with his shorter run from a variable position, made the ball fly viciously and alarmingly at the batsmen and, with Lindwall skidding at them from the other end, life was pleasant only for those in the New South Wales side. Many of the States tried retaliation through medium of their own quickies but they were never quite fast enough and though life could be decidedly uncomfortable it could never compare with the lot of the Queenslanders and South Australians who used to fly in to play their matches but often failed to last the full four days.

Miller was an eye-catching cricketer with long hair, often windswept, and constantly being tossed back like the mane of some gallant thoroughbred. He would do this just before turning to run into bowl then, putting his head down, would lift it again sharply once he had got his bearings. On the bowling crease, and with a magnificent side on action, his left arm would come high in the air before the right arm flashed over with perfect body action and timing. Sometimes the ball would be as fast as one believed humanly possible, at others it would be a wrong 'un or an off spinner or any one of the infinite variety of odd balls he would bowl.

I only ever batted against him once in a Testimonial match at

Melbourne and then only for three short overs. But the thing that impressed me most about him then was his deceptive speed—his arm always seemed to be coming over quickly but the ball always seemed to be arriving at different paces and the forward shot had constantly to be checked and the back stroke hurried.

A measure of their greatness was that they were equally good in Australia and England where conditions vary so much. Their pace probably ensured that they would do well overseas but then there have been plenty of really fast bowlers who have never been able to adjust even to bowling in one country, let alone two. 1948 was their great tour, following on their triumphs of 1946 against England and 1947 against India, but they were still at their peak in 1950–1 and 1951–2 against England and the West Indies.

It was quite significant that their success coincided with some of Australia's greatest years in international cricket and it was certainly no fun for opposing batsmen to have to try and combat the fury of this pair. Furious they could be, as well as fast, and they were never averse to testing the batsmen with the short-pitched delivery, sometimes even to the extent where they were advised by the umpires that their quota of bumpers had been reached, and it would be inadvisable to drop any more short in that particular over.

They were no doubt assisted by the forty-over rule that allowed them frequent recourse to the second new ball but even had they been playing at their peak in 1967 when the eighty-five six-ball over new ball rule was in operation they would still have been a great pair.

In many ways Lindwall was a predictable fast bowler in that in this style of bowling he was unusually accurate. Not many over the years have been able to match him in this particular aspect of bowling and he allied with it the swing and variations of pace that caused the batsmen so much trouble.

Miller, on the other hand, was always inclined to the unorthodox, stretching things so far one day in Georgetown to run up and bowl a wrong'un at Bruce Pairaudeau with the new ball. The astonished batsman, preparing to play off the back foot at what was certainly going to be a vicious, lifting outswinger, suddenly found himself playing two or three shots before the ball reached him and he edged it to 'keeper Maddocks.

This was not unusual for Miller and it was a mark of his greatness that he was so accurate, despite his constant variation in methods. He was a brilliant slip field of the lackadaisical type, standing with arms folded or behind his back often as the bowler brought his arm over, but there was nothing slow in his movements once the ball was on its way towards him.

I saw him take some great catches and though I wouldn't put him in quite the same class as Simpson he was still one of the finest close to the wicket catchers in post-war Australia. His Test record is an enviable one for although, unlike Lindwall, he didn't take 100 wickets in Tests against England, nor score 3,000 runs, his overall figures of 170 wickets and 2,958 runs put him among the very greats to have played for Australia.

He was late getting to the ground in the first Sheffield Shield match I played for New South Wales, not for his usual reason of unpunctuality, but because he had an attack of conjunctivitis the day before and had been to a doctor's surgery on the way to the match to have some special drops put in his eye. With Len Johnson carving a swathe through the New South Wales batting Miller went out and hit a magnificent 52 not out in quick time, in the course of which he played the stroke that is so often used now as a cover picture or a feature picture to illustrate the square cut. The ball from this particular stroke hit the fence just in front of the players' dressing-room at the S.C.G. and I can still see the fieldsman, who had five yards to move to cut it off, making his vain endeavour to do so.

Probably one of his greatest batting moments was when he helped a young left-hander named Harvey to his first Test century against England at Leeds in 1948. This was some eight years before Jim Laker was to tear the heart out of Australian batting line-ups in Leeds and Manchester, and Laker this day, even as a relatively youthful 26-year-old, was troubling Harvey so much early in his innings that Miller strolled down to him with the message that he'd have a look at Jim for a while until Neil got settled. Miller then proceeded to drive Laker so strongly that the off-spinner was removed from the attack and Harvey, gaining in confidence, went on to a magnificent century.

There was nothing tight or confined about Miller's cricket and he was always keen, where the subject was receptive, to offer advice that would be helpful in any of the batting, bowling or fielding spheres of the game. He wasn't a great theorist, believing that the game was played best by those who were natural cricketers rather than forced cricketers, and he himself was the best example of this.

But there were many occasions when he would suggest some

small change in a player who was making a fundamental error in either batting or bowling, and far more thought went into this advice than was apparent in the manner in which it was delivered. Basically a nervous character himself, his suggestions would be proffered boldly but with a characteristic cough and much hand-waving. But the players who took his advice or asked for it invariably benefited.

I always found him a good captain of the unorthodox variety and I learnt a lot from him in this department of the game, particularly by way of trying something a little unusual if all unorthodox methods had failed. He himself produced some unusual moves in the time he was captain of New South Wales, having taken over from Arthur Morris, but there was always plenty of thought behind everything he did.

He was prepared to buy wickets if his bowlers would co-operate and I took many wickets in first-class cricket that in some way could be traced back to a pointer produced by Miller. It may have been a change of pace or some little weakness in a batsman, undetected by myself, or it may have been something to do with the pitch or the amount of zip being gained from the surface. But it happened that his advice suited me because I was always keen to try something a little different.

A couple of years ago I produced a cricket coaching film for Coca-Cola in which I used present day players as well as some of those in the immediate post-war era. Three I chose in the latter section of our cricket were Miller, Lindwall and Morris. There was a very good reason for this for those three, although quite often unorthodox in some of their cricket, were always completely correct in the basic fundamentals of the game and, even when retired, were the most perfect examples of fast bowling and correct batting. In this film Lindwall is just as perfect a model for any aspiring fast bowler as one could wish to see and the straightness of Miller's bat and Morris's dancing footwork provide a fine flashback to their golden days.

Morris and Miller in the time after the war were rivals for the New South Wales captaincy after "Ginty" Lush had taken over for a time when Bill O'Reilly retired. Morris was made captain in 1948 after Miller came to New South Wales in 1947 and once the latter was settled there his attacking brand of cricket brought him many admirers for potential leadership of the State side.

Morris was always a quiet skipper but a very thoughtful one who led the side just as well as did Miller when the latter became captain, but he led it in much less flamboyant manner. Morris's great strength though was in his own batting which, round about the 1948 period, was probably unequalled by any other Australian left-hander in the history of our cricket. He had a wonderful tour of England in that season, scoring 1,900 runs, and in the course of the year bringing up his sixth century in ten Tests against the home country.

Only four players have scored more runs in Test matches for Australia and the fair-haired left-hander scored 2,080 of his runs against England at an average of just over 50, and when he returned from England in 1948 he led the New South Wales side in what was my first Sheffield Shield season. He scored over a thousand runs in this domestic year and the most vivid memory I have of him is in the making of that century before lunch against Queensland and in the manner in which he treated the slow bowlers in opposition sides.

There was no being tied down in the crease for Morris—no defensive pushes to the bowler giving the ball a little air. On the contrary, he was continually dancing down the track and driving through the covers or through mid-wicket. One of the pleasures in one's cricket life was to watch Morris batting against Ian Johnson who, at that time, was a very good exponent of off-spin bowling. Johnson relied mainly on flight and Morris on footwork, and it was always a great battle for the batsman to see how often he could arrive on the spot before the ball had hit the ground. In Morris's heyday this was quite often and although Johnson bowled very well to many other batsmen he never quite seemed to have the answer to Morris.

When Jack Iverson burst on the cricket scene in Australia in 1949–50 Morris and the other tourists in South Africa had hardly heard of him and had not seen him bowl. But of all the well-known players who batted against the freak spinner in the next few years Morris probably played him better than any. I played against Iverson on my first Southern tour and it was only a year later that Morris first saw him and made 182 against him at the Sydney Cricket Ground. I had to watch this game as I had broken a finger in a grade match a few weeks before. Morris slaughtered the Victorian attack this day in what had been billed as a battle between Iverson and the New South Wales batsmen and there was no finer sight than this in the whole of Australian season.

In this same year Iverson took six for 27 in the Third Test

against England on the S.C.G. and no English batsman could fathom him, partly I believe because of their disinclination to move down the pitch to kill the spin—if the occasion ever arose where they were able to pick which way the ball was going to turn.

Morris played for Bill O'Reilly's club in Sydney at a time when Lindwall was on his way up as a promising bowler, and when he first came into grade cricket, whilst Lindwall was always making his name as a fast bowler, Morris was listed as a left-hand unorthodox spinner. He batted well down the list but O'Reilly was too shrewd a judge to miss the latent potential in the slim left-hander and he was soon being put in first when St. George had to bat a second time on Saturday afternoons.

In 1940 he made his debut for New South Wales against Queensland and became the first cricketer ever to score two separate hundreds on his initial first-class appearance, a feat that was later to be matched by Nari Contractor, playing for Gujerat, twelve years later. He spent most of his time during the war in the islands north of Australia, batting in jungle green on indifferent pitches. When he returned to Australia it was obvious that he and Lindwall, also in the same battle area, would be two of Australia's line-up against England in 1946–7. Miller was another, with his fine performances for the Services side, and from the war came these three brilliant exponents of different facets of the game of cricket.

Morris played well against England in his first year, scoring a century in each innings of the Adelaide Test, and then followed it with an even not out century against India in Melbourne the following year. In 1948 he made three hundreds in the Tests and in 1950–1, when he became rather irrationally known as "Bedser's bunny", he picked up 206 against England in Adelaide.

I have always been interested in the manner in which it was claimed that Bedser had something of a hoodoo over Morris and, in fact, it was quite true that Morris found him difficult to play. This was because Bedser switched his attack to Morris's leg stump, with striking results in the first few matches. But no one at this stage played Bedser with any great confidence, so well was he bowling, and in 1953 the big England medium-pacer had his finest season, taking his tally of wickets against Australia past the hundred mark. He got 39 wickets at 17 apiece in this 1953 series and very few of Hassett's side had any real answer to his late swing and movement off the pitch.

Morris though was back the following year in the First Test in Brisbane scoring 153 but thereafter, like all the Australian batsmen of that series, he had no answer either to the fiery pace of Tyson and Statham or the vagaries of the pitches in Sydney and Melbourne.

It is impossible to overestimate the valuable part played in post-war Australian cricket by this trio and a great deal of the success achieved in the five years after the war was due to their efforts with both bat and ball. Certainly they were the answer to any captain's prayer and the most recent Australian skipper, Bill Lawry, must look longingly at the record books and wish that a batsman like Morris and all-rounders like Miller and Lindwall were available to him.

One wet, miserable day in January 1952, the Australian selectors announced their Fifth Test team to play against the West Indies in Sydney. The series was already won against a side that had come to Australia with a great reputation and contained players like Weekes, Worrell and Walcott as well as spinning twins Ramadhin and Valentine. Apparently the selectors had decided that it was time to experiment. Not only was I included but so were Colin McDonald and George Thoms, the Victorian opening pair. Ian Johnson was made twelfth man to make way for me and Arthur Morris was left out of the side.

Quite often cricketers will enjoy playing on their home ground more than on any other in the world and I am no exception in this for I have always been pleased to play top-class cricket at the Sydney Cricket Ground. It was where I made my first-class debut and then this Test debut against the West Indies, and it was where I played my last Test against the South Africans twelve years later.

As cricket grounds go I suppose it is midway between being a stadium and being attractive but it has great tradition and, I believe, the best atmosphere of all grounds for a Test match. Melbourne holds more people, Newlands is prettier, but Sydney, with its expanse of Hill and perfect surface, can be matched but not beaten as a Test venue. It was here, as a nine-year-old schoolboy, I had watched Grimmett and Bradman and O'Reilly, and it was here that I had seen Bradman and Barnes make 234, and Miller 105 the year before, and it was here I walked on the field behind Lindsay Hassett wearing the green cap for the first time.

Miller was playing in this match and so was Lindwall and,

between them, they produced some of the most fiery fast bowling I had ever seen on a pitch that was just made for that type of bowler. It was so green that it was scarcely distinguishable from the rest of the square and they made the most of it. It was perfect for any type of pace bowler and Australia certainly didn't have it all their own way for Worrell and Gomez bowled us out cheaply in the first innings, as well as causing a great deal of trouble in the second. But they had no one really to match Miller, Lindwall and Bill Johnston and eventually the Australians won the game in reasonable comfort.

At that stage of my Test career I had no idea where I was going or what I was going to do and would, in fact, have been happy enough to have played just the one game for Australia. Had I known that cricket in the next twelve years was to take me to every part of the Commonwealth then I would have been even more up in the air than a normal 21-year-old representing his country for the first time.

I think I saw more good things and great things done at the Sydney Cricket Ground than at any other first-class venue in the world. Understandable perhaps in the light of it being my home ground for State matches as well as Test matches.

The bowling of Miller and Lindwall in that initial Test match remains a great memory, as does the batting of Stollmeyer who made a magnificent century against this blistering attack. My own part in the match was as insignificant as had been my Interstate debut, being caught off Gomez for 3 in the first innings and then dismissed for 19 in the second and taking only the wicket of Valentine in the few overs I bowled. But it was a great moment even to be in the same dressing-room as players like Miller, Lindwall and Hassett and one that remains as vivid as does my last Test match on the ground when Australia was so close to defeat against South Africa.

It was just a year later when the South African 1952–3 side was in Australia that a small disaster befell me in the shadow of the Sydney Hill. I had been taken to Brisbane as twelfth man for the First Test and then played in Melbourne, making 45 in the second innings and taking a few wickets, thus ensuring a place in the third match in Sydney. At this stage the Tests stood one all and eventually they were to finish two all, with the South Africans winning the final game in Melbourne.

On the first day of the Third Test in Sydney there was a little early moisture in the pitch and I was fielding very close at short gully to Bill Johnston who was bowling his left-arm spinners over the wicket from the Noble Stand end. Suddenly he let go a quicker ball outside Waite's off stump and the batsman square cut it with tremendous force straight into my mouth.

It was only three years before that I had had my skull fractured trying to hook in Melbourne and this latest incident was just another in what seemed an unending chapter of accidents. It happened that the injury looked much more serious than it was and that shock was the main problem, and I was able to come back on the field and take two wickets and a catch to dismiss Roy McLean, as well as make naught in the first and only innings of the match.

This was the season where Neil Harvey scored 800 runs in the series against the South Africans, 190 of them in this Third Test match at the S.C.G., in one of the finest innings of his career. His driving and cutting that day were absolutely magnificent and a classic example of the great left-hander in action. Harvey had already made runs in the Brisbane Test and in Melbourne, and he made a lot more in Adelaide in the latter part of the series in what was probably his best year in international cricket. He made 650 runs in the West Indies but that year in Australia against South Africa no one could have batted better against the persistent opposition attack that included Hughie Tayfield, at that time, and later, one of the finest bowlers the world has seen.

I didn't play a Test match in Sydney for another two years, when Tyson and Statham were at their top for M.C.C., on a pitch that again gave the fast bowlers every possible assistance. Arthur Morris skippered this side, the Second Test of the series, and Australia had come down from the Brisbane Test full of confidence, having won the game by an innings.

There were no high scores in this game in Sydney though the youthful May and Cowdrey performed well in the grassy conditions.

Ray Lindwall was the spearhead of our attack, but Miller wasn't playing and Lindwall was partnered by Ron Archer, and this pair, with Bill Johnston, ripped through England's first innings batting so quickly that it seemed the game could well be over in four days. But Wardle, hitting briefly and in the manner in which he plays best, in the first innings, and Appleyard in the second, turned the tide with Statham and eventually England set a reasonable fourth innings target for the Australians.

It was one of the most exciting matches in the early part of my career for, although we managed to get a first innings lead, May's and Cowdrey's batting in the second innings set a total that was too much for batsmen who, even at this stage of the tour, were beginning to become a little "punchy" from the effect of the Tyson–Statham onslaught.

Harvey batted magnificently in the second innings of this match, making an unbeaten 92, and at one stage looking almost as though he would win the match single-handed for Arthur Morris who had taken over the captaincy. It happened that I was made vice-captain for this match, with Ian Johnson and Keith Miller not playing, and looking back on it, it was one of the most astonishing things that had ever happened to me. I had been playing Test cricket for only three or four years and there were players like Harvey, Lindwall and Bill Johnston with far more experience than I, and at this stage the only captaincy I had was with my own club side. It was a great thrill to receive the appointment but I must confess to one or two thoughts of what might happen if Arthur Morris were injured during the game and I had to take over. Fortunately nothing of this kind happened and it wasn't until four years later that I had the privilege of captaining the Test side in the first match against England in Brisbane.

On all Test grounds there is always a thrill in walking out on to the field in front of a large crowd but nowhere have I felt this more than in Sydney. The new M.A. Noble Stand towers above the others and the Hill, with the scoreboard, provides a sea of colour with the multi-coloured shirts of the spectators contrasting with the lush green grass of the outfield.

I had a chequered career on this ground, being in winning sides in the first two Tests I played there, then losing in 1954–5 and 1960–1 against the West Indies and drawing in 1958–9. But oh, what memories the ground produces—Harvey's great batting and the bowling of Davidson in 1962–3 when he took five for 25 against England, and even that infamous Fifth Test match of the same series when Ted Dexter and I were opposing captains.

There have, too, been some wonderful State matches, particularly between Victoria and New South Wales, games played in fiery spirit and much the same atmosphere as a traditional Yorkshire–Lancashire match. These were the days when the players snarled at one another on the field and then drank compatibly in the dressing-rooms later on, in the traditional way the game should be played.

In those days New South Wales had the best of the fast bowling brigade in Lindwall and former Victorian Miller. Neither was averse to bowling bumpers at the opposition and they occasionally got back as good as they gave, particularly one day in Sydney when, heartily sick of constantly being on the receiving end, the Victorians gave John Power a free hand in letting Miller have "a few of the best". I was batting at the other end at the time and had also been on the receiving end of three or four bumpers an over, hooking some and managing to escape decapitation with others. When Power started in on Miller there were one or two tense moments on the field, "Nugget" hit on the fingers and throwing his bat down and Ian Johnson saying to Power as he walked back past him, "well bowled—give him another one".

This was all part and parcel of these matches in those days and I related this story to a couple of journalists a few days later. It was merely done in conversation but I suddenly found the story splashed all over the Melbourne *Sporting Globe* the same week—good copy but slightly embarrassing the next time I saw Johnson who was captaining Australia at that time.

Round about 1955 Australian cricket was going through an awkward period, with a number of players reaching the end of their careers, and the defeats in that 1954–5 season did nothing at all for the morale of the side. But we were able to go to the West Indies in 1955 and win the series three nil against bowlers who, if not quite as fast as Tyson and Statham, were still able to provide batsmen with plenty of problems. The 1956 tour was disastrous in the light of these good performances for, although expecting to be confronted by pace in England, we were in fact "done" by spin presented by Laker and Lock.

From that moment on we had a new look Australian side with a battle for the captaincy between Ian Craig and Neil Harvey, the former playing for New South Wales and the latter for Victoria but just about to move to Sydney for business reasons. Sydney was the interesting place at this time for word was filtering through that Craig was to be the next Australian captain and, in fact, he was made skipper of the Australian side to visit New Zealand early in 1957 whilst Harvey was made vice-captain. There were many of us keen to go on this New Zealand trip and many more keen to go to South Africa later in the year for this was to be the start of a revival of our Test cricket performances against England in 1958–9.

There was a long break in Test matches at the Sydney Cricket Ground from 1954–5 to 1958–9, when we played the drawn match against Peter May's M.C.C. side, and I only ever after that time played in five Tests on the great ground before retiring. Ironically we should have lost the last of these against South Africa but the young South African side panicked at the thought of winning the match and settled for a draw late on the last day.

For me it was a sad day to be bowing out of Test cricket on the same ground where I had started but it was one of those occasions where you can look back and be grateful that you have had a good run. I came off the field that afternoon and turned at the gate to have a last look at the scoreboard which in future would dispense with the name Benaud that had stood there for the past 15 years. As I watched the scoreboard attendants had reached the last two names on the board—Simpson and Benaud. There was a touch of irony about this kind of King is dead, long live the King, for I had earlier in the season relinquished the Australian captaincy in favour of Simpson and now on the scoreboard they took my name down and left his in solitary splendour. He had been kind enough to allow me to walk off the field at the head of the team and I thought now that if he could enjoy his next fifteen years on this great ground as I had enjoyed mine then he would indeed be a very happy cricketer.

One of the most resilient things I know in this great game is Australian cricket. The ability to bounce back from a seemingly impossible position or an unaccustomed defeat has been the thing that has kept our cricket near the top over the years. But there always comes a period where a side is rebuilding, where the selectors and captain have almost insurmountable problems, and such a situation arose in Australian cricket around 1962–3.

Our side for the past five years had been particularly stable with McDonald, Burke, Lawry and Simpson attending to the opening batting, and Harvey, Burge, O'Neill and one or two others looking after the middle of the order. I had done the leg spinning with Simpson's assistance since 1957, and Kline and Johnny Martin had made occasional appearances and tours. Mackay was the stock medium-pacer and Davidson the great opening bowler who, though he had a variety of partners, was always pre-eminent in this department.

But in 1962–3 the side had a complete face lift with Harvey, Mackay and Davidson dropping out for business reasons and I announced that I would be retiring at the end of the following season. Grout too, that most brilliant of wicket-keepers, was retiring after the 1965 West Indies tour and there were obviously going to be many gaps in the side. One of the great strengths of Australian cricket in this period, as in many others, was in the number of all-rounders secure in the composition of the side. Players like Davidson, Grout and myself and Mackay, whom we used to bat at number 8 though he was Queensland's top run getter. This was a useful team with Davidson 7, Mackay 8, myself 9, Grout 10, and someone like Meckiff, McKenzie, or another fast bowler at 11.

When all these players retired within a couple of years of one another, and we lost Harvey as well as McDonald, it was obvious that the balance of the side would change. This was perfectly underlined when the Australian side toured South Africa in 1966–7 for there was a tremendous gap in the latter part of the batting order where normally, in recent seasons, we had been so strong. Simpson on this tour was given a young side of relative inexperience and in many ways it was an unbalanced side, a situation that was not really the fault of the selectors but only of the lack of particular talent available.

Burge, Jarman and Walters were unavailable for the tour and O'Neill was omitted, despite the fact that he was averaging 45 in Test matches at that stage. The one that made the big difference to the balance of the side was Walters but he was doing two years' National Service and the first series for which he would be available was Australia in England in 1968. His inclusion at number 6 in this side would have allowed Chappell to go in at number 7 and provide batting strength something along the lines of that available to Australian sides in the five previous seasons.

On the other hand South Africa, with one of their strongest sides in cricket history, were in the wonderful position of having many batsmen who were also useful seam bowlers, and they made the most of this advantage. To see Procter coming in at 8, van der Merwe 9 and du Preez or David Pithey 10 was a sight that reminded me quite vividly of what had only recently been the position in Australian cricket.

This great balance of all-rounders in Australian cricket wasn't solely the prerogative of sides from 1958 to 1963 but it was certainly one of the main reasons that the teams of that era were so successful. From 1946 to 1956 we had all-rounders like Miller and Lindwall, Ian Johnson and Sam Loxton, who compare more than favourably with players from any other era.

On quite a number of occasions Australian batting sides in

trouble have been rescued by great performances from the all-rounders batting towards the end of the list, and in this sense we have often had the advantage over England whose selection methods generally consist of playing five batsmen, one all-rounder, a wicket-keeper and four bowlers. This is not to say that we were right and they wrong but for our particular brand of cricket it was a very happy circumstance that allowed us to collect so many all-rounders in the one side and still retain a top bowling team. It happened that three of the all-rounders, Davidson, Mackay and myself, carried the Australian bowling during most of these five years with various assistance from players brought into the side for a short time. No player is so good that he can be the most important in the side and yet I will always have a sneaking suspicion that without Alan Davidson in that particular era Australian cricket would have been struggling rather than on top.

There would, of course, have been another opening bowler to take his place but unless he had been really great, as was Davidson, our performances would have suffered.

They called him "Al Pal", or the "Mayor of Gosford", and he was one of the finest all-round cricketers the world has seen. Few bowlers could match his late swing and awkward movement off the pitch and there weren't many better fieldsmen in any position in the world. As a batsman he more often than not turned the tide for Australia after the early batsmen had failed.

I first struck him in 1945 when he was playing for Gosford High School and represented Northern High Schools against Combined Metropolitan High Schools in a match at the end of the schools season. In those days he was a hard hitting left-hand batsman and, as always, a brilliant fieldsman but he bowled left-arm unorthodox over the wrist deliveries rather than the ones that later made him famous. We went on our first tour together to England in 1953 and thereafter Davidson never missed a match other than through injury, nor an overseas tour. I played against him for a couple of years in this Combined School cricket and then suddenly he came from Gosford to play with Northern Districts and was an immediate success. So much so that he played his first Sheffield Shield match in 1949, only three years after leaving school cricket.

There are great cricketers in every era and Davidson was one of the greatest Australia has produced, particularly in the period from 1957 to 1963. This was after Miller and Lindwall had left the scene—Lindwall temporarily—thus allowing Davidson full scope with the new ball rather than condemning him to come on when the shine had all but disappeared.

He was injury prone—sometimes real, sometimes imaginary—but he never left the field or stopped bowling for any other than a very real reason. I caught Johnny Waite off him one day in Cape Town in one of those dismissals where fieldsmen and captain work on a certain plan and it happens to come off. Alan had been limping back to bowl and then boring in at the batsmen and moving the ball late, either into or away from them. Then he would limp back and Craig would ask him if he were all right—he would say "no" and get a sympathetic pat on the shoulder and then bore in again with yet another magnificent delivery.

The Cape Town pitch was very slow and I asked Craig if I could come up three yards at gully for the one that flew off the thick edge and wouldn't normally carry. Davo limped back for the next ball and Waite square drove it like a bullet. I caught the red blur, body parallel to the ground, and was just rolling over for the second time when Davo arrived alongside me, saying excitedly "it was the old trap, you know. The old trap." It had taken him just two seconds to get down and the boys thought it was the quickest he had moved all day.

This was the match where, so much was he on the massage table, that we had a copper plaque engraved and nailed on to the massage table and inscribed "The A. K. Davidson Autograph Massage Table."

I saw Waite in South Africa some time later and he recalled this particular incident in the context of Davidson's Test performances and bowling skill. Waite contended that Alan was at his best when not feeling 100 per cent fit. He said the real danger time was when you could see him limping back or looking sorry for himself.

I have never played with or against a more penetrative opening bowler, possibly because of the particular angle in which he came at the batsman, bowling from wide of the return crease to a point just outside the off stump and then swinging late to round about middle stump or middle and leg. He wasn't a big swinger of the ball but he certainly moved it as late as anyone I have seen, and this was one of the prime reasons that he was so successful. He only needed to hold the ball across the seam for variety and deliver it with the same action as for the in-swinger and I will defy any batsman in the world to pick the fact that the ball will continue straight on instead of swinging in.

He used to do this sometimes and at other times he would cut the ball away from the right-hander in a fashion that made him the joy of wicket-keeper Wally Grout and his slip fieldsmen. He and Grout used to refer jocularly to the fact that they had "made" one another, each pointing out that the other would never have done as well without the benefit of either the bowling or wicket-keeping of the other. There was a lot in this for Grout took some magnificent catches off Davidson, both on the off and leg side, and developed a great understanding with him, as well as the ability to pick the way the ball was going to slant.

I think that Grout is one of the finest wicket-keepers of all time, fit to be ranked level with Tallon and Langley in my time, but in many ways he was lucky that he played in the same era as a great fast bowler who could find the edge of the bat as often as did Davidson.

I don't think I ever saw a bowler beat the bat as much as Davidson and this was probably because there are more right- than left-handers in the world and once the shine had gone from the ball he was constantly coming at them from such an angle that even if they played straight it was still possible for them to be beaten. Some said that he didn't like bowling against left-handers but this was fallacy and they went the same way as their right-hand counterparts unless they were really great players.

"Davo" first came into prominence in Australian cricket when the Australian team was in South Africa in 1949–50. At the beginning of that season he was chosen to play against the Victorian Second XI and started proceedings by taking a wicket with his first ball. We then went on the Southern tour under Ron James's captaincy and he trapped big Bob McLean l.b.w. with his second ball in first-class cricket, which, by any standards, was a fair start. In those days he was very raw—who wouldn't be—at the age of 20, opening the bowling in a first-class match, and his performances for the remainder of the season were not as startling as those of some opening bowlers who have made their debuts since that date.

But there was so much tremendous promise there that the Australian selectors must have had his name very high on the list for international honours, and they took the opportunity of blooding him later the same year when an Australian side went to New Zealand with Bill Brown as captain and Phil Ridings vice-captain. Davidson had an excellent tour, his general all-round ability impressing everyone who watched him, and in one match against

Wairarapa scored a century and took all ten wickets. This was a remarkable feat in any class of cricket, particularly so in an important match, and there was no doubt by the end of the tour that Davidson eventually was going to be a force in Australian cricket.

The following season, 1950–1, he had the problem, like all of us, of retaining our places in the New South Wales side now that the South African tourists were back home. Morris, Moroney, Miller, Lindwall, Walker all returned to the side and with the forty-over new ball rule in operation it meant that Davidson first of all would not get the new ball and certainly wouldn't have a great deal of bowling to do. But he was a most valuable member of the side and the first time he bowled in the company of these great names he took seven for 49 in the opening Shield match in Queensland. It was a fine spell of bowling and he raised one or two of the older eyebrows when, on bowling Ken Archer, he exclaimed excitedly to Miller and Lindwall that it was "the best ball he had ever seen bowled". This was typical, youthful enthusiasm and not far from the truth for the ball had started just outside Archer's off stump and then swung late to land in line with leg stump.

Archer half turned his body and shaped to glance it but, landing on the seam, the ball flashed back the other way and neatly removed the off bail. On reflection, I have seen few better deliveries in all the time I played cricket and perhaps only one to equal it when Alec Bedser bowled Lindsay Hassett in the First Test at Trent Bridge in 1953.

Davidson hovered about the fringe of the Test side for the next couple of years but it was this emphasis on new ball bowling that in fact kept him out, though the promise and the skill were there for all to see. The new ball rule had brought on so many fast and medium-pace bowlers that really a youngster like Davidson was a supernumerary. The selectors hadn't forgotten him though and although I beat him for a place in two Test series before he eventually played for Australia this was solely because so many over the wrist spinners had been killed off that there was something of a desperate search for one who could bat and field, as well as show a little promise as a leg spinner.

In 1952–3 when the South Africans were in Australia Davidson had quite a good year, without playing in a Test match, even when Lindwall and Miller both broke down for the Fifth and final Test. In that game, where South Africa squared the series, the selectors preferred Noblet and Ron Archer but then immediately after that match they announced the seventeen names to tour England and Alan was included and Noblet omitted. This was a learning tour for some of us, Davidson included, and though he bowled well in the Test matches it was obvious that his full potential would not be realised for some time. I was in the same position, trying to learn everything possible about leg spinning on this tour, but there is no doubt that the five months' tour of England did the two of us, and Ron Archer, a great deal of good.

Davidson played in three Tests in the 1954–5 series against England and then was chosen to go to the West Indies in 1955 in what was to be the start of a touring career interrupted only by injury. He was badly hurt in Jamaica in 1955, slipping in a bowler's footmark in the first match of the tour, and tore ligaments as well as chipping a bone in his ankle. He didn't play again in any serious cricket on that tour and suffered a recurrence of the injury in the First Test match in 1956 in England.

In between times he had been establishing himself even further with sound all-round performances in Interstate cricket and he was taken to England in 1956 in the dual role of fast medium-pace bowler and left-arm orthodox spinner, as well as brilliant fieldsman and useful middle order bat. He was able to play only in the First and Fifth Test matches but he had so little experience of bowling spinners on a turning pitch that he was not able to be fully effective and, by that stage of the series, Australia had to win the final Test to draw level with England who had just won at Leeds and Manchester.

In 1956–7 in Australia Davidson continued to improve but the selectors, after he had a tough season with New South Wales, wisely left him out of the Australian side to tour New Zealand in March of that year. He was in the 1957–8 side to tour South Africa though and it was around this period that he really came into his own as an opening bowler. Getting the new ball was one reason for this, with Miller and Lindwall both out of the side, and increased opportunity was another, for now he was the main bowler and had to act as spearhead of the attack, as well as stock bowler.

For the five years after 1957–8 whenever the side was in trouble the captain, whether it was Craig, Harvey, or myself, always looked for Davidson and rarely did he fail. There was always the thought that at some stage he might break down but the times when he left the field could be counted on the fingers of one hand and he bowled a lot of overs for Australia and New South Wales. In the Fourth Test in Adelaide in 1962–3 he badly tore a hamstring muscle but still played in the Fifth, and in the first Test I ever captained in high temperature in Brisbane he left the field with heat exhaustion in the first session. There were one or two other occasions when he wasn't feeling too well but it was no wonder, considering the amount of work he was given.

I used him unmercifully because he was the best bowler I had and, in fact, the best bowler in the world at that time, constantly worrying the batsmen and thinking them out even if the pitch were unsympathetic to his type of bowling. He bowled well all over the world, irrespective of conditions, sometimes slowing his pace and cutting the ball and sometimes concentrating on bowling as fast as he could in the initial overs and then bowling within himself with the occasional quick delivery to unsettle the batsmen. And he could be quick too!

He is always listed as a fast medium bowler, and indeed I think of him as such, but he could be really slippery at times and his bumper lifted at the batsman from a spot on the pitch farther up than most. He rarely wasted a bouncer and generally had it about shoulder height at the batsman, and there weren't a great number of bowlers who provided more difficulty with this ball than Davidson. One day in Melbourne, in the second Test in which I captained him, he had three for none in his second over, Richardson caught by Grout, Graveney l.b.w. and Watson bowled, in an astonishing display of swing bowling. Graveney played no stroke at the ball that dismissed him and it came back so late and so quickly that he had only just begun to shuffle across when the ball hit him.

In England in 1961 he was uncertain of being fit for the Second Test at Lord's the day before the match, when Harvey, McDonald and I were settling down to choose the side. He called me across to the massage table and said that he didn't think he'd be able to play, a statement that was a crushing blow in view of the fact that I had just declared myself unavailable to the co-selectors. I said to him that he would have to play as Neil was captaining the side and he'd need every bit of support he could get. Davidson has a great regard for Harvey and immediately said that he'd try for "the little bloke", and he went out the next day and took five for 42, a magnificent display of fast bowling.

Marvellous character, Davo! Two of the things I'll always remember him for are when I took the fluke catch off him at

Western Province that day—and how he changed from an invalid to an athletic broad jumper in two seconds to pump my hand and clap me on the back—and the day I felled him with a "clever" throw. Wes Hall was the batsman at the S.C.G. and he had been playing his shot and running a few yards up the pitch to try and force a throw. I was at mid-wicket and decided to pick the ball up with my back to Wes and throw the stumps down at the batting end next time he tried it. Unfortunately I forgot to tell Davo. The ball hit him in the throat and he went down like a felled steer—gave a final convulsive twitch and we thought he had left us. Up and about 60 seconds later he bored in at Wes and the next delivery was just about the quickest he bowled all day.

Those two performances live in the memory but they were just two of many that set him apart from the ordinary run-of-the-mill fast bowler. In Sydney in 1962–3 he took five for 25 in England's second innings, routing them with an almost unplayable series of in-swingers and away cutters. But I suppose my fondest memory of him is at Manchester in 1961 when he and McKenzie added 98 priceless runs for the last wicket and then Davo shattered Statham's stumps to win the match late on the last day.

I was never fortunate enough to see the greats of the past in action, players like Trumper, Jackson and McCabe, though once, when seeing my first Sheffield Shield match, I caught a glimpse of McCabe that remains now in my memory only as a dancing-footed right-hander who was engaged at the time in something of a duel with Grimmett. I read of them avidly but have to leave it to the older generation to provide the details.

I saw all the modern players though, and of these one of the most attractive was Norman Clifford O'Neill who, tragically, in 1967 announced his retirement from the game. O'Neill, for some time, had been troubled by knee injuries, brought about by a chronic weakness in the thighs, and this in turn induced growths on the knees.

O'Neill was one of the finest batsmen I ever watched, a magnificent player in really good form and a strokeplayer who captivated crowds all over the world. It takes all sorts to make up the batting side of a cricket team—slower players who begin the innings to form some kind of a foundation, the occasional dashing opener, often frowned on as being too venturesome in that particular position, glorious stroke players in the middle of the order and all-rounders who are often hitters towards the bottom of the list.

O'Neill was among the greatest strokeplayers of my time. I put him not far below Harvey in enjoyment provided for the spectators. He was quite often a nervous starter but, more than anything else, he suffered the disservice of being compared with Bradman. "Another Bradman" is a favourite phrase of Australian critics when they believe they have discovered one to match the greatest run-getter of all time and the most merciless slaughterer of bowlers.

When O'Neill appeared Australian batting had just gone through one of its worst periods and the selectors were engaged in a search for young talent. The 1948 side had been so strong in batting that it will always be compared with the great teams of any era but after that, in 1953 and in 1954–5 and 1956, the batting was never quite able to combat England's bowlers although the Australian side did well in the West Indies in 1955.

O'Neill came on the scene in 1956 and at the end of that Australian season went to New Zealand with Ian Craig's side, scoring a brilliant century in his last innings of the tour in the third representative match. I saw quite a bit of that innings from the other end and, having watched him play in Sheffield Shield matches in the five months before, there was no doubt that Australia had the makings of a very fine batsman indeed. He missed the South African tour, to the annoyance of many critics and to his own disappointment, but it wasn't such a bad thing for him for he made over 1,000 runs in Sheffield Shield cricket, becoming only the third Australian player ever to have done so; 175 against Victoria and 233 against the same team in a return match were the two great innings of that season, and he was certainly the most publicised cricketer since Bradman at that particular time in Australia.

One of the biggest problems with publicity for a young player is that it is provided by critics whose job is to boost the performances of young players and, equally, if they fail, their task is to criticise. When England arrived in Australia in 1958–9 the young O'Neill, then aged only 21, came to me and asked if he should accept an invitation to travel to Perth to play against them in the Combined match, the second game of the season. This coincided with the New South Wales match against Queensland and O'Neill was receiving conflicting advice on whether or not he should take his chance with M.C.C.'s bowlers in Perth or be content to wait for them in Sydney later in the tour. My advice to him was to go to Perth and to take his chance there, for I believed he was a good enough player to overcome the problems that might face him in such a meeting.

He had an immense reputation in Australia at this time and even if he failed in Perth I believed his skill was such that he would soon make up for it once the series began. In fact, he was to play ten Test matches against England before notching his first hundred, though in the meantime he made centuries against other countries.

I think he was one of the finest back-foot players I have ever seen and this in itself is remarkable for, though Australians do produce good back-foot players, a lot of the play by batsmen in that country is produced off the front foot. O'Neill played many forcing strokes off the back foot that other players would have discarded or else elected to play defensively off the front foot. It was this more than anything else that made me put him so close to Harvey in the period 1956–63, for it was so difficult to bowl to both of them if the bowler had in mind trying to keep them quiet rather than get them out. In some ways he was in the wrong era for he played his cricket at a time when success was the yardstick rather than skill or an avalanche of strokes to delight the spectator.

The basis I used with him was that I never expected him to make a hundred on any occasion when he batted for me but only ever asked him to play his strokes with as much concentration as possible. This was where he suffered most by inevitable comparison with Bradman for really, if he were to be compared with any other Australian player, it should have been someone like McCabe who was never a run compiler but was a brilliant, stylish batsman whose innings always contained some element of risk and some chance for the bowlers.

Comparison of players in different eras is always difficult but the mere statistics of McCabe and O'Neill in both their career and Test matches make interesting reading. McCabe in his sixty-two Test innings scored 2,748 runs at 48 and O'Neill in his sixty-nine scored 2,779 at 45. But both scored only six centuries at a rate of one every ten or eleven times at the crease and their career records are also remarkably similar, both having scored in excess of 10,000 runs at an average of 50.

There have been plenty of batsmen over the years whose century striking rate is better than this but there haven't been many who have provided any more entertainment than O'Neill—and, I am sure, McCabe. There is no intention here of trying to produce argument with older readers who might contend that

McCabe was the greater player, for not having seen the two in the one era it is really impossible to compare them, but the picture in my mind of O'Neill is that he was the same type of player as McCabe, always carrying the fight to the bowler, not with attrition but with strokeplay.

He was one of the brilliant fieldsmen of any era, a fine close to the wicket catcher that one used almost exclusively at cover or in the outfield because of his magnificent throwing arm—a feature of his athletic ability that at one stage produced an offer from the New York Yankees to try out at Spring training after he had been watched by one of the Club's talent scouts in Australia.

O'Neill first played for New South Wales in 1955 and might well have played for Australia in official Test matches only two years later, and it was an absolute tragedy that he had to retire when he did. He was a most courageous player of fast bowling and one of the hardest hitters of the ball I have ever seen, mostly off the back foot but also possessing the skill and footwork to destroy any slow bowler whose length was anything but perfect.

His career coincided with that of Bob Simpson who made the New South Wales side at the tender age of 16 back in 1953. Simpson was quite unlike O'Neill in his cricket ability though he too had plenty of strokes and was probably a more competent all round the wicket player than his dashing contemporary. My own personal view, obviously not shared by Simpson and the Australian selectors, is that although the latter was a very good opening batsman he would have been even more successful, and of more value to Australia, had he batted at number 4. He turned himself into an opening batsman, partly through necessity and partly through desire to take advantage of the fact that, coinciding with his later career, Australia was somewhat short of good players in that position. At the same time he eliminated some of his strokes to make certain that he became what is popularly termed a safe opening batsman rather than a dashing one.

He is one of the best batsmen, and indeed all-round cricketers, Australia has had and I have never seen his like as a slip fieldsman—and you can throw in any of the old timers you like to try and match him. He started off by being brilliant in the covers and a good throwing arm produced from baseball kept him, for a time, from close to the wicket positions. But by 1954–5, when he played for New South Wales against M.C.C., he was fully established as a promising young slip and, in addition, in that game made a fine 98 in this his first international appearance. I have seen him miss remarkably few chances over the years that he has specialised at first slip and by the time he retired from Test cricket he had taken an astonishing 99 catches in 52 Tests.

Naturally wicket-keepers can provide better records than this but only one modern day player, M. C. Cowdrey, has taken more catches than Simpson and Cowdrey's 113 catches at the end of 1968 had come in 101 Test matches, a comparison that is quite remarkable for English bowlers have exactly the same ability as Australians to find the edge of the bat.

No-one in present day Australian cricket has scored more runs in Tests than Simpson and he approached the 4,000 mark. Only Sir Donald Bradman and Neil Harvey stand ahead of him in the great Test match run-getters in Australian history.

He owes something of a debt to Australia's Cinderella cricket State, Western Australia, for it was there he began what was virtually a comeback, having left New South Wales without ever having made completely certain of a Test match place. He went across there in 1956 and his mammoth scoring, particularly in the 1959–60 season, made him sure of a place in the Test side from that moment on. He made himself into a technique player and is the best Australian player of the bat and pad technique I have ever seen. This really came about through a season in the Lancashire League where, with the ball moving a considerable amount in the air and off the pitch, he found that the defensive push with bat close to the pad paid big dividends.

When he returned to Australia, having missed the Australian tour of India and Pakistan in 1959–60, he was a much tighter player and the bowlers at that time found him just about impossible to dismiss. At one stage in the season he was averaging 300 with a total of 900 runs, in a still incomplete year. Those of us in India and Pakistan knew that he was a good player but doubted that even his Lancashire League experience could have improved him this much. But he proved us all wrong in the final match of the season in making 98 and 161 not out against a full strength New South Wales team.

In many ways he is a remarkable batsman, giving the bowler less chance than most other players I have seen in modern day cricket. It is often thought that he is not at his best against really fast bowling and yet many of his best performances have been turned in against that particular type. He has a rather peculiar method of playing the short-pitched ball but it is one that he has devised himself and he claims that it serves him better than the traditional method of moving inside the line of flight of the bumper. Instead Simpson sways away to the outside, allowing the ball to pass sometimes over the top of his stumps, and very rarely does he move to or outside his off stump in negotiating this type of delivery. He is the only player I have ever seen do this and he does it for the simple reason that he finds it more effective, being a predominantly front foot player. His first movement is to put his left foot forward to the line of the ball.

He is a tough character, forthright in his views on the game and the players, and a very resilient competitor indeed. Back in 1963, after I had informed the Australian selectors that I was unavailable to tour overseas again, Simpson was one of a number of candidates in line to take over the captaincy. Others mentioned in the same breath were O'Neill, Booth and Shepherd, but the latter was handicapped by the fact that although he was a fine skipper and an excellent leader of men he was never quite certain of his place in the Australian side. One of the first requirements in Australia is that the captain should be able to hold his place against all comers and I can never recall any instance where an Australian captain has been played for his captaincy rather than his ability. Out there they believe that out of 11 of the best players in the country you must be able to find one who can captain the side.

It was obvious at the time that New South Wales would provide the lead for the captaincy for Victoria, who have provided a great number of excellent captains over the years, had Bill Lawry skippering at this stage and he was a relative newcomer to the Test side. It was far too early to consider him for the Australian captaincy though he was always my choice for the 1968 side to tour England. New South Wales provided the lead by appointing Simpson as vice-captain for the first match in Brisbane, thereby indicating to the Australian selectors that he would lead the side as soon as I stepped down.

I intended to retire from both the captaincy of New South Wales and the Australian side at an opportune moment during the season but I wanted to play the last year of my career on Australian soil and, if good enough, to continue playing for State and country until the conclusion of that season. As it turned out, I broke a finger in a grade match when trying to take a catch off Doug Walters's bowling, and therefore missed playing in the Second Test against South Africa. I had previously had a long talk with Sir Donald Bradman about the right time to step down and it was agreed that it would be left to me to judge the opportune moment in the light of what went on in the season.

The last thing I wanted to do was throw Simpson in to lead the side at a time when we had been weakened by the loss of Davidson, Harvey and Mackay, and I was hoping that a successful start to the season by both New South Wales and Australia would give me the chance to let him start off on a confident note. He started the season in auspicious style by making 359 against Queensland when we were facing a 613 total—an astonishing innings this, combining strokeplay with immense concentration, and it gave him a great start on the rest of the contenders for the captaincy.

Although I wasn't able to play in the Second Test in Melbourne I covered the match for my newspaper, and it was during this game, at a stage where it was obvious that Simpson was about to lead Australia to victory, that I told Sir Donald I thought this would be an ideal time for Simpson to take over. He proved to be a sound captain for Australia in a period where the selectors were forced to rebuild and to bring on young players as a result of the retirement of Harvey, Davidson, Grout, Mackay and myself. He gave a fine exhibition of captaincy in 1964 in beating England but then went down to both West Indies and South Africa in the 18 months following.

On the latter tour I found some aspects of his captaincy puzzling for it was here he began what seemed almost a fetish with his bowling attack, in that he seemed to have little faith in the use of spin and concentrated almost entirely on pace, particularly in the later Test matches. Sadly unused—or rather, hardly used at all—was Tom Veivers, and there was a striking difference in the amount of use of McKenzie and Renneberg compared to the spinners in the side. At the same time it is worth underlining the fact that there was only one really good bowler in the Australian side on this tour and any captain restricted in this way has a very tough job in front of him. Graham McKenzie took 24 wickets in the series and bowled his heart out in the face of the great demands made on him by his captain.

McKenzie is an outstanding bowler, a strapping six footer who, by the time 1970 has arrived, will, I believe, have passed Freddie Trueman's 307 wickets record for bowlers in all Test matches. At the moment of writing he has taken 187 wickets and is only 61 short of the record I hold. McKenzie first started playing for Western Australia in 1960 and was spotted by former West Indian captain, Sir Frank Worrell, as a promising youngster in the 1960–1 year. The story goes that, never having seen him in action, an Australian selector paid a special visit to Perth just before the 1961 Australian side was chosen—a profitable 4,000 mile trip for once having seen him the youngster was certain of inclusion in that side to tour England. Had he not made the trip and figured in two partnerships realising 102 runs at Lord's and that magnificent partnership of 98 with Davidson at Old Trafford our homegoing would have been much sadder.

In many ways he is an unpredictable bowler but there is no more beautiful action in the game and his great strength and ability to bowl within himself in a spell that also combines some really quick deliveries makes him a very difficult bowler to combat. He is the only genuinely good bowler of real pace in Australia at the moment, with the others all learning their trade, and if anything happens to him before the youngsters realise their promise then Lawry, or his successor, and Australian cricket in general, will be in a sorry state. But it is interesting that he only really got his chance by a selector making a round trip of 4,000 miles to watch him in Perth.

Thorough men our selectors, though in some things they can also be very hard—things like players' fitness for instance! On that score, they have to be hard to satisfy everyone or even get part of the way towards that ideal state. One of their problems comes in making certain that every player chosen for the Australian side is fully fit and quite often they have the task of giving a certain player a fitness test. I went through one of these after breaking a finger in the 1963–4 series against South Africa; this fitness test was before Dudley Seddon in Sydney, and I've seen one or two others like Alan Davidson put through their paces as though they were engaged in a Test match at that time. It can be an exhausting business, for the selectors are putting their reputation on the line by choosing a man who has been under something of a fitness cloud. Jack Ryder once had his suspicions about Len Maddocks and a finger injury after Maddocks had been chosen to play against England in 1955 in Australia. Jack hounded Maddocks everywhere, clapping him on the back and shaking hands with him, giving his injured finger a tremendous squeeze each time. Maddocks steeled himself and no flicker of expression gave away the fact that he was in great pain with each greeting.

Australian cricket is, in many ways, typical of the country itself, harsh and sometimes unyielding, and the cricketers who play the game in Australia delight in the prospect of challenge whether it is a match against England or the West Indies or a game in the park. Schoolboys playing their own matches will invariably be playing for victory rather than just for the exercise and this competitive streak carries right through to the national contests between Australia and other countries.

I have always been a great believer in the benefits of improvisation and, generally, I have found Australian cricketers to be good at this, with the exception of being able to improvise their batting to combat rain affected pitches. This latter disability is because, once reaching the first-class scene in Australia, a cricketer never sees a damp pitch and nowadays even grade pitches are being covered in Sydney and Melbourne in order that a start can be made in matches that would normally be delayed or even abandoned. Whether or not this is a good thing is open to argument but the theory in Australia is that the game should be played on the best possible surface so that batsmen can play their shots with confidence and bowlers have to work hard to dismiss their opponents.

My first knowledge of Test cricket was in 1936–7 when I sat, ear glued to the wireless, listening to Gubby Allen's side run to a two-nil lead over Bradman's Australian team, having twice caught the Australians on rain-affected pitches in Brisbane and Sydney. We talk now about the great series between West Indies and Australia in 1960–1 but what a series that 1936–7 one must have been. I have been back through the cuttings to learn that Allen's side was not particularly favoured by the critics but when Voce, Allen and Verity bowled their side to a two-nil lead few people could have imagined that Australia would win the series. It was during this rubber that the Melbourne Cricket Ground established their world record attendance figures that remained unbroken until the West Indies series in 1961.

Cricket was brought to Australia by the first settlers and then moulded by the Australians themselves to their own liking, and there have been many uneasy passages in cricket history in that country. The first overseas tour was by an aboriginal team led by Charles Lawrence in 1868, but this was more of an oddity than a serious tour and Australian cricket did not come of age until 1882 when Spofforth bowled out England in that famous Oval Test match. Teams from England visited Australia in 1861–2 and 1863–4 but so weak was Australian cricket at this stage that quite often 22 of the locals would be pitted against the England side.

An Association was formed in New South Wales in 1857 and the Victorian Cricket Association was formed in 1875, 18 years later.

The Australian Board of Control came into being in 1905 with the two great rivals, New South Wales and Victoria, being the first members, closely followed by Queensland and South Australia. Tasmania and Western Australia joined in 1907 and 1914 respectively, but the Northern Territory have, so far, not been considered as members. It wasn't the smoothest partnership on record, with disagreements over managers of teams and payments eventually forcing a break in 1912 when leading players Armstrong, Ransford, Trumper, Hill, Cotter and Carter declined to tour England. There have been other ructions over the years but now, so strong is the Board, that there is never any possibility of a real challenge to its authority, other than by constitutional means, and Australian cricket moves steadily along its chosen path with the only problem how to keep spectators interested enough to attend the matches.

The composition of the Board is 13 members with the voting strength three-thirteenths Victoria, New South Wales and South Australia, two-thirteenths Queensland and one-thirteenth Tasmania and Western Australia. Profits from tours are apportioned in this manner with New South Wales taking, say, $39,000 from, say, a tour profit of $100,000, whereas Western Australia would receive only $13,000 from the same tour. Recent Chairmen of the Board of Control have been R. J. Parish, E. G. McMillan, Sir Donald Bradman and W. J. Dowling, all of whom significantly come from the States providing the major representation—New South Wales, Victoria and South Australia—a system that keeps the top position alternating between only three States. I am never able to understand why Queensland, Western Australia and Tasmania should be debarred from having a Board of Control Chairman. I can't believe that no-one in those States is able to act suitably as a Chairman of the Board if he is considered good enough to be a member of the Board.

The Board's influence in Australian cricket has been great from the time the 1912 dispute ensured that authority rather than players should have control of cricket teams and, in general, it has done an excellent job for Australian cricket. It is a non-profit making body, in the sense that it represents the States and passes any profits immediately to them, but one of the big problems that exists in Australia is that few members of the Board have had any real contact with playing problems at first-class level.

AUSTRALIA

I once walked on a "pair" at Hove when I wasn't out and the only reason I publish the picture here is that it gives another slant on the contentious question of walking. It had always been drummed into me that as soon as an appeal is made I must look at the umpire and if he says "out" or "not out" I must obey that decision instantly and without any display of emotion. These were the lessons taught to a young cricketer and, consequently, when the business of "walking" came into vogue it proved a difficult assignment for me and many others who had been brought up under a different style of cricket. In the picture shown here Sobers has bowled to me at the Sydney Cricket Ground after I have made 60 runs and a ball just short of a length on leg stump has got up sharply, forcing me to play a hurried stroke at about rib height. Jarman has caught the ball, has heard a snick and has made a tentative appeal to the umpire—the only raised voice on the ground. For an instant I thought I had hit the ball and started to move to the pavilion, having, in recent times, forced myself to adopt the principles of walking. I was a couple of yards from the crease when I realised it had flicked my shirt—but—there is no going back once you have started to move.

Bradman (*right*) apparently wasn't much of a bowler though he used to take his turn at the nets—I presume more for relaxation than anything else. But he was a pretty useful batsman who brought excitement and colour to the game and made it a wonderful pleasure for spectators present at the various grounds. When I saw him in 1946 he looked a fine batsman, though this was towards the end of his career, but those who talk of him speak of the brilliance of his footwork and perhaps there is something of the secret shown in the picture (*left*). The bowler has just let go of the ball and his left foot, having landed around the batting crease, has come up on to the toe as the right foot prepares to hit the ground. The ball then won't be very far down the pitch but already Bradman is on his way and his bat is a long way off the ground. One of the best tips I have heard came from "The Don" on this very thing—that as the bowler brings his arm over it does no harm to have your bat on its way back just to get a little start for the stroke. But this next picture is perhaps the most ironic ever taken of this great batsman. He is on his way into the Oval in 1938 having broken his ankle when he slipped in the footmarks. England batted on—and on—and on—until word came that in fact his ankle was broken and there was no chance of him getting on the field. Could any batsman be paid a greater compliment?

A great double, Keith Miller *(top)* and Ray Lindwall, pictured here in their prime bowling at the Sydney Cricket Ground. Australia was very fortunate to have them play their cricket together immediately after the war when they developed into one of the finest pace bowling combinations ever to step on to a cricket field.

A line drawing by Russell Drysdale of a Sydney "Hill" barracker.

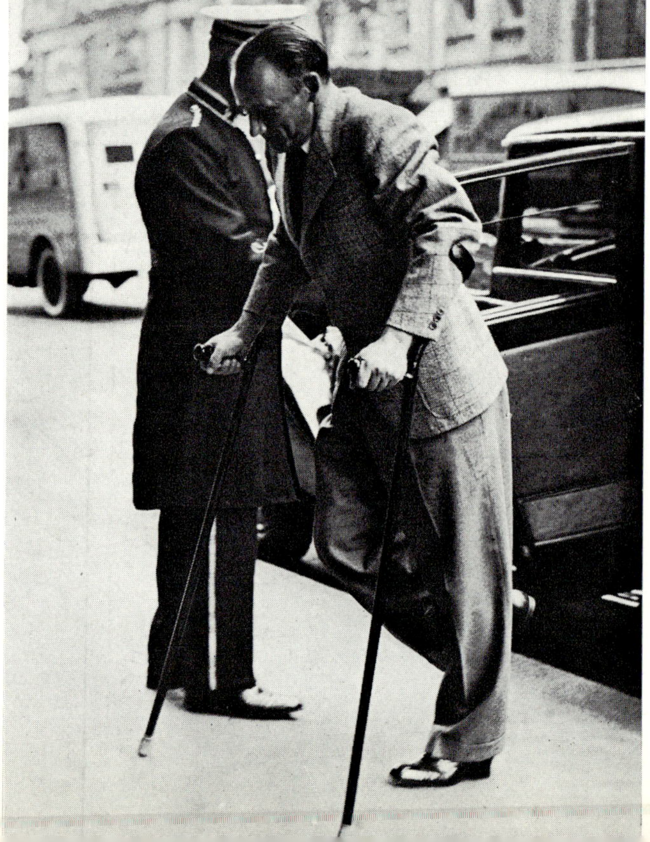

R.D.
"'Ave a go, yer mug!"

There is a set process for administrators becoming a member of the Board. They are, in a way, the same as Managing Directors of a big firm in that, in most cases, their promotion is made on the score of seniority rather than any particular attributes on the cricket field. In New South Wales, for instance, our cricket is split into a number of grades, beginning with country cricket and junior cricket, under the auspices of the N.S.W. Junior Cricket Union in Sydney. There are no delegates to the Cricket Association from individual country areas but there is a country committee within the Association itself. The N.S.W. Junior Cricket Union provides one delegate to the N.S.W.C.A. and the Newcastle District Cricket Association provides another. The 16 affiliated grade clubs within the Sydney metropolitan area each provide two delegates to form the general committee of the Association. From that general committee are appointed an executive committee and a grade committee and the Association itself appoints three members to the Interstate Cricket Conference and the Australian Board of Control.

If that might seem complicated on paper it works well in practice, but it is quite a different system from the one operated by M.C.C. in England where players and ex-players have a great deal to do with the administration of the game. In Australia at the moment only Sir Donald Bradman on the Board of Control is a former Test cricketer. Other members have played first-class cricket but it is an extremely difficult thing for any player or ex-player to become a force in cricket administration in Australia. This is because of the particular system whereby delegates to, say, the N.S.W.C.A. must come from grade clubs and, it follows, that players representing their State and Australia, and absent for long periods of time, find it impossible to represent their club satisfactorily on a committee of this kind.

I have long been a believer in the fact that there should be a committee of players and ex-players formed in each State to keep Australian cricket administrators in touch with what goes on in the middle in first-class cricket—players' thoughts on the game and possible changes in the structure of cricket that would be of benefit to the game. For instance, very few members of the Board of Control, or of State Associations, have seen cricket played in an overseas country although, where possible, a Board member is appointed as manager of a touring team. I believe that the game could be assisted in Australia by the mutual discussion of ideas between players, ex-players and administrators, for in these modern times it is important that every section of the game should be canvassed for up to date ideas.

Whilst the basis of Australian cricket is, and always will be, cricket of lesser standard than first-class, it is the Sheffield Shield competition that has continually stimulated the game over the years. Players who take part in that competition of necessity come from grade and junior cricket ranks and the small clubs in these spheres do a tremendous job for the game. But the formation in 1892–3 of the Sheffield Shield competition, sponsored by Lord Sheffield in the form of a farewell present to the Cricket Council, is the thing that has provided the sense of challenge for Australian domestic cricket.

Victoria were the first winners of the Shield and over the years it has been Victoria and New South Wales who have dominated the competition, New South Wales winning 36 times, Victoria 19 and South Australia 8. In the 40 years Queensland have participated they have not won the Shield and Western Australia won it the first year they entered, playing on a restricted basis. Tasmania and Western Australia have been the Cinderellas of Australian cricket, playing only occasional minor representative matches for many years, but Western Australia now has a very strong side and, having in recent years, several times been on the verge of winning the Shield without ever quite being able to win the vital match, at last emerged triumphant in 1967–8.

There is a vast difference between cricket in Australia and cricket in any other country, partly because of the size of the grounds, with a ground record of 93,000 being established in Melbourne and crowds approaching 60,000 having watched Test matches in Sydney. These vast seas of spectators—often noisy spectators—make cricket a completely different game from the comparative gentility of say, an English cricket scene, and different in fact from any other country where the game is played. In general, the Australian spectator is a barracker, and often a vociferous one at that. To go to a cricket match and remain still and quiet during the day would seem a waste of time to most Australians who work on the basis that they have paid their admission money to see their heroes, or, in many cases, the selectors' choices with whom they do not fully agree.

The two grounds with, to my mind, the greatest character in Australia are Sydney and Adelaide, though neither holds the same number of spectators as can Melbourne. But to play before a capacity house in Sydney is to play before the most exciting and appreciative cricket crowd in the world on a ground that, if the pitch is true and fast, cannot be bettered in any country. To play in Melbourne is an experience akin to performing in the Coliseum for it is a huge arena where the spectators tower seemingly miles from the players, and this can be, at times, a terrifying experience for a player young to the game. Adelaide is a beautiful ground with the Cathedral and the hills in the background and trees all round, and a capacity of something like 45,000 spectators.

I first saw the Sydney Cricket Ground on a Saturday in 1940 when there were 30,400 spectators present to see Bradman and O'Reilly in battle. In all nearly 76,000 people saw that game but I only saw the one day; my father was not playing cricket on the Saturday. I then saw some wartime matches but it wasn't until 1946–7 that I saw a Test match between England and Australia. My great hope in this game was to see Lindwall in action but he had to cry off because of illness, and it was Miller and Freer who opened the bowling for Australia. Ian Johnson did the damage in this match, which was comfortably won by Australia, and I saw the Fifth Test match of the same series where Wright bowled so well to Bradman on the last day of the match.

I didn't see a great deal of cricket from then until 1949 when I first played first-class cricket, for I was almost continually engaged in playing club matches, or some form of organised cricket, when the big games were on. From 1949 onwards my one ambition was to play for Australia and, if possible, to play on the Sydney Cricket Ground. When it came about it was the most wonderful thing that had ever happened to me in the game, walking out into the centre wearing a green cap and playing before a crowd stretching from the tip of the Hill to the back of the Members' Stand.

The crowd on the Hill is a cosmopolitan sea of faces and bare torsos when the weather permits—a babble of sound, punctuated with shouts of advice, and a blanket of silence the instant each ball is delivered.

The start of a Test match at the Sydney Cricket Ground is the most wonderful experience imaginable for a player—the umpires have been welcomed, the field set and the bowler at his run up mark. A sudden hush comes over the 50,000 spectators, a hush that must be as close as possible to the one in the famous poem where there was "a breathless hush in the close tonight", and then the ground breathes out as the first ball is delivered or explodes into sound if it happens that the batsman has scored from it.

If I had to single out any one moment in my cricket career as being the saddest, it would perhaps naturally be the day I last walked off a Test match field at the S.C.G. The most enjoyable and exciting was to lead Australia on to the field on the same ground where I had played most of my cricket in a Test match against England. This was the first time I had captained an Australian team on this great ground and words cannot convey the heart-throbbing excitement of stepping into the sunshine out of the old Members' Stand and looking at the sea of faces in front of me. As far as Test matches go, it was not difficult to have this as my most enjoyable S.C.G. day up to that time, for other matches had produced little of any real consequence as a player. Test matches against the West Indies, South Africa and England in 1954–5 had produced few wickets, few runs and a hit in the mouth that saw me taken to hospital after an attempt to take a catch in the gully.

This was the start of a five year span of captaining Australia but it was a span that encompassed only moderate success in Sydney. The Third Test of the 1958–9 series was drawn, Australia lost the Third Test of the 1960–1 series against the West Indies, and won the Third Test played in 1962–3 against England, only to see the last one drawn.

The 1958–9 M.C.C. side came to Australia with a blazing reputation that was not quite carried on to the field. Before the team left English shores it was written that it was probably the finest combination ever to tour Australia and yet Australia, by the time the Adelaide Test was concluded, had regained the Ashes. With a bowling attack of Trueman, Statham, Tyson, Loader and Bailey, together with Laker and Lock, there seemed no doubt when the tour started that M.C.C. had only to make runs to be assured of success in the series. But their run getters let them down and the bowlers in the end were not quite equal to the occasion as they were in 1954–5 when England held the Ashes. England skipper Peter May was criticised during the series for his captaincy and yet he did all the same things that had previously won matches for his country.

One of the biggest problems facing England on this tour was their rate of scoring and in the First Test in Brisbane they got off to a bad start by batting first on an extremely grassy surface. I think I can safely put that match down as one of the worst I have ever played in, with an absolute minimum of runs made by batsmen of both sides in conditions that were far from ideal for bowling. Trevor Bailey batted for what seemed like days, failing to score off 388 of the 428 balls he received, and in one session only 19 runs were scored. The real feature of this series was the superb catching that assisted Australia as much to regain the Ashes as it had done England to hold them in 1956 when close to the wicket catching made such a tremendous difference to Laker and Lock.

It was the Sydney Cricket Ground that provided my first real problems in captaincy, in the middle of a series that had seen less positive cricket than most others in which I had played. We had a first innings lead of 138 on a pitch taking an increasing amount of spin and, with May and Cowdrey in full flight and the chance of being caught on a real "turner", I decided if possible to close up the game. There were some who immediately assumed that word had come from higher up in the persons of the selectors, that a two-nil lead in the series should not be squandered by any Australian generosity. But I am afraid the decision was my own to bowl Davidson and Mackay for long periods with five men on the on side, using off spinner Slater, with his low trajectory, as a change bowler. I thought Davidson bowled very well that afternoon and he certainly bowled to instructions, keeping the ball straight in line with the middle and leg stumps at reduced pace, in much the same way as he had seen many English bowlers do over the years.

It was not a game I can look back on with a great deal of pleasure, nor was the one in 1962–3 when the scoring rate of both sides was not a great deal faster than that iniquitous Brisbane game of 1958. Overall in that 1958 series, there was not a great deal of difference in the scoring rate of both sides, Australia scoring five runs per hundred balls quicker than the opposition, and only once in the series was 100 runs scored in the session—and the spectators had to wait until the Fifth Test for that.

I found captaining Australia a fascinating business from the time I was announced as skipper for the First Test of that series, though before this I had little experience of captaincy in the higher realms of cricket. It has often been said that I was a lively captain, or a go-ahead captain, and it has often been written that I was an attacking captain. But, above all, I wanted to be a winning captain and everything I did on the field was aimed at that desirable state. That, I believe, is the way to play cricket and if the sense of providing a spectacle overrides the desire to win then the game really becomes only an exhibition. Win first and provide the spectacle second—even though it runs a very close second—should be the aim of all captains. There are though many things that can be done to provide good cricket, as distinct from exhibition cricket, and it is the captain, with the assistance of his players, who should plan that way.

In 1958 I have already related how the captaincy came my way but it was most necessary then, and in every match until the end of my career, to have the team playing for me. There again, success is the yardstick for what players are interested in following a captain who is an incessant loser, albeit a good one? A losing team is always changed at some stage by the selectors and the players justifiably, in addition to blaming themselves, can also blame the captain for his tactics that lost the game.

The night before the First Test match in 1958 the Australian side had a team meeting at which I expounded my policies on captaincy, which were very brief and, I hoped, to the point, that I wanted to regain the Ashes that had been lost in 1953, 1954–5 and 1956 and that I thought our best chance of winning was to attack at all times until we got into a dangerous position, and only then to fall back on defence. Hence the falling back on defence in the Third Test in Sydney and hence the almost incessant attack for the remainder of the five matches. As many men as possible in catching positions and get through the overs quickly were the two main instructions, and an extra one was added that everyone should pick up as many singles as possible against what I believed would be a tight, restricting attack. It was an extremely restricting attack but it was a bowlers' series where England, with the exception of May and Cowdrey who batted well throughout and Graveney in Adelaide, had to go through the rubber without making 300 in an innings. The same system was used in 1961 where the rubber was decided in the Manchester Test after Harvey had led Australia to victory at Lord's.

I went back to the Sydney Cricket Ground just before coming to England in 1967—a nostalgic visit when the ground was empty. The centre had been levelled and the grass had grown again, and it was the most beautiful sight imaginable. I wandered around the old Members' bar where Harold Larwood sometimes stands watching the modern day players cavort in the centre and I wandered around to the Sheridan Stand where I had sat on a stairway in 1940 because there are not enough seats for a ten-year-old boy. Even empty it is a beautiful ground, conveying at a glance to one who has played there, all the feelings of a cricket match and the nostalgia that goes with retirement.

One of the prettiest grounds in the cricket world is the Adelaide Oval, particularly when viewed from the Members' section or the Players' Dressing Rooms, where there is the sight of green trees allied to the Cathedral and the Mount Lofty's.

I played three Test series against England on this famous ground and two of the matches turned out to be the deciding Tests of the 1954–5 rubber and then again in the series against Peter May's side in 1958–9. Australia has a good record against England on this particular ground, having won ten out of the 18 matches played with two drawn, and no game has given me more pleasure than the one in 1958 to regain the Ashes that had been lost in 1953. The series against Hutton's side four years before had provided results in the first four of the five Tests, and only rain saved Australia from defeat in the Fifth after Graveney had played a magnificent innings on the fourth day of the match.

In this series Hutton superbly harnessed his fast bowling attack, leaving out Bedser and concentrating on Tyson and Statham, then at the height of their powers, together with the admirable medium pace of Bailey. It was the more remarkable that this series should be decided in the Fourth Test for Australia had won the first conclusively by an innings and 154 runs and then England had just scraped in in the Second on a fiery pitch in Sydney. But a resounding victory in the Third Test in Melbourne and an equally good one in Adelaide kept the Ashes in England where they stayed for the next four years.

But no matter what games are mentioned in connection with Adelaide Oval there can never have been a more exciting one than the Fourth Test match between West Indies and Australia in 1961. West Indies had won the toss and made 393, including a glorious century from Kanhai, and Australia had replied by getting within 27 of that total. The West Indies second innings of 432 for six declared, with Kanhai again making a century, set Australia a task that had never before been achieved in the fourth innings of a Test on this ground. With an hour to play and nine wickets down any reputable bookmaking firm should have been prepared to offer 10,000–1 about the game being saved.

The match had followed the pattern set by the earlier games, with good strokeplay and effervescent bowling and fielding drawing hundreds of thousands of people to the matches and causing an upsurge in cricket interest throughout the country. The excitement of the tied Test will never die out, and if the next two matches in Melbourne and Sydney had produced more clearcut victories for both sides, the Fourth Test in Adelaide had still promised a great deal for it was very nearly the deciding match of the series. Davidson, who took 33 wickets in the four games he played, was not available for this Adelaide Test and Hoare had taken his place to open the attack with Misson. By the time the last day came, with Gibbs having taken a hat-trick in the first innings and Hall ripping through the early batsmen on the fourth evening, I had gone in as nightwatchman and remained not out with O'Neill at the other end.

The next morning was one of the most fiery episodes I had ever gone through, with Hall bowling at express speed and, for a lot of the time, well short of a length. It was Sobers though who dismissed me and when O'Neill fell not long after in mid-afternoon, there seemed little chance of saving the game. Hoare, Misson and Grout went quickly and by the time I was out of my creams and ready to shower Kline was walking down from the players' balcony to go out and join Mackay.

Kline wasn't the greatest left-hand batsman Australia has ever produced but he was keen and had a sound defence. In order to get a sight of the ball, he had just been to the nets at the back of the ground to have some practice against Johnny Martin, the left-hand spinner, so that he could simulate batting against Sobers. So many times was he beaten and dismissed by Martin in the nets that eventually he came upstairs again, hoping that he would not be needed, and now, as he passed me, he said "What would you like?" I said "I'd like you to be there at six o'clock" and continued on into the shower without the slightest hope that the optimistic suggestion would be carried out. By the time I had showered and dressed it was ten past five and I sat down quietly at the back of the players' balcony to watch the last rites being enacted.

Things obviously weren't good at this moment and there was no doubt that in a few minutes the crowd would be converging on the players on the ground. The victorious West Indies would then be leading two-one in the series with only the one match to play and they would be very difficult indeed to peg back from this position. Still, we would have Davidson back for the Fifth Test and that would immeasurably strengthen our bowling attack which, although hard trying in the present game in Adelaide, had obviously missed the thrust of the great left-hander.

O'Neill had made a lot of runs during the series and, in general, our batting had stood up quite well to the battering from Hall and the crafty, medium pace and spin of Sobers and Gibbs. What was really needed in Melbourne in the Fifth Test match was to attack, for it was quite obvious that the only way to beat the West Indians was to attack more than they did—all these things were going through my mind as Mackay and Kline quietly played out the next ten minutes. But it was a pity that we hadn't been able to do better in this Adelaide match—even a draw would have been most acceptable. At any rate, looking at it philosophically, we had been beaten in this game by a better side that had led us on the first innings, though only just, and then had taken our bowling attack to pieces with the glorious strokeplay of Kanhai, Alexander and Worrell. No use crying over the proverbial spilt milk but better to look ahead and hope for better things in the final Test.

Mackay and Kline were still pushing stolidly down the line and the West Indians were still moving quickly between their overs, eager to get it done with and get back to a celebration beer in the dressing room next to ours. Alongside me Wally Grout said "They don't look like getting out, do they?", and all he got from the rest of the players was a long, hard look. But, in fact, Mackay and Kline didn't look like getting out though, of course, one of them would before very long, for against them in the centre were Hall, Worrell, Valentine, Sobers and Gibbs, all fine bowlers, and if they were finding Mackay a tough nut to crack then they had only to have a go at Kline and the game would soon be over. But Kline, despite his agonising experience in the nets an hour before, was still playing very straight, the blade of the bat well behind the handle, and keeping the ball out of the reach of the clutching fieldsmen. Suddenly someone said "It'd be funny if they managed to stay there" and, ridiculous though it seemed, from that moment on we counted the minutes.

The Adelaide clock moves faster in the 30 minutes from hour to half hour than it does on the upward swing, and suddenly the clock seemed to take over in the West Indians' minds as being just as important as the batsmen in the centre. They began to hurry even more between overs and then more and more between deliveries, working on the basis that the more deliveries they got in the more chance they had of getting one of these wickets. There was now a hush in the players' section as the tremendous possibilities became apparent but there was still half an hour to go. Worrell bowled to Mackay and then to Kline, but he and Valentine and Gibbs got little past either batsman and the hands of the clock still kept moving slowly upwards.

In the end it was real panic that had the West Indians scurrying everywhere, in contrasting style to their relative calm that had prevailed in the tied Test, and when Kline played out the second last over it left Mackay to face Hall for the final over of the match. There could not have been a better man to play out a maiden over, nor a more characteristic manner of playing the last delivery. Mackay said later he reasoned that it would be a bumper but probably one at which he would have to play, and he reasoned also that the best way to play it was to let it hit him, keeping his bat close to the ground in case the ball happened to keep low. The fieldsmen were still crouching around him when the ball struck him on the body and fell to the ground to bring about one of the most astonishing drawn matches in cricket history.

I will always remember this match above all when I think about Adelaide Oval, in the same way as I will think of the tied Test match against the same side whenever Brisbane is mentioned but there could hardly be two more contrasting cricket grounds than Adelaide and Brisbane. The one gloriously situated with a magnificent view—the other set in what can be depressing surroundings, with sprawling stands for the spectators and less atmosphere than any of the big grounds throughout the rest of Australia.

There were only 4,000 people who saw the tie on the last day of the First Test in 1960, hundreds of thousands of others saw it on television and millions heard it on the radio throughout the country. It was a great cricket match all the way through, producing one of the best innings ever played, when Gary Sobers made 132 on the first day in the West Indies 453 total, and then O'Neill making a brilliant 181 as part of his record aggregate in a series against the West Indies. Set 233 to win on the last day, I firmly believed that we had an easy task and would go to Melbourne for the Second Test one up. But Wes Hall wrecked the early part of our batting and, with six for 92 before tea, it looked as though the reverse could easily apply and we might well be one down when we flew out of Brisbane.

Mackay and Davidson added some stability to the innings and then Davidson and I shared in a valuable partnership that took us within striking distance of the runs needed. At the start of this series we had determined to play good, positive cricket, knowing that we would be met half way by the opposition, and when Sir Donald Bradman asked me at tea on that last day what the plans were for the afternoon I was able to tell him that we were going for a win, with a draw only as a last resort.

The events of that last hour have been well chronicled by some who were there, and some who weren't, but it was certainly the most exciting 30 minutes I have ever gone through on a cricket field. Davidson was thrown out by Solomon and I was out off the second ball of the final over, with Hunte saving a third run shortly after and throwing out Grout from deep square leg. Kline, who was later to figure in the Adelaide Test, had Meckiff as his partner when he pushed a single—or what he thought was a single—wide of Solomon at forward square leg from the second last ball of the match. The picture showing Solomon's throw hitting the stumps tells its own story—the story of a match that was not only a tie in the record books but a remarkably even and exciting contest, and one that was to set the stage for a wonderful series between the two sides.

In my mind that was the finest cricket series I have ever seen and certainly the finest that has ever been played in Australia, both from the participating point of view and the entertainment provided for the spectators. It has not always been like that in Australian cricket, nor will it be in the future, for a cricket series such as that is, in many ways, a fluke. England in 1962–3 and in 1965–6 played some fine cricket, as did South Africa in 1963–4, but each of those three series was drawn one all with three drawn matches, and there is nothing the cricket public in Australia likes less than drawn series after the excitement they witnessed in 1960–1.

Cricket in Australia at the moment is going through a transition period, with many young players on the way up striving to take the place of the established Test players who have retired only a few years ago. Simpson took the Australian side to England in 1964 to win the series one-nil, with four drawn matches, but, that series apart, nothing conclusive has come from Australian cricket in the past three or four years. This is only a passing phase and I believe that by the time Australia plays England in 1968 both teams will have established themselves back at the top of the international table. Certainly England got there early in that year when they beat the West Indies by Sobers' declaration in the Trinidad Test and the side Australia took to England was so chock full of youth and potential brilliance that I can't see anything but a great team coming from it in the near future. There are plenty of good, young cricketers on the way up in Australia, despite the fact that for the first time Test series were lost against South Africa and New Zealand, but it is a question of how quickly the young cricketers can establish themselves and gain permanent places in the Australian Test side.

There was much promise shown by young players in South Africa and it was evident when the New Zealand and South African touring team representatives played one another in Melbourne for the Tasmanian Bush Fire Fund in April 1967, that there were a number of youngsters who would be making their presence felt within 12 months. One of the best of these is Doug Walters who, following his astonishing debut against England in 1965, did two years' National Service, coming out of the Army only days before the 1968 England tour was due to begin. He is the best young cricketer I have seen since Neil Harvey burst on to the scene in the Bradman era, and it was my view before the 1968 season in England that he would thrill English audiences in the same way as he had Australia. That he did not do so in no way diminishes my admiration for him.

Unfortunately O'Neill has retired but I rate Walters as just as exciting a player as O'Neill, and probably with more solidity about his batting. He is, too, a brilliant field and a more than useful medium pace bowler. No other country but Australia had seen him in action for he was not chosen to go to the West Indies and was unavailable for South Africa before 1968. I am sure he will be back in England in 1972, taking advantage of all the lessons he learnt on his first trip.

One other I believe would have been very useful in England with the ball is Graeme Watson who eventually finished up playing Lancashire League in the same season the Australians were in England. I thought he bowled particularly well in South Africa, without ever being given a great deal of work, and in the Combined match between the two teams in Melbourne at the end of that tour he showed that he had come on a lot as a result of the tour. Watson had some flaws in batting technique that may have debarred him from making many runs in England but his bowling would have been handy. In the end five seam bowlers were taken on the tour and, with Walters there to make up the sixth, there was scarcely room for the young Victorian.

These are only two of the promising youngsters on the way up but, although Australian cricket at the time of writing is, on paper, less strong than in the past, I am a firm believer in the resiliency shown by our cricket in times such as these. The point is often made that there is a lot wrong with cricket in England, and in Australia it has been said in recent years that the game has slipped.

The game though in Australia is, as everywhere else, in the hands of the players and I am confident that the harsh, and at times brash, style of cricket played out there will again come to the top. For this to happen great co-operation is needed between players, captains and administrators, and again I make a plea for a closer liaison between these groups. Over the years I have been in close touch with administrators, by virtue of my position as captain, but not all players are so fortunate and it would do Australian cricket a great deal of good if all sections of the game were able to get together and work harder for its future.

3

West Indies

Take one of sweet, two of sour, mix the required ingredients with a dash of spice and you have one form of West Indian punch that is such a popular drink in the Caribbean. There are as many varieties of this recipe as there are varieties of cricket in that area and today they stand collectively as the most exciting players in the world—a tag that they held for many years without ever attaining the required consistency to go with it. It wasn't until they were taken over by Sir Frank Worrell that the West Indies began to play as a cricket team and the wayward genius that was with so many of their players came to fruition.

Cricket is one of the main exports of the West Indian islands, a scattered chain in the Mexican Gulf, and it is the export by which they have become best known since the turn of the century. Ever since I first saw them play, their cricket has been fiery and, for the most part, inconsistent, though from 1960 onwards this inconsistency changed to a superb blending of strokeplay, lightning fast bowling and determination.

I played my first Test match in Sydney against the 1952 side but unfortunately only played against them on two other occasions, in 1955 and 1960–1. I saw quite a bit of the 1951–2 series and gained a good insight into their methods of playing cricket at that time when they were under the captaincy of John Goddard, an enthusiastic leader who also skippered Barbados in the West Indies. In the first State match against the tourists in 1951 New South Wales were 96 for seven when I went in to join a youngster named Ray Flockton who, at that stage, was reckoned to be one of the finest young players on the threshold of a Test career. Prior Jones and Gerry Gomez, with Alf Valentine as a second string, had done the damage and then Flockton and I added a hundred in 43 minutes to take the total in the end past the 200 mark. There wasn't one sour look from the West Indian players, who needed a victory at this stage—instead it was all congratulations on the strokeplay that had been produced to better an awkward situation.

They had just arrived in Australia after a wonderful tour of England in 1950 where Ramadhin and Valentine had bowled their country to victory in three Test matches out of four. Weekes, Worrell and Walcott on that tour became the Three W's and in full flight they were almost impossible to bowl at. When English pitches recovered in that year from an exceedingly wet May, the West Indian batsmen came into their own and it was quite obvious that England would have to produce a strong bowling attack if they wished to bowl them out twice in the one Test.

In addition, Ramadhin and Valentine had established themselves by the time the First Test arrived as a fine spin pair; Valentine the orthodox performer, using his wrist spin as well as finger spin that ripped the callous from the index finger of his left hand. Ramadhin, with an action that ended in a flurry of arm and shirt-sleeve, often appeared to be bowling leg spinners and the ball would spin from the off—then his real leg spinner would have the batsmen groping ineffectually down the pitch. The promise shown by this side was not realised in the First Test at Old Trafford, where England won by 202 runs, but then the West Indies stormed through the next three, winning them by 326 runs, ten wickets and an innings and 56 runs—which is just about as conclusive a way to win a series as one could wish to see.

It was with this sort of record behind them that a West Indies tour of Australia was hurriedly organised so that they were able to arrive in Sydney to take advantage of a blank season in 1951–2. The tour, in fact, was poorly organised, the West Indians beginning their matches in New South Wales and not being given as much time as other touring sides to accustom themselves to Australian conditions. They had very much the same balance in the team for that tour, with Williams, Trestrail, Pierre and Johnson being left out and Ferguson, Atkinson and Trim included, but the essential balance of the side was much the same as the one that had thrashed England.

Looking back on it, it is almost impossible to understand why they did not do better even though Australian cricket was of a very high standard at that time. The essential brilliance was there in the batting, Ramadhin and Valentine knew what it was to bowl on rock hard pitches, and they had, in Gomez, one of the best all-rounders to play Test cricket for any country. The real secret I suppose was that, great batsmen as they were, they were not at

WEST INDIES

It used to be the Three W's but now there is a new breed of West Indian cricketer exciting crowds throughout the world. What could be better to watch, for instance, than Kanhai executing a sweep shot from the middle of his back or, if you like your cricket in more orthodox fashion, Butcher square cutting with delightful artistry. On the bowling side nothing could be more perfect than the action shot of Wes Hall, left arm well up and eyes looking over the left shoulder, left side to the batsman, in a pose that could be used for ever as a model for young cricketers. Lance Gibbs is the best spinner in the world at the moment and has been a force in West Indian cricket since the day he took over from Ramadhin during the 1960/61 West Indies tour of Australia.

Weekes (*left*), Walcott (*centre*), and Worrell (*right*) made a great impact on world cricket and when they visited England in 1950 each one took full toll of both county attacks and the England side when it was in the field.

But more than anything else on that tour West Indian success evolved around Ramadhin and Valentine who so often came to John Goddard's rescue when the team was in trouble.

It was Frank Worrell who provided the catalyst so badly needed by West Indies individual cricketers—he welded them into a team and led them into their greatest era. There is no doubt in my mind that he is the most important cricketer ever to play the game in the Caribbean, as well as one of the finest men ever to grace the game. He is pictured here with Australia's former Prime Minister, at a time when it was Mr. Worrell and Mr. Menzies, during the 1960/61 tour. Later both were knighted and Frank passed away in March 1967.

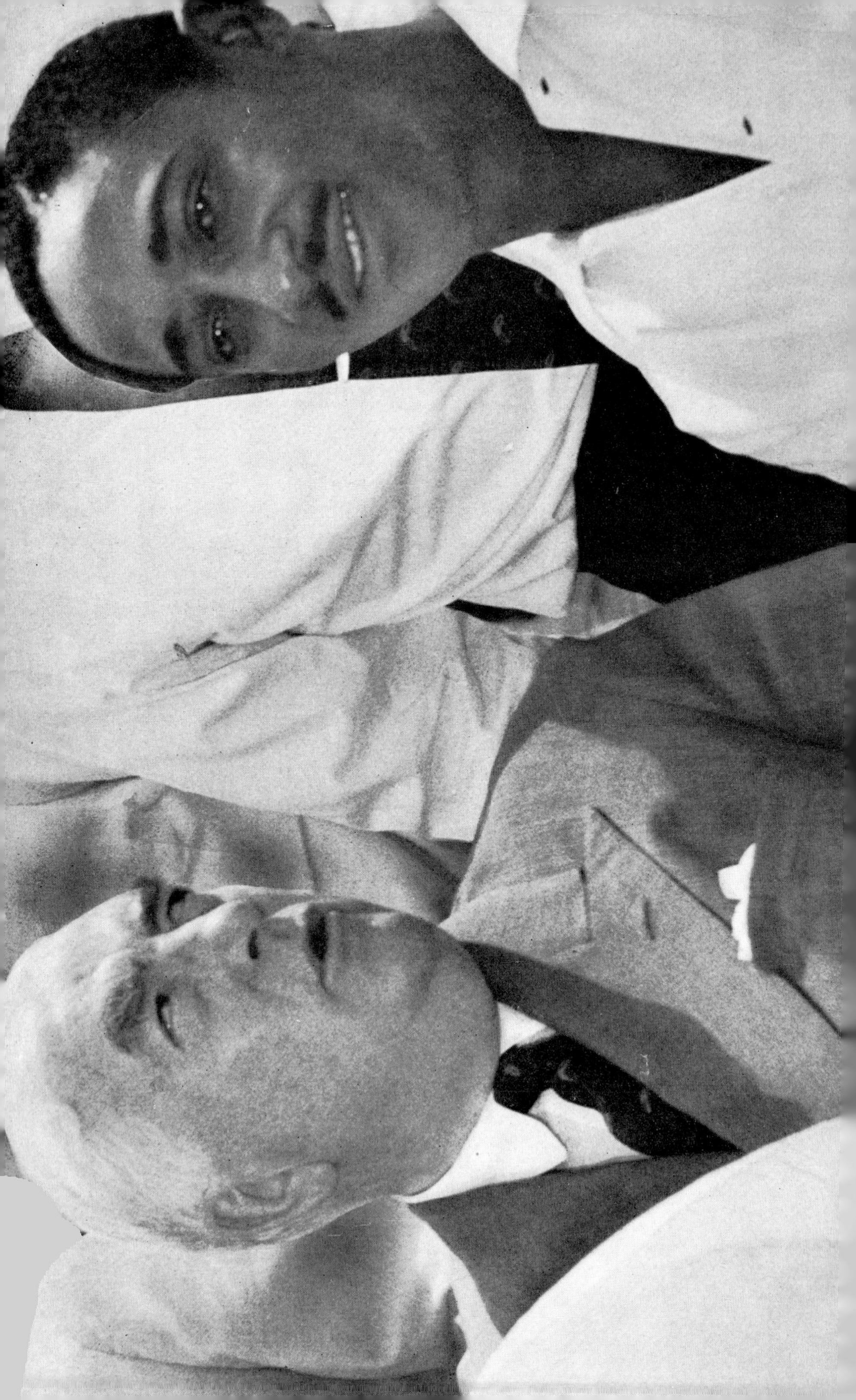

their best against really good fast bowling and, for that matter, I don't know anyone who is.

The West Indies could have won the First Test in Brisbane, going down by only three wickets in a tight game where very few of the Australians were able to make anything of Ramadhin and found that only very quick footwork could help them against him. This was an extremely low scoring match, 245 by the West Indies in their second innings being the best total in the five days, and Australia had many uneasy moments before hitting off the winning runs at the end of the match. In the Test series Lindwall took 21 wickets and Miller 20, and their figures were not a great deal better than the opposition bowlers, but they had that wonderful ability to rip through the early batsmen and produce something extra when any of the Three W's came to the crease. In the end the thing that carried Australia to victory was the decision of the Australian batsmen to attack Ramadhin not just occasionally but all the time.

The West Indies were two Test matches down by the time the Third Test in Adelaide came along, and they won this on an uneven pitch by six wickets to give themselves a chance in the series. They should then have won the fourth game in Melbourne but temperament played its part here and when Ring and Bill Johnston, in their own individual styles, took control of the match in its dying minutes the West Indians seemed to go to pieces. This was in extreme contrast to the way their temperament reacted to the excitement of the tied Test in Brisbane in 1960–1 and it seems to me that ten years before they were something akin to teenagers in life and only came of age in that later series.

Although, on paper, they lost the 1951–2 series by four Tests to one, it was only the Fifth Test, and a 202 run victory after the rubber was decided, that gave Australia an obvious edge on their opponents. Even then it was clear that, with more determination and firmness, in years to come the West Indies were going to be a real force in world cricket and not just a variable, exciting side.

That this was done was due entirely to the late Sir Frank Worrell who, having been one of the great names of West Indies cricket for many years, was given the captaincy over Gerry Alexander who remained in the side but stepped down from the leadership. M.C.C. had just beaten the West Indies in 1959–60, despite some very fast bowling from Hall and Watson, together with a third player, Stayers, who, in the island matches, gave England's batsmen plenty of practice at playing the ball short of a length. No one could have imagined then when Worrell's side arrived in Australia that they were likely to be any better or any different from other West Indian teams of the past—at all times brilliant but never completely reliable.

Worrell proved himself a remarkable man on this tour when, at 36 years of age and captaining the team for the first time, he moulded them into a tight-knit, competent group destined to provide, with Australia, some of the most exciting results in the history of cricket. Worrell was the graceful player of the Three W's, a cultured strokemaker never appearing to possess the damaging intent of Weekes and Walcott but, at the same time, scoring just as quickly and always in a manner likely to evoke memories of the great stylists of the past.

Walcott, on the other hand, was a massive striker of the ball and Weekes a tremendous cutter and hooker, whom I thought to be the best of the three until a wasted leg muscle destroyed his footwork. Neither Weekes nor Walcott came to Australia in 1960 but there were two players new to Australian cricket, Sobers and Kanhai, to take their place. Sobers these days is classed as the greatest all-rounder the world has seen and there are few better batsmen in the world than Kanhai when he is in form. But, more than anything else, West Indian cricket will be remembered for the Three W's and their contribution to the game—a contribution always appreciated by spectators, even if not by opposing bowlers.

There was never any doubt that Worrell would be a good captain for his players looked up to him and he, in turn, made it quite obvious that he would do anything for them. Life had not always been as good as this though for Frank and he had at one stage of his West Indian career left Barbados to live in Jamaica. He never lost his love for his native island though and had, in fact, in later life intended to settle back there when suddenly he was struck down in 1967 by his tragic and fatal illness.

I saw the very best of Weekes and Walcott in the West Indies in 1955—despite Weekes' bad leg muscle—and although Worrell didn't make a great number of runs he was always wonderful to watch. The other pair absolutely murdered the Australian attack on many occasions and I particularly remember the Trinidad Test match of that year where both scored centuries and turned on some of the most blazing batting I have ever seen.

Walcott, in fact, had an astonishing series, scoring 827 runs in the five Test matches—well ahead of Neil Harvey's 650—but Harvey had fewer chances, batting only seven times for his runs whereas Walcott had ten innings. I have never seen a more powerful batsman than Walcott, who started his career as a batsman-wicket-keeper, and when he was "going" it was almost impossible to bowl a length to him. He was a good 6ft. 2ins. in height and broadly built, and the most powerful striker off the back foot in my memory.

In Australia in 1951–2 the grassy pitches seemed to find him out and he was often caught behind or caught at slip trying to force the ball off the back foot through the covers. On West Indies pitches though, where there was less movement, it was quite a task to try and stop him scoring off any delivery for he had no real weakness, particularly against slow bowling. Anything a little short was smashed in the arc between cover and mid wicket and his long reach allowed him to destroy the length of almost any bowler. Most batsmen reach a peak at some stage and Walcott's was probably in the period from 1952 to 1956 where he slaughtered bowling attacks from both England and Australia. He was an individual player, of a style I have never seen before or since, with a pronounced flurry in his backlift that sometimes took the bat forward in a semi-circle through mid off before bringing it down with a full face to meet the ball.

Weekes, on the other hand, was completely orthodox in his basic technique, though often quite unorthodox in his execution. He was a magnificent hooker and cutter and a glorious driver, said by many Australians who saw him in action to be the closest in style to the pre-war Bradman, whose batting turned the thoughts of so many bowlers to other more pleasurable tasks.

Very few cricket countries have been fortunate enough in any era to have a trio of the calibre of Weekes, Worrell and Walcott and when they came to Australia in 1951 the crowds poured into the grounds to watch them. Weekes' 70 in the First Test match of the series was described to me later by Ray Lindwall as one of the greatest innings he had ever seen where a batsman did not make a century, and he compared it later with Dexter's 76 at Old Trafford in 1961. The latter's 70 at Lord's against the West Indies in 1963 was also, I suppose, a similar type of innings and it was always a fearsome and challenging task for bowlers pitted against players of the ability of these West Indian stars.

In Trinidad in 1955, on a beautiful batting pitch, where one's reflection shone back at a bowler careless enough to look down, I fielded at gully for Weekes and Walcott in the West Indies second innings. I have never seen cutting like it! They started on Miller and Lindwall before tea and when they took the new ball after tea the West Indian pair absolutely massacred them. There wasn't a great deal of bounce in the pitch and because of this I had to field closer than normal at gully and after tea that day was the only time in my life I have ever fielded kitted as though for batting with an abdominal protector. Australia had high hopes of winning that match, having declared at 600 for nine in reply to the West Indies' 382, but such was the devastating batting produced by Weekes and Walcott that they had 273 for four on the board when the game was concluded.

One of the most pleasant things I have ever done was to go on a tour to New Zealand and the Far East with Everton Weekes—a most rewarding experience. He has a tremendous knowledge of cricket and, apart from being one of the greats of all time on the field, is a wonderful ambassador for his country and one of the finest of team mates. "Father" Weekes we called him and I should imagine that his sage advice and pleasantly helpful manner are invaluable assets to Barbados cricket, where at the moment he reigns as coach. It always surprised me that he never captained West Indies, though I suppose if he had stayed in the game then the honour would certainly have come his way, such is his popularity in his own country.

Frank Worrell was knighted in 1964 for his services to cricket—a far-reaching nomination but one that was very well deserved. He was only 42 years of age when he passed away in 1967, a terrible loss not only to his family and country but, as well, to the game he graced. I remember him best for his work in the 1960–1 series in Australia where it was his influence that inspired the side to play as a team and not as the brilliantly erratic group of individuals that had toured our country nine years earlier. When he retired from the game Frank was the only one of the W's to average less than 50 in Tests, and that was only by ·52 per innings, and he was the only one not to have scored ten Test match centuries. But I think it indicative of his batting, and his attitude to the game, that he made many more half centuries than did the others and there never seemed in his graceful approach to the game the same urgency or certainty of making three figures.

I went out for my newspaper to interview him at the airport in 1960 when he arrived in Sydney on his way through to Perth and he said he hoped that we had an enjoyable season. When he left four months later he had contributed much of the enjoyment himself by leading his men in such a way that, although they lost the series, they received a tumultuous farewell from a quarter of a million people in Melbourne streets.

There were others alive to the chance of an enjoyable and challenging Test series that year and I had already had a meeting with Sir Donald Bradman, in the course of which we had agreed that this could be one of the great years of all time. So keen was Sir Donald on the prospects that he made a point of asking if he could sit in on the team meeting the Australian side always held before the beginning of a Test series. Traditionally, the First Test in Australia is played in Brisbane in a five Test series, and I agreed that he should come and talk to the players at the start of the meeting then leaving us to discuss tactics and other matters later in the evening.

His message was quite short and to the point, and gives an insight into his knowledge of the game and his reading of the possibilities in a series between two national sides. "This could be one of the great years of all time" he said. "I think it is most important that we try and play good cricket all the time, even to the point where the result becomes immaterial. I am not suggesting that defeat would be as pleasant as success but this is a most important year for Australian cricket and for the watching public." Sir Donald was convinced that the West Indies would reciprocate to attacking gestures provided by the Australians and this proved to be so throughout the great series.

If Worrell had not been captain that year I think Australia would have won the series quite handsomely and certainly would have won the tied Test in Brisbane. When I think back to the lack of temperament shown by other West Indies sides over the years, it seems remarkable that one man could hold them together in the way Worrell did. At one stage on the last day of the tied game the West Indies were in the box seat for victory and yet not so long after, when Davidson and I were in partnership, it looked as though they would be beaten. There was a certain amount of good fortune about the eventual tie, as there must be in a result of this kind, and not the least fortunate happenings, from the West Indies point of view, was Solomon's ability to throw down the stumps from side on and off balance on two occasions.

But it is Worrell I will never forget for his leadership on that last day when his side was threatening to show the variable temperament that had previously caused West Indian teams so much bother. Perhaps the most astonishing sight on that great afternoon was Hall charging from his bowling follow through to square leg to knock over Kanhai who was waiting under a mistimed hook that had flown from the top edge of Grout's bat. It was a simple catch and the dropping of it might well have meant the loss of the Test match, but it was something of a tragicomic sight to see the 6ft. 3ins. Hall hurtling into the tiny Kanhai at that crucial moment of the game.

The temptation for a captain to put his head in his hands at that instant must have been all but impossible to repress but Worrell quietly went round his players saying "relax fellows, just relax and settle down and we'll be all right". The hands stopped waving and the team settled down to play with such purpose that the final result was achieved, and it was Australia who, in the closing minutes, suffered panic and two run outs instead of getting the extra run needed for victory.

As a batsman on that tour Worrell was past his peak but still played some fine innings, always in the strictly orthodox vein that made him such a delight to the eye of a purist. I very rarely saw him play a bad stroke, in fact he seemed not to know how to hit across the ball and always to be playing with a bat that was completely straight.

Apart from the Three W's, West Indian cricket after the war was well served by Ramadhin and Valentine, both of whom took over 100 wickets for their country, although Ramadhin was never quite the success in Australia that he had been in England. He was at something of a loss when attacked by quick-footed batsmen but his figures in Test matches stand comparison with any. Valentine was still a fine bowler when he came to Australia in 1960–1 but both these players enjoyed their best years round about the time the Three W's were at the height of their powers. Apart from anything else, it must have been useful for spin bowlers to have such batsmen in the side to give them runs to play with and they took full advantage of this.

Another of the best of the West Indian cricketers, apart from the W's, was Jeffrey Stollmeyer who opened the batting in 31 of his 32 Test matches for his country. He was never as heavy a scorer as his more illustrious team mates but was an extremely sound player on all types of pitches.

West Indian cricket, though, really only came of age in 1960–1 and I say that with due deference to the great players who represented their country in the years before that. They needed only a catalyst to weld them together and Frank Worrell was this catalyst, at a time where they again had some wonderful individual players in the side. Conrad Hunte, for instance, was as good a Test opener as any side could wish for and made over 3,000 runs in the 44 games he played after taking over the opening spot around 1959.

It is the all round strength of the West Indies these days, together with the inimitable Sobers, that makes them the formidable side they are. Sobers is such a versatile cricketer that he is almost worth two players in the side, in the sense that he allows the selectors to leave out an extra bowler for he himself can bowl four varieties of fast and slow deliveries under any pitch conditions that might be encountered. In England he often bowls orthodox finger spin and he does this occasionally in the West Indies as well and will often take the new ball at the start of an innings, or when the required number of overs has been reached, and can as well bowl medium pace cutters and unorthodox over the wrist spin. He is a great batsman in his own right, holding the world record Test score as a sideline, and if there has ever been a more complete cricketer then I haven't seen him.

Sobers made his first appearance against Australia in 1955 and rarely have I seen a more brilliant 40 than the one he made in the Barbados Test of that series. He was promoted to open that day and hit 43 in 15 minutes against Miller and Lindwall and then, in the final Test of the series, 35 not out and 64. In those days he was already classed as an all-rounder and he bowled mainly orthodox spin, but there was no doubt that here on show was a great cricketer in the making.

By the time he came to Australia in 1960–61 he had made his world record Test score of 365 not out and had massacred bowlers from all over the world with scant regard to reputation or skill. He is delightfully orthodox in his batting and yet, at the same time, is a wonderful improviser against the ball that, for a fraction of a second, looks as though it will beat him. He has devised his own whippy shot through mid wicket for a ball not necessarily short of a good length and very frustrating it is to a bowler to see what *he* might consider a good delivery, hit away through this gap.

His century against Australia in Brisbane in 1960 must rank with the great ones ever played and it was here that I had my first taste of his talent for improvising. I bowled him this day when he was in the forties what I thought was the perfect top spinner on a good length on middle and off stumps. He came back to hit it through mid-wicket but when the ball straightened instead of turning towards the on side he changed his stroke in mid back lift and hit it past mid-off for four. What can you do but clap a stroke of that kind even though, in a fraction of a second, you see a wicket taken from you? Frank Worrell called on him for prodigious efforts with the ball during that series but it never seemed to affect his batting. Apart from being the greatest all-rounder in the world he is also one of the hardest workers. When he played for South Australia in the Sheffield Shield he created new records by taking 50 wickets and scoring a thousand runs in a season and in only 23 matches he scored more than 2,000 runs and took over a hundred wickets for the State, and was, as well, the prime reason that South Australia won the Shield competition in 1963–4—only the second time they had achieved this since World War II.

When West Indies came to Australia there was something of a battle between Sobers and Kanhai to decide the world's best batsman, and it says much for Kanhai that, batting alone, I thought he just shaded Sobers in that series. Sobers, with his other abilities, was even then the best all-rounder in the world and they were a terrible pair to bowl against at that time. The only two slight weaknesses were in the opening batting and opening bowling positions where Cammie Smith, a great striker of the ball but slightly inconsistent, partnered Conrad Hunte, and where Frank Worrell himself opened the bowling instead of using either Chester Watson or Sobers. The balance of the side seemed best served by leaving Watson out for it allowed an extra batsman to be played, but he and Hall made it obvious in Melbourne that they would provide our early batsmen with plenty of problems every time they came together.

Back in 1955 Wesley Winfield Hall worked in the Post Office when the Australians played in Barbados and had the chance to watch Lindwall and Miller in full cry during the Test match on that island. By the time we saw him in Australia he had already played with indifferent success in England in 1957 where, despite his pace, his apparent rawness kept him out of the Test side. In that series Gilchrist provided great problems for England's batsmen but soon after he dropped out of Test cricket and 12 months later, when Frank Worrell was unable to go to India, Hall was chosen to go in his place.

It was the start of a great career for a man of astonishingly good temper who has turned out to be one of the biggest-hearted bowlers any country has ever produced. I have never seen him bowl with anything but the maximum effort except once in

Queensland where, troubled by a back injury, he bowled off a short run and still took wickets at a decidedly quick pace. He was a magnificent bowler in Australia in 1960–61, the fastest I had ever seen apart from Tyson and Lindwall at his very top, and although he was not a great swinger of the ball he was so tall that batsmen were constantly fending him away from their ribs, even when the delivery was of good length.

In the First Test in Brisbane he was at his magnificent best but I thought perhaps that long spells of bowling during the tour sapped his energy towards the end of the Test matches. Needing 258 to win the final Test of that series, I sent Bobby Simpson out with strict instructions to get after Hall and to fling the bat at everything on the second last afternoon. He was not out 50 at the close and it was a match-winning effort wherein he played some glorious strokes, as well as some chancy ones, and gave a selfless display of batting, carrying on the next day to 92.

A great character Wes—and a great one for a chat. One day in Brisbane during the lunch break he slipped into the old Members' stand to have a chat with some friends, expressing his various points with much waving of arms, until suddenly the group realised that the players were on the field and Ken Mackay had been forced to share the new ball with Harry Fisher. Wes made it to the centre in a few seconds, mumbling something about having forgotten Queensland had to field after the interval.

The West Indies have always been well served by their fast bowlers and never more so than in recent years when Hall and Griffith have provided such a great combination of speed. Hall was somewhat dwarfed by Griffith's pace in 1965 in the West Indies when the Australians returned there but he never gave anything but maximum effort to Gary Sobers, captaining the side for the first time, and his bowling on the dead pitch in Trinidad was some of the finest I have ever seen from a fast bowler.

In newspaper articles and on television I made it quite clear at the time that I thought Griffith to be contravening the throwing law, and certainly photographs of him in mid-action indicated that his delivery had in it at some stage an arm that was anything but straight. The throwing law is always a matter of interpretation and the umpires' view was that, in that series, never once did Griffith bowl anything but a completely legitimate delivery. It would be idle to say that my statements on Griffith's action were well received by all parties, but I was pleased to see that in 1966, when the West Indies came to England, the same bowler had made great endeavours to alter both his final yard of delivery and actual bowling action.

I first wrote about Griffith's action in Jamaica on the rest day of the First Test and it has since been suggested to me by interested parties that the timing of this was all wrong and that the matter should have been left in abeyance until the end of the series. I have also been told, by one prominent in West Indian affairs, that by publishing the pictures I had taken myself and writing as I did of Griffith's action, I kept him in the game three or four years longer than would ordinarily have been the case. The theory expressed here to me, and an extremely confident one it was too, was that the West Indians themselves intended to leave him out because of their own doubts about his action, but that an outsider, having jumped on the bandwagon, it was then impossible for them to make any move. I can't accept that for I don't believe any West Indian selector or official would have chosen him to play in such an important series if they had the slightest doubt about the legitimacy of his delivery.

It was in this series that the West Indies became the new champions of the cricket world, and a well deserved victory it was too for they outbatted and outbowled Australia and, though some of the Australian players had contrary opinions, I didn't believe at the time, and still don't, that Griffith was the difference between the two sides. The West Indians had then the strongest team in the world but it is possible that, in the same way as Australia reached a peak with a great side, they too may at the moment have approached theirs, and their losses against England and Australia underlines this possibility—in fact, turns it into a probability!

One of the difficulties of having a great team is that players on the fringe can be given no experience of Test cricket until it is too late, and I fear that this may well happen in the West Indies where some of the most talented players in the world are unable to get into the national team. In Barbados in 1965 I saw players in the island side and in the Colts team who looked real Test cricketers in the making and I saw some more in the other islands. But only one or two of these will ever play for the West Indies, simply because they, as a country, are so strong in every department of the game in this particular era.

The astonishing thing is that they have been unable to find a full time opening batsman to go in first with Conrad Hunte, and Hunte's own performances were the more remarkable for this.

He had a wide variety of partners in recent years—Davis, Nurse, Bynoe, Smith, Solomon, J. K. Holt, Rodriguez, Lashley, McMorris and Carew have all joined him at one time or another to form combinations that have been unsuccessful enough for the West Indies selectors to continue their search. I am surprised they never fully went on with the experiment of opening with Nurse, for, to me, he looks a superbly-equipped player and one who could readily have formed a fine combination with Hunte, thus allowing one of the younger batsmen to come in in the middle of the batting order.

One of the weaknesses in early West Indian teams was the fielding and there was some bad catching on the 1951–2 tour of Australia and again when the Australians went to the West Indies in 1955. But the present team can be direct opposite of that with Hunte brilliant around the boundary, Sobers able to field in any position and one of the great close-to-the-wicket catchers of all time, Kanhai a magnificent cover and a good slip, as well as Gibbs, surprisingly quick in the field for one who is also the best spin bowler in the world.

One of the great players to come from the West Indies since the Three W's were in full cry is Rohan Kanhai who is a complete individualist with the bat but at the same time, when the bowler is good enough, is a highly orthodox batsman. In defence he is very straight and if he has a weakness it is that he sometimes chooses the wrong ball for attack—a ball that other batsmen of lesser confidence would play with the greatest care. He was virtually unknown when he came to England in 1957 with something of a reputation as the second wicket-keeping string to Clyde Walcott but although much was expected of him he was unable to live up to the talk that had preceded the team.

But it was after this tour that he really began to make a name in world batting lists and by the time he came to Australia in 1960–1 to play on a series of good batting pitches he was reckoned to be one of the best players in the world. By the time the tour was over there were many in Australia who listed him as the best! He began to play well in the early part of the tour in Perth and Adelaide and then made a magnificent double century against Victoria in the State match in Melbourne. He failed in Sydney in the State match and then in the First and Second Tests gave occasional glimpses of the magnificent player that was to appear later in the season. He made two centuries in the one Test in Adelaide and then two thirties in the Fifth Test in Melbourne; four innings that will always remain in the memory of those who saw them.

The most vital point about his batting is his ability, like Sobers, to hit not only the bad ball for four but also the one the bowler considers to be a good delivery. An example of the bad ball is the full toss I bowled him first ball after lunch in Adelaide—he hit it for six from around ankle height where most batsmen would have been having a sighter and pushing it past mid on for two. There were plenty of good deliveries that series that went flashing to the boundary, deliveries from Davidson, myself, Meckiff, Martin and Kline, and at team meetings before and after each Test match one of the main points of discussion would be "whether or not it was possible to keep Kanhai quiet". The best way we found of keeping him quiet was to attack and try and get him out because when he is in the mood I doubt if there is any bowler who could keep him quiet by defensive means. To me the best method of stopping his run getting is to dismiss him and although this doesn't happen very often at least he does give the bowler a chance by attacking from the moment he comes into bat.

I thought after the 1960–1 series that his batting slipped a little and when the Australian side went to the West Indies in 1965 he was palpably out of form at the start of the tour. By the end of the series though he was back in touch, making runs and making the bowlers' life miserable, and his form in 1966 in the series in England left me in no doubt that he would continue to be a great run getter for the West Indies for many years. And I think this despite the poor form he showed in the last series against Australia.

He is not the most consistent of Test batsmen, in the sense that an injudicious shot played to the wrong ball is always likely to cut short an innings that was threatening to be a real showpiece. But over a period he has averaged as well as most in world cricket these days and I will defy anyone to produce me a more exciting cricketer when things are running for him. Sobers is one of the most brilliant in the world and Kanhai loses nothing by comparison with him, but it is an indication of his approach to the game that whilst he has scored 19 half centuries in Test cricket he has only scored 12 hundreds in almost a hundred Test innings. His play, I am certain, must be along the lines of Bradman but Bradman allied consistency to devastation and scored a century once every three times at bat.

It is true that England took cricket to the West Indies, in the same way as they took it to Australia and all other parts of the world, but cricket played in the West Indies from the time the game began there is vastly different from the game as played in England. Barbados is an island around 20 square miles and you can see the whole of the sugar cane plantations and villages in a day. But, per head of population, nowhere in the world has produced more and better sportsmen than this tiny strip of land where cricket, sugar and rum punch provides the best possible public relations with other countries.

Worrell, Walcott, Weekes, Sobers and Hall were all born in the 21 miles long, 15 miles wide area, where something like 300,000 people have recently achieved independence. There are plenty of others like Charlie Griffith, David Holford, Hunte, Nurse, Lashley and Allan, together with the great names of the past, who have in these modern times lifted West Indian cricket right to the very top. Early West Indian cricket was always flattering to deceive with teams being built up and rated as the equal of any others in the world, only for them to fail when faced by Test series against other countries. There were always good fast bowlers about and there were always good attacking batsmen and the occasional spinners, but the sides never seemed to be able to weld together as good teams whether they were on tour or playing at home.

In 1935 West Indies beat England by two Tests to one, winning the last and deciding Test by an innings and 161 runs, and in 1939 suffered a reverse in the one match of a three Test series that was able to be decided. It was really after the Second World War that West Indian cricket came in its own when in 1947–8 in their own country they beat England in two Tests out of four—the first two of the series having been drawn. This was the start of a great run where, in 1950, West Indies won three Tests to one and were accordingly given recognition by being allowed five Test match series, a compliment to which they responded by winning the first two Tests against Len Hutton's side in 1953–4. England though won two of the next three by nine wickets and then in England in 1957 England won three of the five matches by an innings.

This gives an indication of the variable cricket played by West Indies sides and possibly confirms that one of their biggest problems over the years has been that of leadership. Sir Frank Worrell was the first regular dark-skinned captain of the West Indies and it is only since he took over that there has been any noticeable difference in team spirit—a difference that has continued in the leadership of Gary Sobers who always seems to have his team behind him. When Australia was in the West Indies in 1955 the home side was popularly preferred to the tourists in any local discussions about the outcome of the series. Tyson and Statham had just steamrollered their way through the Australians and on the fast West Indies pitches it was generally thought that the Australian batsmen would be in just as much trouble against anything of pace that could be produced out there. But, in fact, there was very little pace bowling that season and the attack was generally opened by Frank King who wasn't to be heard of again after that series, and he had as his opening partner Dewdney, Butler and any others who managed to catch the West Indian selectors' eyes at around medium pace. The West Indies relied on that tour on spin and Ramadhin and Valentine had one of their worst tours from the result point of view though they always bowled steadily in conditions very much in favour of batting. This was the last time the West Indies were to be short of pace bowling for on the horizon they had Hall, Gilchrist, Watson and then, even later, Griffith, to take up from where Francis, Martindale and Constantine had left off.

West Indies hold a unique position in the game at the moment for they play far more cricket out of their own country than they do inside it. When the West Indies season is on the players return to play in Shell tournaments, with a view to gaining selection in whichever tour is coming up at that particular time, but for the rest of the year most of the good ones have made a practice of spending their time in the Lancashire League. Constantine was the first top player to play Lancashire League but since then the W's, Sobers, Kanhai and all the other leading players of the present era have played league cricket in the north of England and have made cricket a full time job.

The side has a tremendous appeal on a tour of England for a percentage of the spectators are themselves West Indians who have settled in England and who provide noisy and discerning appreciation of the game, irrespective of how it may be progressing. They have beaten England twice in recent times, in 1963 and 1966, and the 1963 tour in particular did a great deal for cricket. Some of the great moments in the history of the game have come in those two tours and in the 1960–61 series.

The first two West Indian sides in that small era were captained by Frank Worrell and the third by Gary Sobers. But it would appear, from what Sobers has said in print, that the 1966 tour was not as happy a venture as the others. In a newspaper article in 1967 he was bitter about the reception afforded his side in England and said that, whilst the tour should have been one of his great moments in cricket, he found it most disappointing because of various incidents.

One of these involved controversial fast bowler Charlie Griffith and former South African Basil D'Oliveira. So incensed, says Sobers, were the West Indians at D'Oliveira's non-dismissal at Leeds that they refused to clap him when he left the field at the end of a brilliant innings. From the sidelines in the Press box it seemed to me that this tour was, in fact, not as pleasant as some the West Indies had undertaken and, certainly, there seemed to be less goodwill between the teams than three years before when Worrell's side had won the series. Sobers said in his newspaper article that the West Indians were convinced D'Oliveira was caught at mid-wicket by Hunte but then was given not out by umpire Elliott on appeal. D'Oliveira himself had no doubt that he wasn't out and told Sobers so when the West Indian captain questioned him saying "Why didn't you go?" D'Oliveira in this series was playing for England for the first time, having been refused admittance to the South African side in his own country and having decided to settle in England and play cricket for a living. The reply I understand he gave to Sobers at Leeds was not exactly the one that appeared in the West Indian captain's newspaper story, but it does reflect great credit on D'Oliveira for possessing the gift of brisk repartee, as well as a sound knowledge of the Australian idiom.

There are one or two other stories—confirmed by the players concerned—about that series that reflected little credit on the principals. One of the nicest fellows in cricket is Colin Cowdrey and whether or not he is a forceful enough character has nothing to do with the situation in which he found himself at Leeds with one of the West Indian players in the West Indian dressing-room. Much of the trouble in that match had come about because umpire Elliott had warned fast bowler Charlie Griffith for throwing after a bumper had brushed Graveney's collar on its way through to the wicket-keeper. When the over ended umpire Elliott told Griffith, "I consider that delivery contravened the laws, and if it happens again I will call you."

Sobers says in print that Griffith then complained bitterly that the umpire's warning had only come about because of the English batsmen's attitude and that the umpire was being influenced by them. Sobers adds that he then went to Elliott and asked him if this were so, warning him that if it were he would report him to M.C.C. I have the greatest admiration for Sobers as a cricketer and captain, and like him very much as a person, but this is one of the most presumptuous things I have read from any international captain in the time I have been in the game. Fortunately the umpire, and umpires in general, are renowned for keeping their heads in situations such as this and captains threatening them with an unfavourable report usually get very short shrift indeed.

Griffith has been a contentious bowler since coming to England in 1963 after playing in a series against India in his own country in 1962. He was unfortunate in that he was the bowler concerned in a bad injury to Indian captain Nari Contractor in the Barbados island match that year, an injury that put Contractor out of cricket and necessitated an emergency operation. That had nothing to do with Griffith's bowling action for it is the sort of thing that can happen to any fast bowler who occasionally drops one short. In 1965 Graham McKenzie laid out Jackie Hendriks in the Fourth Test Match and Hendriks was on the danger list for two days before word came through that his condition was improving. I have seen plenty of bowlers hit batsmen when the batsmen either try and duck out of the road of the delivery or play a misjudged hook, and, in fact, I spent two weeks in hospital myself in 1949 having been hit by a bumper when playing for the New South Wales Second XI against Victoria.

But Griffith has been under fire because various people in various cricket countries consider that his action doesn't always conform to the laws. He is not the first bowler to have this charge levelled at him and I doubt if he will be the last because bowlers' actions always remain a matter of opinion rather than of fact, although it is possible to produce photographic support for the fact that a bowler's arm does not remain straight until the moment of delivery. The law over the years has been loosely worded and when I came out in 1965 and pointed out that Griffith's arm was at first bent and then straightened, it caused some consternation in the West Indies.

The fact remains that Griffith, to his own credit and that of his advisers, for some reason changed his action enough in 1966 to satisfy most of the people most of the time. It resulted in performances that were far short of those he produced in the earlier series but the fact that he saw fit to change his action and if he continues to do so is worthy only of the highest praise in an era where there is so much spotlight on this particular type of bowling. He took 14 wickets in the 1966 series and 49 wickets on the whole tour compared to 119 in 1963, but in between times managed to play something of an important part in the 1965 series against Australia. He has been a more controversial figure than Hall but, for me, there will never be a greater West Indian bowler than Hall who personifies everything that is perfect in fast bowling. Not always was his run to the wicket judged meticulously, not always was everything in unison in the first ten yards of his run, but there is no more beautiful sight on slow motion film than this man in full cry against a batsman 22 yards away.

I have often wondered how another off spinner would have bowled in conditions in 1956 in England when Jim Laker had such a remarkable year against the Australians. Over the years there have been a number of very good English off spinners, very good in their own conditions and occasionally not quite so good when bowling overseas. An exception to this was Laker, who was one of the great bowlers I have ever seen in any conditions, rivalled only in his craft by the flight and magnificent control of Tayfield, the South African, when he came to Australia in 1952–3. But I have no doubt that Lance Gibbs, the West Indian off spinner, would have provided England in 1956 with as many problems as Laker was able to provide for the hapless Australians who were unable to find any sort of method to counter him. It is very difficult to compare bowlers of different eras but, having seen Gibbs bowl in England, I found it slightly amusing that English batsmen were able to show little better technique against him on a turning pitch than overseas batsmen are when caught in the same conditions by English off-spinners.

Ramadhin was in a different category for he was something of a mystery bowler with the batsmen unable on most English days to decipher the direction of turn. Gibbs was more straightforward in the sense that he was an orthodox off-spinner, possessed of the same tantalising flight as Laker where the batsmen were never quite able to get to the pitch of the ball. I batted against Gibbs a number of times and, whilst I set myself up only as a latter order batsman, I have played against a number of off-spinners over the years with only a moderate amount of trouble. Laker though, I found terribly difficult to handle and so too Gibbs for, although wanting to attack them at all times, I was never quite able to get through to carry out the job, and this problem was one admitted to by many other Australian batsmen as well. Gibbs is a very tall off-spinner but will turn a little even on a good batting surface and turns a lot given any assistance from the pitch.

At Manchester in 1966 he was almost completely responsible for England's disintegration when facing a large West Indies first innings total, and it was ironic to see England's batsmen committing the same faults as the Australians had done in 1956 on pitches that turned even more. But the mark of a great bowler is his ability to bowl on good surfaces and you can't find better batting surfaces than in the West Indies. On these Gibbs is head and shoulders above any other spin bowler in the world and he forms a most important part of any West Indian attack these days.

Gibbs has learnt his craft under the most rigorous conditions and his pinnacle of skill has been reached only through hour after hour of the hardest work imaginable. But all this could have been lost to international competition if the county registration rules had been firmly applied with regard to Gibbs when he sought release to play for West Indies against England in 1967–8. The county rules themselves were quite specific, making it clear that if Gibbs went overseas for any length of time he would have to restart his registration period. It was soon realised however that to deprive the West Indies of the use of Gibbs' services would hardly be in the best traditions of the game and, accordingly, he was given special leave and allowed to take his place in the Caribbean.

From 1960 onwards I have considered him to be the best of any type of spinner in international cricket and I doubt if we will see a better until the turn of the decade when one of the younger West Indian spinners has served his apprenticeship. It was on Sir Frank Worrell's tour of Australia that he first came of age, taking over from Ramadhin after the Second Test and bowling West Indies to victory in the Third Test Match of that series on a turning Sydney pitch. It was a great start and one that was continued for much of the time under the guidance of Worrell until he retired from Test cricket.

It is strange how, when the West Indies success is talked about, one always seems to come back to Worrell but it appears such a logical thing to do. It doesn't detract from the performances of the West Indian greats to repeat that they were of variable temperament, unable to weld together to play as a team, either through their own subconscious wishes or through the lack of a leader to weld them. Worrell brought them together because he knew that it was cricket that was common to every West Indian island whereas politics and concerted thinking was not. There have been few greater men in cricket than Sir Frank and, for me, it will always be this man more than any other who has brought West Indian cricket to the position it holds at the moment and to the esteem in which it is held throughout the world.

4

The Names

Cricket is a game peculiar in the fact that, although personal performances always show up in statistics over the years, it is only rarely that an individual can be very outstanding within the team for which he plays. There have been some able to do this like Trumper and Bradman and, more recently, Sobers. Perhaps Worrell, too, could be included in this group of great names, not so much for his batting or bowling but because of the marked influence he had on cricket in his own country.

Trumper I never saw. He must have been a wonderful cricketer and all those fortunate enough to see him in action at his peak speak his name nowadays with some reverence. He played for New South Wales for 20 years, making his debut at 17 in 1894, but was only 37 years of age when illness struck him down and denied him the chance to enrich even further the game of cricket. A glance at his figures cannot possibly tell the tale of what must have been superb batting for he averaged only 44 throughout the whole of his career in first-class cricket and in Test matches was fractionally under 40. It would appear though that he had the marvellous co-ordination of a natural athlete as well as the ability to see the ball and make up his mind as to the stroke to be played quicker than normal batsmen. Many have said he was a genius with the bat and that I can believe, having both listened to and read of his deeds over the years.

In 1902, in what was apparently a very wet season in England, he took part in a triumphant Australian tour where the touring side lost only two matches and ended the season with the best record of any Australian team to that date. The weather in *Wisden*'s 1903 edition is described as "abnormal and deplorable" and Trumper's batting is given the rating "marvellous". On that tour he was obviously pre-eminent as a batsman and made 2,570 runs in varying conditions where games were played on hard, true pitches on some days and then on strips made most difficult after overnight rain. I like the phrase in *Wisden* of that year where Trumper is credited with having reduced England's bowlers on at least two occasions "to the level of the village green".

A wonderful eye and supreme confidence, and also magnificently quick reflexes, seem to have been the answer for this remarkable player. Apparently he was also stylish and made his runs with an easy grace that was always a pleasure to the eye, not being prepared to sacrifice attractive batting for the sake of making runs. In 1968 it reads strangely that there was widespread pleasure in England that year at the failure of efforts to secure Trumper as a player for an English county. *Wisden* says "it would have been a paltry and unworthy thing to deprive Australia by means of a money bribe of her finest batsman". At this very moment county clubs in England are looking all over the world for overseas players who may be able to assist in bringing crowds back to watch county cricket.

In the same way, Sobers is very much in demand at the moment, being unquestionably the finest all-rounder in the world today and, quite possibly, the finest all-rounder the world has ever seen. He is one who has the ability in these modern days to tower above team performances and, with his captaincy added to his remarkable all-round ability, he is a name player indeed. Bradman as a young man had the magic to bring crowds pouring back to the game—probably more so than any other cricketer in the history of the game. Even at the end of his career many people would go to a game just to see Bradman in action and quite often would leave the ground if he were dismissed early. The other three, Trumper, Sobers and Worrell, probably did not have the same influence though I am sure these days there are many who would go to a cricket match simply for the purpose of seeing Sobers in action.

Worrell was a slightly different proposition and, when I suggest that his main gift to cricket was from the point of view of lifting the game in his own country, I make no suggestion that the others did not do the same thing. But Worrell's emergence as a captain coincided with the emergence of West Indies as the cricket power on the international scene in the 1960s and I doubt if any other player from the Caribbean could have done the job he did at that particular moment in West Indian cricket history.

The three modern day players, Bradman, Worrell and Sobers, all led their country and led it in the most successful fashion imaginable. Sir Donald captained Australia first in 1936–7 and was unbeaten in a Test series at his retirement in 1948. Sir Frank lost the series in Australia by a whisker in 1960–1 but was remarkably successful firstly from the point of view of results and, more important still, in the building up of a team spirit and affinity within his side. Bradman and Sobers were more remarkable individual players than any I have ever known in that more often than not their own performances controlled the destiny of the match.

I have seen Sobers time and again come in late for the West Indies and bolster the side with a dedicated innings that first of all steadied the opposing attack and then took it apart, with the other players in his side gaining confidence all the time he was there. So too with his bowling—the lithe action and fantastic ability to bowl two types of spin and another two of pace often made him the key to West Indian success, whether it be achieved by a breakthrough with the new ball or a middle innings collapse or by spinning the opposition out. In the all-round sense he had the edge on Bradman simply because of his bowling but, good though Sobers is as a batsman, I can't really imagine anyone having been as good as "The Don" in that field.

Bradman batted only 80 times for Australia and scored just under 7,000 runs and no doubt Sobers will one day pass this. Already he has made over 6,000 batting on over 100 occasions. But it is not my purpose here in any way to try and compare their cricket ability for I believe that there are very few great players ever to have played the game, though there are a lot of very good ones. The great ones would have been great in any era and, in fact, we are extremely fortunate that the careers of Sobers and Bradman did not coincide and that instead we have been able to watch their genius at work at different times in cricket history.

I doubt that there has ever been a batsman of more value to any side than Bradman, even up to the moment of his retirement in 1948. As an old bowler it makes my fingers itch to think of bowling at the opposition with 500 and 600 run totals at my back, and the knowledge that once in every three times he went to bat Bradman made a hundred. Over the years there have been comparisons made with Trumper, Hobbs, Hammond and Macartney. Remarkably only twice did Australia win Test matches in which Bradman did not score a century and I can only say that it must have been a joy to be in the same side as him, even if some of the glory that would normally go to the other ten players would find its way on to Bradman's shoulders. The story goes the rounds that in the timeless Test in 1938 at the Oval England had made 903 for seven by tea on the third day. But the only reason the closure was applied was that Bradman broke his ankle and had declared himself unfit to bat—simply because 903 might not have been sufficient for victory had he been able to get on the field. The authority for that—*Wisden*—and, whilst believing that the writers of this great cricket journal have a good sense of humour, I am prepared to believe that on this occasion they are deadly serious.

I first saw Bradman in that already mentioned match of 1940 when he batted late in the day and then was dismissed by O'Reilly the following day. I should think I was too young then really to be able to define genius whether with bat or ball and it is true that Grimmett impressed me more in that match than did Bradman. I little thought then that when I grew older I would come under his eagle eye as a selector and critic and eventually be sitting over the dinner table with him discussing the merits of a 1963 Henscke claret. I really know very little about him as a cricketer for his greatest days were over when I began watching Test matches in 1946 and he retired from the game when the 1948 side came back from England in the same season as, possessed of a keen eye and high backlift, I made my own debut in first-class cricket. More's the pity! I'd have given a lot to play in a side under Bradman and to be able to watch the master at work, whether with bat or in the field of captaincy, but I have managed the next best thing and picked up a lot about the game from him off the field.

I find him a remarkable man. I have heard a number of stories from not disinterested parties that indicate when young he was of cold and uncompromising disposition but, as one who generally likes to make up his own mind about things, I balanced this with conversations with people who knew him just as well as the anti-brigade. I have no doubt that in his young days he was at times most uncommunicative and I am sure that he must have been under tremendous pressure from the time he came into the game to the start of the Second War. He was *the* batsman, in fact *the* cricketer in the world, and everyone wanted to know him, write about him and be associated with him in some way. Some of the players of his own early era leave no doubt that their feelings for him are less than lukewarm and I can imagine that his emergence as the one great cricketer of his time, with the rest slightly behind, would scarcely have endeared him to any lacking the backbone to accept this situation. No doubt some of the acid had a basis in fact for I can't imagine a young Bradman, or a young anyone for that matter, doing all the right things all the time. He could well have been a difficult man but I scarcely think that anyone could be as difficult as he has been credited with being and still make as many friends as he has done.

There are very few cricketers who have ever played the game who have had a particular method of attack devised purely to keep them in check. Only one, Bradman, has ever had an attack such as Bodyline devised—an attack that was to have repercussions throughout the empire in all fields, not just on the cricket field. I never saw Bodyline but I have read a number of accounts of it and I should think it is the most unfair method of playing the game ever produced by any cricket team. I have read the brilliant book by J. H. Fingleton written in 1946 wherein he leaves little doubt that he considered Bradman's methods of countering Bodyline well divorced from those that should have been used by any tenacious Australian batsmen. *Wisden* at the same time said of Bodyline "a method of bowling was evolved—mainly with the idea of curbing the scoring propensities of Bradman—which met with almost general condemnation among Australian cricketers and spectators, and which when something of the real truth was ultimately known in this country, caused people at home—and many of them famous in the game—to wonder if the winning of the rubber was, after all, worth this strife". Bradman in that Test series made 0, 103 not out, 8, 66, 76, 24, 48 and 71 and, if he had made them in 1968 as a normal batsman, would no doubt have been congratulated on having a great series. He averaged over 50 which is the norm these days but, by his own standards, he had failed. I know of Bodyline only what I have been told and I am delighted never to have seen it in modern day cricket.

All this was pre-war stuff and, apart from that one Sheffield Shield match in 1940, I didn't see Bradman play until the England–Australia Test series in Australia in 1946. He had been dogged by ill-health and it was very doubtful if he would turn out for Australia in that series—eventually he did so, as usual with tremendous success. I would think his decision to play cricket in 1946 was probably one of the hardest he ever had to make in his career. He had tremendous offers from newspapers all over the world to cover the Test series but in the end it became a question of duty to him and Australian cricket got the benefit of his decision. I can remember reading stories of that 1946–7 tour, and reading the accounts of the play from journalists and ex internationals, and wondering at the "edge" to some of the comments made about this man I had never met but had always thought of as the greatest player in the world.

His career ended in 1948 just as mine was beginning and I first met him in the 1949 season. That he should have gone to England in 1948 at all was in itself a rather remarkable thing. Johnny Moyes tells how, when the team was to be chosen at the end of the Fifth Test match in Melbourne, he and Bill Jeanes were with Bradman in his room when he produced from his pocket a statement indicating that he was available for the English tour but that on his return he would retire from cricket of all grades.

The 1948–9 season then was to be the first since 1928 that had got under way without Bradman's playing influence. There was no real reason for him to go to England but, in conversation with him, I am certain that he felt he owed something to the game in both Australia and England and that his form was probably good enough to get through the tour. I am equally certain he had no real desire to spend six months playing cricket six days a week and that he could have commanded a tremendous fee just for sitting in the Press box writing about the players he had instead decided to lead. He did write on the 1953 and 1956 tours after he had led that 1948 team on an unbeaten tour where Australia easily retained the Ashes. That would have been a most important thing for Bradman simply because he was keen on winning and he believed that the game should always be played hard and fairly. But he must have also derived great satisfaction from the tremendous boost to the game in England and could satisfactorily retire at the end of that tour knowing the job he had set out to do had been completed successfully in every way.

There must have been great pressure on him as a player throughout his career, never more so, I would imagine, than when he made his comeback in 1946. At 28 in the Brisbane Test match the Englishmen thought he was caught at gully by Ikin off Voce. There was enormous publicity given to this incident where apparently the umpire said immediately "not out" to the appeals for a catch. Reading back on the incident, it seems very similar to the day Kline caught Cowdrey in Brisbane when those who wrote of the incident were in the new Press box. This is in a much better position than the old Press box which was in the old stand, a long way from the actual play. In the 1958 Cowdrey incident Cowdrey didn't believe he had been caught at short backward square leg

I

off Meckiff but, on appeal, and after McInnes had consulted square leg umpire Hoy, he was given out. Hoy was standing a few yards from where Kline took the catch. We were playing five on the on side to Meckiff at this stage and I was at deep mid on with another player at short mid wicket covering the single. From where I was I had no chance of seeing whether or not Kline had taken the catch and, with Cowdrey dragging his bat and looking over his shoulder, I moved in quickly to ask Kline and Grout if it had been a fair catch. Kline confirmed he had caught the ball and Grout said it had been deflected directly into the fieldsman's hands—but there were still a large number of those watching from the Press box who would have it that the ball had hit the ground, and they were twice as far away as I was at mid on.

But this was only a minor incident compared to anything concerning Bradman and his 1946 comeback was made even bigger news, with a variety of people insisting that it had not been a bump ball caught at gully by Ikin. In fact, everything Bradman did was big news from the time he stepped on to a cricket field to make his first first-class century. Nowadays he lives in a pleasant home in Adelaide where he is President of the South Australian Cricket Association. He plays golf off a handicap of three, frequently being under the card and taking golf balls off hapless interstate visitors almost at will. He is a director of a number of companies but no longer has a seat on the Stock Exchange where he was in business for a number of years. At weekends occasionally he goes to a small farm in the Mount Lofty hills where he will clear scrub and trees, partly for the obvious purpose of clearing them but also to retain the fitness that he never seems quite to have lost. I commented to him one day recently about the length of his drives on the golf course and he put this down largely to the physical work he had been doing. He is a sound judge of good wine, occasionally producing a special bottle of some obscure claret for dinner guests, but much of his time now is taken up in the business of helping run Australian and South Australian cricket. He was always something of a perfectionist as a batsman, even in an unorthodox way, and he strives for perfection in administration as well.

Some 20 years ago a writer with some foresight suggested that once Bradman retired from the game there would be an inevitable slump. Perhaps this accounts in some measure for the desperate search since his retirement for "another Bradman". Harvey never filled the bill because he was a left-hander, they talked of Craig, who may have been another Jackson but never in a million years would be another Bradman, and they grasped O'Neill as the one most likely to follow the great man. Since then Walters and Sheahan have come on the scene and borne the same comparisons, particularly after Walters made a century in each of his first two Tests against England.

All the talk of who was the greatest player the world has ever seen seems to centre round players like Bradman, Trumper, Hobbs, Macartney and Hammond, but it is interesting that young players are rarely described as, say, another Hobbs or another Macartney, or even another Trumper. The thing the public and publicity mediums desperately want is only another Bradman and not another anyone else. I think probably over the years feelings have changed greatly towards players who are star turns in the game. If Bradman were playing now I have a feeling that he would be far more welcome in any team than when he was in his own heyday. Modern day players may or may not be as good as those who have gone before and I am not prepared to argue that now or with any of the good players of the past. But, from what I have heard and from what I have read, the fact that Bradman was pre-eminent in his era did not necessarily make him the most popular man in the side.

I have a feeling that in modern days there is more effort made to make sure a team runs smoothly and team members themselves are treated as a godsend that they should have one great player in a side able to make more runs than anyone else, and therefore get the team more publicity and win them more matches. I know one young cricketer in Australia, a potentially great player, who in recent years has got more than his share of publicity, sometimes deservedly and sometimes not. I also know that his team treats him as a valuable commodity and that team mates and others have been eager to help in making sure that his future in the game is secure. I mark this down as good teamwork and correct appreciation of a player's skill.

I am always amused by criticisms of the better players and often have a quiet chuckle when anti-Bradman hour begins. The ones who produce the remarks and tell the tales could be thought nothing but paragons of virtue themselves from the way the stories go. I have never heard a Bradman critic, for instance, tell much of a story against himself so I can only assume that those who like to produce the information and story that blasts the Don have themselves led nothing more nor less than blameless cricket lives.

It is not so, of course, and I suppose the fact that even 20 years after his retirement there are those willing to have a dash at him indicates that he is still a large-sized figure in the cricket world. On figures anyway, he is the most remarkable player there has ever been and I doubt very much that anyone will ever approach him. But, in the time I have known him, he is a very human person who has never objected to adverse criticism if it is factual. If it is personal and impinges on his private life then he does as I would, or, as his critics would, and rightly resents it.

They say he has made a lot of money out of cricket and I have no doubt that he has made more money out of the game than most other individuals who have played. He has also put back in ten times as much money in gate receipts and, at the same time, has sacrificed a great deal for the game. I suppose he could have got £12,000 sterling to cover the 1948 series for a paper and could have done the same in 1946–7 when M.C.C. visited Australia. The same applied in 1961 but he had other things to do for each tour, all of them connected with the welfare of Australian cricket and, in the case of the 1948 team, the welfare of English cricket as well. He has a remarkably analytical mind with regard to cricket and I presume he was the same in business otherwise he would hardly have been successful on the Stock Exchange.

One of the most important things I find with him is that he is not dogmatic either with regard to players or situations in the game. None of this business I hear so often of "so and so's not much good" or "Bill Smith will never make a really good player". He is always prepared to look for the best from every player and to look at him in the light of his value to a team rather than whether or not he is a star. It is the same with situations, in that there is no dogmatic statement of right or wrong, but he is prepared to approach both sides of a question and then give an opinion, instead of coming out with a blunt one sentence verdict that brooks no argument. Lesser lights in the administration world in Australia will condemn a young cricketer to oblivion in a few short words, whether it be for a lack of technique or purpose. They would listen to Bradman occasionally giving a run-down on the player's ability in each department of the game and then drawing a line on his lack of skill in others. The latter is always accompanied by the provision that he might well improve "if we can concentrate on helping him in some particular way".

A remarkable man—I have no doubt he has always been a

remarkable man—but, in the time I have known him, he has added much to my knowledge of cricket and to my enjoyment of the game.

* * *

If Bradman had an extraordinary effect on cricket in Australia then, in his own way, so too did Worrell in the West Indies. He was not the top run-getter in West Indian history, nor was he probably the best player, but, as luck would have it, he became the best and best-known captain ever to leave the islands. He was known as "Petit Garçon" when he played his first match in short pants for his school against a team of policemen but it wasn't until 1960 that he became one of the most important men ever born in the West Indian islands. He was born on August 1st, 1924, in Barbados and tragically he died in 1967, aged only 42, and still with much to do for Caribbean cricket. Worrell himself said that Barbados was an extraordinary place—in that it is the only place in the world without a local hero. It seems that he had plenty of reverses as a youngster living in Barbados and so too, apparently, had Weekes and Walcott who, with Frank, were to make the phrase "the Three W's" famous throughout the cricket world.

He played his early cricket with Barbados but when I first met him in 1955 he was playing with Jamaica. On that tour it was Walcott who held the stage and Weekes and Worrell who took a back seat, both of them partly through injury but also partly through loss of form. His great year, and the great year of the other W's, was undoubtedly in England in 1950 when Ramadhin and Valentine were introduced to Test cricket. The trio made nearly 6,000 runs between them on that tour in first-class matches and in the Test matches they made 1,100 at an average of over 60 an innings. The West Indians themselves started that tour on the basis of being good practice for England who were preparing to go to Australia the following year. If it is true that Ramadhin and Valentine won the Test matches because of their tremendous bowling skill, it is probably equally true that they were provided by the Three W's with the opportunity of bowling at large totals, with almost inevitable success.

Worrell as a player, to me, always pales beside Worrell the captain. I believe too, as I have already suggested, that Everton Weekes would have been a good captain but he had retired from Test cricket at a time when Worrell decided to carry on. Australia in the West Indies in 1955 didn't see Worrell at his best and saw only glimpses of him in Australia in 1951–2. Nine years between West Indian tours is a long time and when Frank's side came to Australia in 1960 it was with the hope that they would provide some good and interesting cricket for Australian spectators who, only two years before, had gone through the anguish of watching Bailey and others bat for an interminable period in Brisbane and other places. Worrell on this tour was a captain of great quality, probably the only man able in that period to get the best out of his team. He had a wide knowledge of cricket and an even wider knowledge of people, and this was to start the West Indies on what is still their most successful era in international cricket.

Worrell himself returned moderate figures, by his own great standards, but it was in the welding of team spirit that he gets full marks from me. West Indians form the most individual team of cricketers in the world, and certainly the most volatile, and I should think it is a much more difficult task to control them and combine them as a team should be combined, than it is with any other country. No player could have done a better job than Frank and it is for this reason that I class him as the most important West Indian to play the game. I shouldn't think that West Indian cricket is easy to administer, simply because the players virtually come from different countries. Jamaica, Trinidad, Barbados and Guyana have all gone for independence and other players from the Leeward and Windward islands are many miles away from the hub of Caribbean cricket. Each island has its own characteristics and trade and the one thing that commonly seems to bind them together is cricket and a love of music. Cricket, though, is their most saleable commodity and it was Worrell who bound them together in such a way that they could sell it to the world and make the West Indies known as a great cricket nation even in places where the game was little played.

His era of captaincy was short but tremendously important, spanning the years from 1960 to 1963 and bringing the West Indies nothing but success and well-deserved fame. He was something of a philosopher about the game, with a remarkable insight into what made every one of his players tick. When problems cropped up, as they always will in cricket teams and teams containing any number of variable characters, he was quick to know how to adjust them and the problems soon disappeared. I had hoped that he would long be a force in West Indian cricket, despite the fact that one occasionally found people in his own country who thought him over-rated. I didn't think him over-rated at all and in a way I felt very sorry for Gary Sobers when he had to take over from Frank on the latter's retirement. Sobers, incidentally, was Worrell's own nominee for the job and, in view of Gary's success with the side and his own increased stature in the cricket world, it gives a further indication of Worrell's foresight.

If there are those in the West Indies who think Worrell over-rated by these sentiments (and there are some to whom I have spoken) then they should consider where West Indian cricket would be but for his great and charming influence in his three years of captaincy and of leadership. I suspect they would be in much the same position as they were for many years—a side containing probably the best group of cricketers in the world, unable to weld themselves together because they had no catalyst to combine them. Worrell did this and there is no doubt in my mind that he is the most important cricketer ever to play the game in the Caribbean.

* * *

West Indian cricket is the most publicised in the world at the time of writing, simply because their players are in more demand than any others. Australia could have West Indies touring teams every two or three years and our administrators believe the game would continue to flourish. I don't entirely go along with this because I think competition between two countries can prove something of an anti-climax unless spectators' wishes coincide with the actual play on every occasion. If West Indies came to Australia very frequently but failed to provide the same entertainment as provided in the 1960–1 series spectators and cricket followers would be inclined to be critical—and there is no more critical band than paying cricket spectators and followers! At the same time, it is patently poor public relations to have them in Australia in 1951, 1960 and 1968—three tours in 17 years. Everyone has their obligations to other countries like India, Pakistan and New Zealand—heaven knows, Australian administration has badly neglected New Zealand cricket over the years—but the arrangement of tours should ride with the times.

Sobers is captaining the West Indies in Australia in 1968–9, despite the fact that he has accepted a three-year engagement with Nottinghamshire, and his very presence in my country engenders tremendous interest in the game. Garfield St. Aubrun Sobers

SOUTH AFRICA

South Africa's Graeme Pollock is undoubtedly the finest batsman to play for his country for many years but there are others like Roy McLean (*top left*) and Eddie Barlow (*top right*) who, in their own particular eras, have made great contributions to South Africa's cricket success. So too have the two bowlers Neil Adcock (*left*) and Hugh Tayfield (*right*)—Adcock fast and very dangerous, though sometimes inclined to bowl too short to be fully effective. Tayfield, an off spinner to rank with the best, and a fine bowler who, whenever circumstances were difficult and the pitches in favour of batting, was at his best.

INDIA

Often in recent times India's captain, the Nawab of Pataudi, has had to fight a lone battle when his side's batting has broken down. Such was the case in England in 1967 and, after he recovered from injury in Australia in 1967/68, it was the same story. When only half fit he played many memorable strokes in innings in Melbourne and Brisbane—a typical one is pictured here as he hits Hawke off the back foot at the S.C.G., the ball landing just inside the boundary at long on. A brilliant player, "Tiger" Pataudi, who certainly would have been even greater had he not sustained damage to an eye in a car accident some years ago.

NEW ZEALAND

One of the tragedies of Australian cricket is that New Zealand has been so neglected over the years that players like Bert Sutcliffe have never had the chance to take part in a full tour of Australia. He was one of the great players of New Zealand a left-hander who would have deservedly won a place in any Test side when at his top.

THE CAPTAINS

An unusual photograph showing five Test Captains together. From the left Ted Dexter, the author, Frank Worrell, Jackie McGlew and the Nawab of Pataudi.

Haig

was born in Barbados in July 1936 and is the greatest all-rounder I have ever seen. So far in 65 Test matches he has made over 6,000 runs and taken over 150 wickets, as well as innumerable catches, and has cut off hundreds of runs in the field. Statistics can be a bit of a trap with players of any generation but occasionally with all-rounders, even more so than players of any individual capacity, they will give a good indication of talent. I saw him in 1955 when, in the first Test in Port-of-Spain ever to be played on turf, he made 47 and 8 not out and took none for ten in three overs. In his next Test match he made 12 and 11 and took three for 20 and then, opening the innings in the Fourth Test in Bridgetown, hit a brilliant 43 against Miller and Lindwall at their top. In the last Test of that series he made 35 not out and 64, finishing with useful batting figures of 231 runs at an average of 38·50 per innings. Nothing really to excite the cricket world but an indication that there was some ability present in this young player.

There have been a number of great all-rounders in cricket history, most of whom have escaped my first-hand knowledge over the years. Grace and other players of that vintage, then Wilfred Rhodes, Frank Woolley, Walter Hammond and others were obviously marvellous players in their own eras. But I find it impossible to visualise a better cricketer than Sobers. He could play in any Test match side today in any department—as a batsman, swing and seam bowler, orthodox spinner and back of the hand spinner with the old ball. His fielding is magnificent and he plays equally well in all conditions, whether it be on flint hard West Indian pitches or on the more variable pitches in England. In between times, he has created records in Australia where he scored 1,000 runs and took 50 wickets in a first-class season—a phenomenal performance this—and he repeated it the following year.

He is undoubtedly the most exciting cricketer in the world today, though matching him in batting is Graeme Pollock, the South African—but Pollock is not in the same class as a fieldsman and does not bowl. No doubt Davidson could match him with the ball and Simpson as a close-to-the-wicket catcher and Bland in the covers, but, when you think that the West Indian captain rolls the four of them into one cricketing life, it gives some indication of what a player he really is. He has led the West Indies since Frank Worrell's retirement in 1963 and has done a sound job in captaincy, though on a different plane from the one Worrell employed. Sobers has led by personal deeds and time and again has extricated the West Indies from awkward positions with a fine innings or a great bowling spell, or a couple of superb catches that have turned the tide of a Test match.

He is always as fit as a Test cricketer should be, though in recent times he has had some trouble with a knee similar to the injury that has forced Conrad Hunte out of Test cricket. But while he continues to play for the West Indies they will be a great force in world cricket and he himself will be the greatest drawcard in the game. He is rated as the most valuable cricketer in the world today; a listing with which I thoroughly agree, and I am happy he will continue to grace the game for many years. His sojourn with Nottinghamshire will make no difference to his international commitments for West Indies for he would have been playing League cricket in England anyway and he had already decided long ago that professional cricket was to be his career.

If there is such a thing, his is the perfect professional approach in that he has wonderful natural ability and is constantly endeavouring to be the best in each particular department of the game. He gives of everything whilst playing and his performances speak for themselves, marking him down as one of the greats from the time cricket began. The West Indies are fortunate to have him to follow on from Sir Frank and I rate him, with the latter and Sir Donald Bradman, as completing a trio of the most remarkable people I have known in cricket.

5

South Africa

No cricket country deserves the tag "Cinderella" more than South Africa where, over the years, the game has developed to the stage where the Springboks possess a team to be compared with the West Indies and England. England's great victory in the Caribbean in 1968 produced a piquant situation with England needing only to beat Australia at home in 1968 to be, in theory anyway, once again on top of the cricket table. In the event, of course, they drew the series.

South Africa, according to the pre-arranged schedule of international tours, then had the task of holding England in 1968–9 and, with the West Indies touring Australia at the same time and bidding to retrieve their prestige, cricket had much to offer when the last English season closed. Then, in September, following the selection of the M.C.C. side to visit South Africa, there blew up what will always be known as the D'Oliveira affair, with the immediate dire and tragic consequence of M.C.C.'s tour being cancelled. It was sad enough for South Africa, even before that time, that only three other countries were able to meet players like the Pollock brothers on the Test field because of the laws of the land that preclude competition against India, Pakistan and West Indies. Now England, after the pronouncement of South Africa's Prime Minister, have also been "forbidden". Just how long this situation will last, and whether Australia and New Zealand come out, as it were, in sympathy with M.C.C., is a problem that will require all the diplomacy—and, I hope, good sense—that cricket's administrators can muster.

I write this having seen most of the Test series played since 1964 in England, Australia, South Africa and the West Indies, and having witnessed South Africa winning their first Test series against Australia. Now this was a "Cinderella" performance if ever there was one. South Africa had never before beaten Australia in a series and had, in fact, never before won a Test match or any other game against an Australian touring side. Perhaps the writing was on the wall in the early part of the tour when Transvaal inflicted the first ever defeat on Bobby Simpson's side, and by the time the series was over there was no question as to which was the better side.

The most pointed thing I found about South African cricket when I was there in 1967 was that now they had some great cricketers as well as a good team, whereas previously it was almost exclusively team effort that produced their success. I think here in particular of Graeme Pollock and Denis Lindsay, two of the finest players in the world at this moment.

Peter Pollock is a regular selection in Rest of the World sides with his younger brother and, though he is not as brilliant in method he still has the best wicket-taking rate of any modern day fast bowler. But, for me, the young Pollock is always the *pièce de résistance* of any cricket match in which he takes part.

I don't know if there is a Graeme Pollock Fan Club in existence but I think I'd probably qualify for President for he is one of the few players in the world I would make a special trip to watch. Sobers and Kanhai of course, the Australian O'Neill, now retired, but, as far as I am concerned, Pollock at the time of writing is the best batsman in the world. I don't take into account anything else but batting here for if I were to talk about cricketers in the all-round sense then it would have to be Sobers who is without peer in the combined departments of the game.

It is not usual for South Africa to produce such a strokeplayer as this gifted left-hander for much of their batting is along English lines—a necessary follow-up to the fact that there are many English coaches who spend the winters in South Africa. There are exceptions like McLean and Pollock who are obviously natural strokeplayers and have been allowed to go their way, with significant success, but much of South Africa's batting in the time I have seen it has been solid and courageous rather than sparkling and brilliant. That, I hasten to say, was up to 1963 when Goddard's side came to Australia and would have won a Test series if they hadn't in the end been too concerned with not being beaten.

In 1952–3 in Australia the young McLean had caught the imagination of the Australian public and, with Funston, McGlew and Endean, had been partly responsible for South Africa drawing the series against an Australian side that, until then, had been unbeaten since the war. There was though something of a lapse in strokeplay and when I went to South Africa in 1957–8 the South Africans squandered any chance they had in the Tests by defensive batting that allowed the Australian bowlers to be on top for most of each Test match.

I first saw Graeme Pollock in 1963 and it was a slightly unnerving experience. He was only a youngster and in the second innings of a match against Ron Roberts' Cavaliers side in Port Elizabeth he was dropped before scoring off Des Hoare, the former Australian fast bowler. He proceeded to make 209 exhilarating runs, showing a fondness for off-side stroking that indicated that, though he was obviously a potentially great player, he might have a weakness around leg stump. Not so nowadays for he is magnificently strong on both sides of the wicket and keeps on improving more and more every time I see him bat.

He went to Australia with Goddard's side in 1963–4, making a hundred in Perth in the match against the Combined XI, and what a glorious hundred it was. Sir Donald Bradman had travelled from Adelaide to see the game and said to him later: "If you're ever going to bat like that again let me know and I'll make a point of being there."

He said later to me "This boy could be a wonderful player because he is only a baby as yet—I think we might see some great batting this year." Prophetic words indeed! Pollock's innings in Sydney and Adelaide that season were rated by old-timers as two of the finest ever seen in Australia and then, two years later in South Africa against the Australian side, he gave our bowlers another taste of what they might well be receiving for a number of years.

In the meantime I had seen him play one of the great centuries I have ever witnessed—125 at Nottingham in the match won by South Africa to give them the Test series against England in 1965. This was on a pitch soft like Plasticine and reckoned by many experts to be too slow for strokeplay. The England bowlers, concentrating just short of a length, had South Africa so much on the defensive that it looked almost impossible to score runs until young Pollock came in. His shots off the back foot that day are amongst the most memorable in my experience and he made a nonsense of the claims that the ball wasn't coming on to the bat and that the batsmen couldn't play their strokes because of the surface. In South Africa the following year he made a double century, a century and a 90 in the Test matches and the most glorious hundred imaginable in the one day fixture at the end of the tour, and

Australia's bowlers were ready to concede that already he is a great player. All the more tragic therefore is the clipping of his wings due to recent events.

I first saw South African cricket in 1952–3, meeting the players for the first time at a reception at the N.S.W. Cricket Association where President Mr. Sydney Smith gave the welcoming speech. Prior publicity for the side had been moderate indeed and it had been written in South Africa that the wise thing to do would be to cancel the tour, so weak was Jack Cheetham's side in all departments. As an afterthought it was conceded that they could hold their own in the field but it was reckoned that the batting and bowling was so weak that the tour would be a massacre. Much the same was said about Australia's side that went to South Africa in 1957–8 and there was a relatively similar result from both tours. In 1957–8 Australia won three-nil to preserve the unbeaten record in South Africa but Cheetham's team's performance in 1952–3 was just as good for they halved the series against what, at that time, was reckoned to be the best side in the world.

When welcoming Jack Cheetham and manager Ken Viljoen, Mr. Smith that evening in Sydney said he hoped the side would do better than some other South African sides that had been out there, notably the one in 1931–2 which had been beaten by an innings and 163, an innings and 155, 169, ten wickets and then an innings and 72, adding that in the final match South Africa could make only 36 and 45 in Melbourne. Cheetham, ever the diplomat, veered away from the subject a little in thanking Mr. Smith for his remarks, commenting on the fact that the pitch they played on in Melbourne was composed of Bulli soil and drawing a nice comparison between that and a load of "bull" that had once been transported to South Africa.

It was hardly a good note for the 1952–3 South African side to begin the serious part of their tour but, as they rightly said, what really mattered was what happened on the field and they were as determined as any side I have ever seen to make sure that their performances would force the critics to eat their words. They did this with what was essentially an ordinary bowling attack, with the exception of one great bowler in Hugh Tayfield, some steady and at times brilliant batting and some of the greatest fielding that has ever been witnessed on Australian cricket grounds.

The feature of South African cricket over the years has been their tremendous fighting qualities and they often seem at their best when in trouble. Time and again in 1952–3 courageous batting would bring about a recovery after the early breakthrough had been achieved by Australia, and much the same has applied in their matches since that time though now they are just as likely to hit 200 in even time in a slightly different method of recovery.

The game was first played in South Africa around 1800, probably introduced by the Army, and most of the early cricket out there was played on matting placed on top of an antbed. Turf was used for the first time as late as 1926–7 in Currie Cup matches and it wasn't until 1930–1 that Percy Chapman's side played a Test match on turf for the first time in South Africa. Their successes have been spasmodic, despite the fact that they have had some great players over the years, and they have won only five Test matches in 44 played in England since the time their competition began. They have played 11 series against Australia and hadn't won one until 1966–7 but they have beaten New Zealand three times in five Test series with the other two being drawn.

It is not an imposing record and it is for this reason that I class them as a Cinderella cricket country, adding that, subject to the present discontents being healed, I think their best days are in front of them. Certainly in 1967 they had, to all intents and purposes, the nucleus of a top Test team for many years to come with not only the Test side itself being strong but also the reserve strength of young players unable to make the side that season. One of these, Ackerman, has decided to throw in his lot with Northamptonshire in English county cricket and may therefore be lost to South Africa—a pity this because on the score of his performances against the Australians in 1966–7 he could well have been a South African Test player for years to come.

One of the younger players, Procter, was an outstanding success with the ball in the Test matches and though he didn't achieve very much with the bat he is one of the most promising batsmen in the land who, I believe, will in the future become one of the finest all-rounders ever to play for South Africa. But the pick of those who didn't play in the Tests was Barry Richards, a brilliant right-hander who plays very straight and hits the ball very hard with perfect timing. He is one of the best young players I have ever seen and I have no doubt that he will make a great name in international cricket in the next few years. With South Africa so successful in the season the Australians were there, there was little chance to ease Richards into the side though there were quite a few Australians, myself included, who would have taken the opportunity to play him at some stage of the series. He played beautifully in the match in East London when a South African XI played Australia and gave a fine exhibition of strokeplay in both the Natal match and the South African XI game at 'Maritzburg later in the season. His brilliant promise was amply confirmed when he joined Hampshire in 1968 and scored more than 2,000 runs—more than any man in the country—in his first full season of first-class cricket. His runs moreover were always scored at a healthy pace and he must have been as disappointed as his supporters that he could not do battle with England's bowlers the following winter.

Even before the unfortunate happenings of September 1968, one of the major problems facing South African cricketers was that they played in competition against only a small number of countries. The problem now, of course, has become more acute, and this, in the end, might well be to the disadvantage of young players who, under normal circumstances, would become seasoned Test cricketers in a matter of two or three years. Take young Ackerman for instance—if he were an Australian playing in Sheffield Shield cricket and Test matches every season, or rather every six months, either in his own country or overseas, then, if good enough, he would be a remarkably fine cricketer in the space of three years. But now in South Africa, the Australians, having been there in 1966–7, are unlikely to return for nearly ten years and although, in the meantime, South Africa will presumably come to Australia, it doesn't leave as much room for development as in other countries of the cricket world. I don't know Ackerman's thoughts on the matter for I haven't spoken to him, but he is a typical young South African cricketer on the verge of stardom who, it seems, has decided that he wants to play regular cricket rather than occasional cricket against other countries.

One of the best things from the South African point of view is that in recent years there has been a wonderful upsurge of interest in the Afrikaans section of the community and the game is now played in a lot of Afrikaans schools. This is quite a change from when I was in South Africa in 1957–8, 1960 and 1963, when there was very little interest in this section which had football as a part-sport, part-religion for 12 months of the year. But the fighting qualities of the South African cricket team and their success changed all this and it remains to be seen whether or not a failure in the future will reverse the process. I don't think so, for once the interest is in the schools and in the young people then it will go through the whole community and I shall be very surprised if we don't see some good Afrikaans cricketers come from this policy.

Certainly in South Africa the treatment of young players is remarkably good and the benefit is being shown already in the way they are producing promising Test players and near Test players just out of their teens. The South African schools organisation and the universities have recently sent teams to England and, as I write this, have scheduled a tour of Australia for a group of schoolboys destined to play against Australia's top schools. Young players have had the chance to come to England in Fezela, schools and university sides, and from these has come the nucleus of the present team that has lifted South Africa to the top.

Despite West Indies' loss against England I would still rate those two sides and South Africa as the top three in Test cricket, and would be loth to separate them and name one as being far and away better than the others. Before the West Indies–England series I would have chosen the West Indies to win a world series because of their strength in bowling and the versatility of any attack that could be put in the field. But it was obvious that, though Sobers and Gibbs retained their skill, the years and injury were catching up with Hall and Griffith and, with few young fast bowlers on the horizon out there, Sobers will have his problems in the immediate future in finding a combination to shake the opposition with sheer speed. Now it will need to be a more subtle attack!

The South Africans, on the other hand, possessed an attack based almost entirely on speed when I was there a few years ago. The Springboks have produced some fine spin bowlers over the years but when the Australians were there in 1966–7 the conditions favoured seam bowlers rather than sheer pace or spin. The South African attack was ideally suited by this although, if the Australians had been good enough, they too could have used the conditions as successfully. But there was an obvious lack of spin potential in the country when I was there and this is why I believe they lacked the West Indies penetration in all types of conditions and, of course, they lack someone of the calibre of Sobers, able to take part in every aspect of the attack. But the way they played against Australia led me to believe that they were as yet nowhere near their peak and, *given intense competition*, they could have a very good side indeed for the next ten years. They had, when the Australian side arrived in South Africa, the most terrible barrier to overcome of having never won a Test match against Australia in their own country. Neither had they won a Province match against Australia but once they had done this in the early part of the tour they then believed in themselves and became vastly different players.

Ten years ago they also had a very good side that didn't really believe in itself although it had a lot of very good cricketers, rather like the West Indies in earlier years. A bowling attack that starts off with Adcock, Heine and Tayfield can never be anything but good and this is what the Australians faced in 1957 against a side that had just drawn a series against England after being two down. But they had their own internal problems then, and injuries didn't help either, though having played a drawn Test in Johannesburg in the first contest of the series no-one would have supposed Australia would win three out of the next four.

As a pair of fast bowlers go, I don't know that there were any better than Adcock and Heine. Miller and Lindwall were great, so were Tyson and Statham, and I presume McDonald and Gregory fell in the same category, but I would place Adcock and Heine right in the top bracket. Both were tall, around the 6ft. 2 or 3 in. mark, but were quite dissimilar in method, Adcock being possessed of a very high action whilst Heine was more of the round arm variety. Both were militant customers who, seemingly on the field, derived great pleasure from seeing the batsman weaving out of the road of fast, climbing deliveries and, like the other bowling combinations mentioned, they were never averse to dropping one or two short and glaring at the competitor at the other end.

I first struck them in Johannesburg on a green, fast pitch that gave them some help but also allowed the batsman to play his shots—and heavens they were fast! Adcock, though he was so high in action, had a somewhat strange delivery that in itself was smooth enough but gave a rather windmilling appearance as he came boring in from his long run. He ran to the crease faster than any other pace bowler I have seen and although he gathered momentum on the way he was moving quicker in the first ten yards than is customary for any fast bowler. When he got near the crease he would transfer the ball to his bowling hand and begin a series of loops with his bowling arm that sound awkward on paper but by sight was quite attractive, culminating finally in a complete circle to propel the ball at the batsman from a position just above his right ear. Practically all the time he was cutting his fingers across the ball, not in the accepted way of right-handers where the ball would swing out or perhaps cut back, but more in the manner of a medium pacer bowling leg cutters, and this was one of the reasons he was so difficult to play. He swung the ball both ways but it was this fast leg cutter that really made him difficult at the pace at which he bowled, and the only thing I could ever find wrong with his bowling was the fact that he, at times, bowled too short in a bid to be too hostile.

There was very little front foot play needed against either him or Heine and I found it easier in South Africa to be prepared to play them off the back foot in the first instance, relying on the fact that for most of the time they were aiming to have the batsman play them at around rib height. This was much the same as batting against Hall in 1960–1 where we all thought that he bowled consistently too short. The three of them were effective, and magnificently so, with their own method but I have always felt that had they given the ball a little more room to swing then they may have been even more effective.

It was fortunate for Australia in 1957–8 when they played South Africa that there was a defensive strain in South African cricket, particularly in the batting, and emphasised even more after the First Test Match where South Africa dominated the first part of that game by making 470 for nine declared. The Third Test match in Durban should have been an easy South African victory after Australia had won the Second in Cape Town, but instead South Africa took so long over scoring 384 they left themselves insufficient time to bowl us out in the second innings. McGlew in that match made 105 in 575 minutes and Waite achieved his century in 414 minutes. McGlew's is the slowest Test century on record and a feature of the match was the fact that there seemed to be so many different opinions on the South African side of how the game should be won that in the end their vacillating cost them the match. This seemed to be part of South African cricket at this particular stage, and it was all the more strange because they had done well previously through going on to the attack and they have done remarkably well since for the same reason.

I often compared the two series (1957 and 1967) when watching a year ago in South Africa and when South Africa got into trouble in the latter series they got out of it by attack, and generally brilliant attack by players like Pollock and Lindsay, in much the same way as they had done in 1963–4 in Australia. The last two or three years has been marked by selections in South African cricket with the emphasis on attack, and this was particularly so when they came to Australia in 1963. Goddard, Barlow, Graeme Pollock and Lindsay were a fine group of attacking batsmen and if this lesson has been hammered home, as I am sure it has, I have no doubt they will never revert again to a defensive outlook in the game and will be the better for it.

They have one problem coming up in the choice of a future captain. They have had a number of leaders in recent years, the most successful of whom was van der Merwe, himself an ordinary but most courageous cricketer, who has now retired. McGlew and van Reyneveld skippered the side in 1957–8 and McGlew carried on in 1960 and then Goddard took over for two years against England and Australia. Now it seems the captaincy will lie between Barlow, who was vice-captain for the series against Australia, Graeme Pollock and Bacher who captains Transvaal above Barlow in the Currie Cup. There seems no doubt that the Test selectors have Barlow in mind for the future captaincy, having lifted him above Bacher, who also played in the Test series against Australia, and I am sure he would do a good job—ebullient character that he is—in any game of cricket from a park pick-up match to a Test arena.

Personally though, as an outsider, I would choose Graeme Pollock whom I class as the most brilliant player in the world today, and leave Barlow to get on with his all-round job in the side, playing him as vice-captain. I think that would be the ideal combination. I have always been impressed with Pollock's grasp of the game and his outlook, but in South Africa they say that they don't think he would make an outstanding captain. I have seen nothing to justify this line of thinking in the encounters I have had with Pollock who is a quiet enthusiast and one whom I think would get a tremendous amount out of his players. It is only a personal opinion and I have a very high regard for Barlow and his cricket, as well as his great enthusiasm which makes itself evident on and off the field. Whichever of them captains South Africa in the future will do a good job for both are attacking cricketers with attacking thoughts and they will never be guilty of letting South African cricket slip back into its defensive vein.

Captains all over the world have plenty of problems once the game gets under way so there's no real point in adding to them. Never take another's word for the state of the pitch, for instance, as did Sid Barnes one day when he arrived a little later than usual at the ground to toss. The opposing captain asked if he wanted to see the pitch but Sid said "No thanks, I guess it's the same as usual—a good batting track." He won the toss and batted but the pitch, in fact, was soft and difficult, rain having fallen overnight, and the New South Wales side was in trouble. Sid's answer was to make a century, but he never took anyone's word about the state of the pitch after that.

In the same bracket of advice is the request not to be as finicky in your captaincy as one Australian who had the habit of putting a man wherever the ball had just gone. At the end of one particularly exasperating over his wicket-keeper was constrained to tell him in rather terse manner that he could do what he liked with the fieldsmen, but would he mind allowing the custodian of the gauntlets to work out his own salvation.

One of the great successes of recent years was Denis Lindsay, son of former South African wicket-keeper Johnny Lindsay. The younger wicket-keeper-batsman took over from Waite during the Australian tour in 1963–4 and proved just as competent as this fine cricketer and then brilliantly successful against Simpson's side three years later. Whether or not he will ever have another season as good as the one he enjoyed last year is a matter of conjecture, but I believe that anything a player does once he can do again and there was nothing flukey about Lindsay's performances that season. He began attacking the moment he went in to bat and I found it fascinating watching and trying to work out some method of countering his vicious strokeplay that wasn't restricted to any particular part of the field. Bacher was extremely strong on the on side and could perhaps be contained by bowling at his off stump, though he was quite likely to cart the bowler to the on side given half a chance. But Lindsay seemed to be strong in every department of his batting and 606 runs at 86 in seven innings gives some idea of his dominance over the Australian attack.

But I did find myself wondering if he would make the same number of runs against a steady England seam attack, concentrating solely on bowling short of a good length and directly at the middle stump. Possibly he would, but if denied the chance to hook —and he is a brilliant hooker—then that would be one of his frequent run-getting strokes cut out. I also wondered why the Australian bowlers—the medium pacers that is—persisted in bowling short at him rather than keep on a good length at his off stump, trying to move the ball into his body. The reason for this was that like O'Neill, the Australian, Lindsay, when he cuts, often gives himself room for the shot and cuts much finer than most other batsmen I have seen who are strong in this stroke. Taber and McKenzie, very belatedly, decided to try him with this in Port Elizabeth in the Fifth Test and they picked him up at second slip from just such a stroke where he drew away slightly to the leg stump to give himself room and cut the ball straight to Redpath. All that is merely conjecture and I expect him to be very successful in years to come and a worthy successor to Waite, who is justifiably listed as one of the greats of South African cricket.

But I hope that players like Lindsay will always be encouraged in South African cricket for they made the tour of South Africa the more enjoyable because of their refusal to be tied down by any bowler, and I'd like to think that they will continue in this vein in the future. They beat Australia on their merits in 1966–7, simply because of attacking cricket and the fact that they were always prepared to take a risk even when the going was tough—and that is a policy which has paid off in more cricket teams than the South Africans.

One of the problems faced by future South African team selection is that some of the players—and the best players at that—have either finished their career or are coming to the end of it. There is no doubt about the Pollock brothers, Lindsay or Barlow being available for any future Test series and certainly Procter and Richards are young players on the fringe of great things. Bacher is a pugnacious character who, until his eye deserts him, will be a force in South African cricket and Lance is an all-rounder, much better than he himself believes. But Peter van der Merwe's irrevocable decision to retire from first-class cricket means that the search for a new captain is on, and, although Trevor Goddard has made a successful comeback, it remains to be seen how long the desire to pursue new fields will be with him. Atholl McKinnon and David Pithey achieved only moderate success as spinners in the series against the Australians and Colin Bland, after being out of form early in the tour, injured a knee and had to undergo an operation that could certainly come against him in future years. Dumbrill achieved little with either bat or ball and though a useful all-rounder is unlikely again to be preferred to Richards. The best leg spinning prospect in South Africa is du Preez who is also a useful batsman, though not making any runs in the series against Australia.

All this adds up to the fact that the future of South African Test cricket will depend, assuming that the problems of politics can be solved, on a small nucleus of players of some experience, together with the ability of other young players, if retained in the country, to lift themselves to the standard required in Test series against England, Australia and New Zealand. I would think that Lindsay, the two Pollocks, Lance, Bacher, Barlow, Procter and Richards will be eight certainties in the side for some time to come and that there is a great chance for four attacking young players to force their way on to the Test scene and remain there for many years. A lot though depends on the approach of South Africa's administrators and selectors and whether or not they continue to pursue their successful attacking way.

Much will depend also on the choice of captain, for in van der Merwe South Africa, for that stage of their cricket development had just about the ideal man. He is quite an unassuming character and I saw him one day in Port Elizabeth allow his bowlers and fieldsmen to waste time unashamedly in a bid to stop Australia winning a Province match. But he lost no points in captaining the side against Bobby Simpson, and it would have been a good thing for South African cricket had he continued in the game rather than announce his retirement. He was a much better batsman than he looked, for, being possessed of a rather ungainly style, with great preference for the leg glance from almost any position in the batting crease, he often gave an impression of being fallible, particularly against spin. But having seen him in Australia when the side was often in trouble, I knew that any lack of ability was more than made up for by stern dedication, and this proved to be a pretty accurate summing up when the Australians were in South Africa. South African cricket owes him quite a debt and the one who takes over from him has the big problem of following on from a successful captain—in fact, almost the only victoriously successful South African captain of all time.

But I firmly believe that the one player to whom South Africa owes most gratitude these days is Graeme Pollock whom I class as being the best batsman in the world at the time of writing. Now that, in truth, is a very glowing description of any player for there are some great individual players in the world today in all countries. I have told how the first time I saw the young Pollock he was playing in a match against a composite Cavaliers side and, after an indifferent start, made a double century. I am quite prepared to believe the old timers who grasp me by the arm and peer rheumily into the distance, telling me at the same time that in their day there were plenty of others as good as Pollock. Perhaps so, but I prefer to live in the present and this boy, for me, is one of the great cricketers ever to appear on the international scene and one who will get better and better as times go on.

I never saw Bradman play at his peak and, consequently, I am in no position to make any sort of comparison and, in any case, I believe, having seen the Don in later years and listened to his team mates and contemporary opposition talk of his prowess, that it would be very difficult to find one to compare with him. Pollock, for instance, is obviously not as light on his feet and is not quite as strong on the on side as the off. But I marvel every time I see the youngster play that anyone can be as good, having played as little international cricket as he has done. When I wrote this he had played just 19 Test matches in four years. Yet in that time he had made nearly 2,000 runs at an average of just under 60, as well as six centuries and eight half centuries in Test matches. Pollock is a superb athlete, standing six feet tall and a magnificent build, with a complete dedication to attacking batting and subjecting the bowler to the maximum amount of punishment over the longest period possible.

There is something of the cavalier about his batting, which is basically built on orthodox lines, but he has that tremendous advantage given to only the great players of always appearing to be on top of the bowling no matter what the situation of the game. In Adelaide in 1964 he batted magnificently—there was only one bad ball in the 22 runs he took off an over from Bob Simpson. I have never yet seen a great player who is not a back foot player and Pollock is tremendously strong in this department and no bowler can ever successfully tie him down by bowling what is commonly known as short of a good length. This in itself is something of a loose phrase for it indicates only roughly a position for the ball to land somewhere short of a driving length. The player who concentrates solely on a front foot movement to begin with is likely to find himself tied down through not being able to drive, but Pollock is such a fine athlete and such a wonderful batsman that he never condemns himself to a forward movement before instinctively knowing exactly where the ball is going to land.

A bowler knows when he is pitted against a great batsman simply because his good deliveries are hit for four or, even if intercepted by a fieldsman, an attacking stroke has been played to them. The bowler also knows when he can tie a batsman down and this is one of the most enjoyable parts of bowling, to try and gauge the ability of the opponent and either work on the fact that he is weak in some particular department or keep him so strokeless that he will eventually play an injudicious shot. Players like Pollock though, where there is no real weakness, have to be dismissed and this is the real purpose of cricket in that it provides a tremendous battle between bat and ball. Over the years when I played Test cricket there were only a handful of players one had to attack from the word go—or perish! This, in a sense, assists the batsman for he is likely to get more loose deliveries from an attacking bowler than from one concentrating on tying down his strokes.

I didn't play a great deal against Pollock—only the one series plus a couple of minor games—and all the honours went to him in one of the most enthralling bowling episodes of my life. It was for this reason in 1966–7 that I watched him with even more pleasure than normal to see how his game had improved since the days when I was on the field as an opponent. He is obviously a thinker about the game for the slight weakness he had shown around leg stump a couple of years previously had disappeared and he was now as close to a complete all-round batsman as one was likely to find. Even now his strength is on the off side, particularly off the back foot, and for those searching these lines in the hope of finding some method to dismiss him, I can proffer little hope other than the advice to keep on attacking because there will be a reciprocal gesture from the other end that will give any bowler his best hope of success.

The most important thing with Pollock is that first of all he believes in his own ability in a quiet modest way, and secondly he has a very firm conviction that cricket is a wonderful game and that the bowler and the ball are there for hitting. He has an unassailable confidence in his ability, again in the most modest fashion imaginable, and a belief in South African cricket that is one of the best things to happen to the game in that country in the post-war era. Not all batsmen are possessed of his ability and the bowlers at that point might give a small sigh of relief, but I for one look forward to even more improvement from him in the years to come and have no hesitation in claiming that there will be few, if any, better players walk on to a Test arena in the time I am permitted to watch cricket.

As often happens with brothers, Graeme and his brother Peter are quite dissimilar in cricketing styles, and in temperament, but they make up one of the great family pairs of all time in first-class cricket. Peter came with Graeme to Australia in 1963–4 as a handy batsman, useful fieldsman and fast bowler, and confirmed his ability in that series and has now taken a hundred wickets in Test matches at a faster rate than most other contemporary bowlers. He has taken five wickets in an innings eight times and has his 101 wickets from some 5,800 deliveries, despite having slightly fallen away in form in recent times.

One of his biggest problems is that there has been no really fast bowler at the other end in his time—rather has South Africa been content with a series of medium pacers to use the new ball whilst using the older Pollock as a spearhead of the attack. In the series against the Australians Trimborn, Goddard, Procter, Barlow, Lance and Dumbrill shared the other end and, whilst they are all useful medium pacers, it stands to reason that a combination of, say, Miller and Lindwall is always going to be more effective than, say, Lindwall and "Slasher" Mackay or Lindwall and Neil Hawke. The fastest of the supporting bowlers on show in recent times has been Procter, an interesting prospect who bowls off the wrong foot, but I believe that Procter will eventually become a top South African all-rounder, rather than an opening bowler, and that the search for another bowler of real pace must go on on the veldt.

Any one of the bowlers mentioned earlier can act as a third seamer and, indeed, Barlow, Lance or Procter would be the ideal for this, assuming always that Goddard at some stage must come to the end of his illustrious Test career. Peter Pollock though is a good bowler who will be an even better one if only the selectors can find a real quickie to partner him and, of course, they must still produce two spinners of international class if they are to be completely successful against Australia and England.

The system of selection in South Africa at the moment lends itself to encouragement of youth and I know of no better system for the good of cricket in any country. Already it has lifted the Cinderella cricket country to the stage of knowing how to win, as distinct from merely desperately wanting to win, and for them I foresee a great future, albeit a restricted one, in international cricket. I trust they will be allowed to prove me right.

6

India

I thought for many years that in Australia there existed the most enthusiastic cricket followers in the world but having toured India and Pakistan I am convinced now that the accolade must go to the supporters of those two countries. I first saw Indian cricket in 1956 on the way back from the England tour where Australia had lost the series to Peter May's side and I was astonished at the enthusiasm and the big crowds present at every game we played on that short tour of the sub-continent. On their own pitches Indian cricketers can hold their own with anyone in the world but they have never been as successful when touring overseas and their best performance against Australia was in 1964–5 when at home they drew a series against Bobby Simpson's side. Prior to that Australia had won a series four-nil in Australia and then two-nil in India in 1956–7 and two–one in India in 1959–60.

The astonishing thing about Indian cricket is the spectators. They throng to the grounds in their thousands and, over a full Test match, in their hundreds of thousands, cheerfully sitting in cramped space having bought legitimate and at times non-existent tickets after months of saving for the great day. They engender wonderful enthusiasm in these home matches, an enthusiasm that is transmitted to the players and seems to lift India's cricketers to a peak that they are never quite able to reach when playing out of their own country.

Back in 1947–8 an Indian side came to Australia to do battle with Bradman's team, with players intent on gaining places in the Australian side to visit England in 1948. They struck Bradman at his peak, making 715 runs including four centuries, and other players like Harvey, Morris, Barnes and Hassett, all preparing to take England by storm the following year. The Indians were brushed aside, despite some excellent performances by Armanath, Mankad, Hazare and Phadkar, but unfortunately too much depended on this small group in conditions that suited the Australians down to the ground. In 1952 it was Trueman and Bedser who did all the damage and this was the start of Trueman's illustrious career in Test cricket where, in the First Test at Leeds, he was the spearhead of the England attack that took the first four Indian second innings wickets for no runs and made it possible for England to win the Test by seven wickets.

In 1956 Australia had gone through their disappointing series against England and then distinguished themselves by making 80 in almost a whole day against Pakistan on the mat in Karachi before arriving in Madras for the First Test against India. This was very much the era of the low scoring day and on this first day in Madras India, having won the toss, made just over the hundred for the loss of five wickets, despite the fact that the Australian side was weakened by illness and injury. It happened that it was also one of the hottest periods of the year in India and it coincided with the moment where I made the decision that was to change my bowling style for the rest of my career. In Karachi I had bowled off my normal run on the mat, a run that was slightly longer than normal for a slow spin bowler, and one that was not at all suitable for the hot conditions in either India or Pakistan.

At practice the day before the match I tried a shorter run, merely to save a bit of strength for the morrow, and it happened that I bowled quite well to Neil Harvey and Jimmy Burke. Having done this for half an hour I thought it might be worth spending a bit of time on a shortened and changed run up as it certainly looked as though I was intended to do a fair amount of bowling in the three Test matches to come. Instead of taking 12 paces and running in fairly straight, I shortened my run to six paces and came from a slight angle and at the end of the practice session, which went for a couple of hours longer than I had originally expected, I felt that I was getting somewhere. I was still dead scared at the thought of using it in the match but, on the basis of nothing ventured nothing gained, I tried it in the first innings of the Test and took seven for 71! I'd like to be able to write that I bowled well but, in fact, I bowled very moderately, picking up the tail-enders to assist the average. However, I felt at least that there was something to work on here and it was from this time on that I operated with the shorter run that I used for the next eight years in Test cricket.

This 1956 series in India, consisting of only three Tests, produced remarkably little attractive cricket, but the thing that sticks in my mind is the fervent enthusiasm of the spectators who paid their money and saw a minimum number of runs scored each day. Australia won the First Test in Madras and the Second was drawn in Bombay, and then the Third, played on an extraordinary surface in Calcutta, was completely dominated by spin to the extent that neither India nor Australia could reach a team total of 200 in any of the four innings.

When we arrived there local officials said the ground had been flooded and certainly the pitch on which we were to play looked as though it had been covered with silt. I have never seen a pitch spin like this one and it was almost impossible I found to bowl a right-hander for the ball would have to be pitched two feet outside leg stump to have any chance at all. I bowled to three slips in this game, the only time in my life I have ever done so, and Ghulam Ahmed, the Indian off-spinner, was almost unplayable. The game was finished with a day and a half to spare, which was a great pity for every day saw packed stands and vocally enthusiastic spectators desperately keen to see as much good cricket as possible.

In 1959–60 Australia undertook a 13-week tour to India and Pakistan, the Indian section of which included five Test matches, of which two were drawn and one lost. Australia won the First at New Delhi, the focal point of which was whether or not we could find 11 fit players to get on the field. I myself was unable to practise the day before the start of the Test and was only able to have the services of a local doctor for as much time as he could spare from five or six of the other players also suffering from stomach ailments. We won the match on a pitch that took increasing spin over the four days' play, even though India had first use of the pitch. I took eight wickets in the match, Kline five and Davidson three, but this gave no insight into the tremendous achievement of the Indian side in the following Test when, having won the toss, India gained their first ever victory over Australia by 119 runs on a newly-laid turf pitch. It was a victory entirely on merit for Australia led by 67 on the first innings and we were then unable to make 225 for victory in the last part of the match, collapsing against Jasu Patel who took 14 wickets for 124 in the game. This game was played at Kanpur and was one of the most interesting cricket matches in which I had taken part to that moment. Prior to this, matches in Kanpur had been played on the mat and big scores were the order of the day with very few games being decided. The surface for this game in 1959 though, was one that was obviously going to take spin and, in fact, Alan Davidson chopped down his run and bowled slow medium-paced spinners and cutters throughout the match taking 12 for 124, almost to match Patel's wonderful return.

There was an extremely interesting happening at the end of this game that had repercussions later in the tour at Bombay, where I was to come into conflict with one of India's top administrators who was also a working journalist. At the close of the game, after we had been beaten, the Indian side did a victory lap of the ground, the only untoward incident here being the felling of Nadkarni with an unripe guava fired from a catapult from the midst of the students' stand where the youthful spectators were cheering Ramchand's side. Both teams got on very well during this series, as has always happened in Test series between Australia and India, and I said to "Ram" when the sides were leaving the ground that if all or any of his players felt like a drink later we would be delighted to welcome them at the Retreat where we were staying. The administrator/journalist, mentioned earlier, wrote two articles at the end of the match, one for local consumption which extolled the playing virtues of the Indian side and the sporting virtues of the Australian side, emphasising that never had he seen a team lose with better spirit than the Australians. Unfortunately, though, he wrote a second article for a paper a long way from Kanpur, extolling the playing virtues of the Indian side and saying that the Australians were the worst and most ungracious bunch of sportsmen ever to come to India.

Even more unfortunate was the fact that a journalist friend of mine sent me the second article which, as I say, bore no relation to the first and which raised one or two eyebrows in the Australian camp. When challenged in Bombay about this seeming lack of co-ordination in his writing, he claimed that he had been misquoted and then demanded that I apologise to him for having challenged his integrity. It was a sticky moment, particularly when both I and the manager, Sam Loxton, made it quite plain that not only was there no intention of apologising but that until he was able to proffer some better explanation for the difference in his thoughts, spoken and written, we would prefer to do any of our future entertaining without his assistance.

This Bombay Test was significant for a fine piece of batting from Harvey and O'Neill and a great fightback by India in their second innings to draw the game and carry the series at one-all to the Test at Madras.

I have started some Test matches in strange circumstances all over the world but nothing as bizarre as the Fourth Test of this series at Madras where, when the players walked out to have a look at the pitch the afternoon before the game began, it was found that the surface on which we were to play, whilst being perfectly flat and well rolled, was as rough as a piece of sandpaper. Harvey called me over to have a look at it, adding in puzzled fashion that he had never seen anything quite like this and what did I think it was on top of the pitch.

We looked at it for a long time and finally decided, astonishing though it was, that there were tiny pieces of wood pitted all over the surface of the pitch and I then went looking for someone in charge who could try and clear up for us just what we would be playing on on the morrow. It took a long time to get to the point but eventually we found that a load of sawdust had been rolled into the pitch "to hold it together". If you had made a film of the game no-one would have believed it for 13 different balls were used in the time that Australia made 342 and then bowled out India for 149 and 138. In the end we obtained a box of brand new balls plus several sheets of sandpaper and sanded all the shine off, as well as roughening the stitches, and kept on throwing out a new ball each time the one in use disintegrated. There was nothing wrong with the bounce of the pitch—it was entirely even but a magnificent surface for the spinners—and the game again finished early and goes down as one of the strangest games in which I have played.

India went to Australia again 1967–8, 20 years after their first full tour of our country—a time lapse that is completely unjustified by performances over the years. I have long been anti the system of Australian teams going to India without reciprocal visits being made, simply because I believe that the Australian Board of Control has taken advantage of the fact that India finds it difficult to get full tours of their own country by opposition teams. M.C.C. often sends sides to India but Australia has made only one full scale tour, that of 1959–60, on a basis that produced a great deal of money for Australian cricket.

Each of the five Tests in India and the three in Pakistan of that tour provided Australian cricket with something like £A7,000 in guaranteed gate money, a total of nearly £A60,000 in all. I am well aware of the fact that India is not the strongest cricket country in the world but I do believe that they have been badly done by in the fact that they have not visited Australia since

1947–8 and yet they have visited England and the West Indies in that time on a number of occasions. I am happy that it seems now that reciprocal visits will be more frequent, even if on a shorter tour basis, whereby Australia can still play its Sheffield Shield matches throughout the season and India can then go on and play matches against New Zealand to supplement the tour.

The biggest problem India faces in this age is not lack of players, and good players at that, for they have quite a number in both batting and spin bowling spheres to match anyone in the world. But it is their pitches that cause them most trouble, slow grassless surfaces that mean the early demise of fast bowlers almost before they are even able to mark out a 20 yard run. The fastest bowler I ever saw in India was Desai who, for his pace, was a remarkably small man and one who was rarely able, enthusiastic though he was, to force an opening batsman on to the back foot.

In England in 1967 there were no fast bowlers at all, only two medium pacers, Guha and Mohol, and when these two broke down it became one of the strangest-looking opening attacks of all time in Test cricket. I can't really see any chance of young fast bowlers earning a place in an Indian side whilst pitches remain as they are with no bounce to lift the ball above stump height and no pace to enthuse a youngster desperately wanting to force a batsman on to the defensive. Nor can I see any chance of India becoming a real cricket power in the world outside their own country unless they get some fast bowlers, so it seems nothing but an impossible circle. Their bowlers out there are brought up to spin the ball, and this they do very well indeed, not only on their own pitches but on overseas surfaces as well, but there is a tremendous psychological lift for opposition opening batsmen, and indeed anyone early in the order, when they know that there is no pace to overcome before getting down to the spinners.

Good bowlers as they were, Chandrasekhar and Bedi in England in 1967 suffered greatly from the lack of support in pace bowling in the side, and it must have been a nightmare for the Indian captain, the Nawab of Pataudi. Their performances in England last season on a shortened tour were far below what I expected from them, even allowing for the lack of drive in their opening bowling, and, even though this could be partly attributed to a terribly wet May, the fact remained that although they promised much at the start of the tour they were well short of England's standard in the three Test matches played. They are so unused to meeting pace bowling that they were unable to combat Snow, as leader of the England attack, and, though they get plenty of practice against spin, Illingworth's accuracy and professional approach sorely tried them in the three major matches. I am told by Indian players and officials that they are unlikely to produce any fast bowlers in the near future and I am afraid this will always stand against them when they come into competition with other countries who possess bowlers of this type.

Back in 1947–8, their most successful bowlers were Mankad and Armanath and over the years there have been some fine cricketers come from India, players like Hazare, who was a brilliant cricketer in Australia on that tour. In recent times Borde has hit centuries against the West Indies and has scored nearly 3,000 runs in Test matches to be the leading contemporary batsman of the country. The Nawab of Pataudi is a brilliant strokeplayer and only one very gifted could have played the type of innings he did in the second innings of the First Test at Leeds in 1967. This was one of the best Test innings in modern times, played in the context of a game that could only be saved and not won, and over after over he defied anything England captain Brian Close could produce for him, striking the loose ball firmly and playing soundly in defence against all else.

Chandrasekhar, the medium pace spinner with the withered arm, is a world class bowler. But, looking at it from outside, he is the only bowler who is really a full time attacking performer and he certainly needs someone at the other end, not just to tie the batsmen down but to gain the breakthrough and give him as much attacking assistance as possible.

I was most impressed with Pataudi's captaincy in England and there is no doubt that he is the man who can inspire Indian cricket to greater heights than they have reached in recent years and, despite the fact that he plays under the most awkward handicap of lacking full sight in one eye. He is a slightly built righthander and a dashing strokeplayer who can take apart any attack when in the mood and, as well, defend against the best bowlers from any side India might be playing. He took over the captaincy after Contractor was tragically injured on the West Indies tour in 1962 and has played quite a bit of cricket in England —an experience that obviously benefited him when the side came to this country in 1967. Far too often though he was committed to coming in to bat in a crisis for the earlier batsmen had never been able to get on top of England's bowling, with the exception of a short period in the First Test at Leeds when Engineer and Wadekar shared a fine strokeplaying partnership.

There are plenty of young players on the fringe of very important things in India but they need experience and need it quickly if they are to prosper on tours of all other cricket countries. Hanumant Singh is one of the most promising young players in the world and Wadekar improved tremendously match by match as he gained in experience on all types of pitches and against all types of bowling. Sardesai's injury was a crushing blow for it meant that with Engineer and Kunderan opening the innings—two players completely intent on strokeplay—there was always the chance of an early breakthrough. Sardesai looked a very good all-round player in all conditions and if India could find another steady player to go in first with him, and bat Engineer lower in the list, they would have a far stronger batting side and one that would allow the later batsmen every chance to play their natural game.

In Test matches in which I have taken part against India there has been an emphasis on defensive play at times and second-hand information seems to point to the same problem in matches against other countries played in India on the slow pitches prevailing out there. In 15 Test matches between India and Pakistan only three have been decided and, though there may be something in the claim that national pride is something to do with this, I lean towards the slow and unproductive surfaces as the real reason. I have seen plenty of Indian cricketers who are fine attacking players and I know how difficult it can be to play attacking shots to balls that consistently rise only to knee height and come off the pitch at sluggish pace.

These days there is a little more bounce in Bombay than in the other centres now that the pitch has been relaid, but I doubt if Indian cricket, and Pakistan cricket too for that matter, will ever flourish overseas until batsmen and bowlers from those countries are given the chance to gain experience on more lively pitches at home. There will always be success around the corner in matches at Madras, Kanpur and Karachi but ground authorities and administrators in both India and Pakistan do their own players and national prestige a disservice by not producing fast pitches for all their domestic cricket. It is no good a batsman being able to bat for hours in India against bowlers subjugated by a dead pitch if next month the same bowlers will be able to bowl out the same opposition in another country. There are too many good cricketers in India for their talents to be wasted and their promise on overseas tours to be dissipated, and I hope administrators in India will look to the problem and find some solution for the good of their own cricket.

7
Pakistan

Pakistan cricket is the youngest in the world on the international scene for they have only been playing Test matches since 1952, after achieving partition in 1947. There is nothing half-hearted about their endeavours though and they set great store by a military-type efficiency, rather in keeping with their style of government that operates at the moment. They toured England on the split tour basis with India in 1967, losing two Test matches and drawing one, but giving a reasonable account of themselves, though this was partly due to the fact that they used in their Test side four players who were playing cricket in England.

I first saw Pakistan cricket in 1956 when the Australian side, on its way back from England, stopped off at Karachi to play a Test match. The game features in *Wisden*, but not in any complimentary sense, for it is listed as the lowest Test score ever made in one full day's play—Australia 80 all out, Pakistan 15 for two. On the fourth day of the same game there were 112 runs scored, Australia making 49 out of these and Pakistan 63 for one. I don't think I will ever forget the match itself, not just for this slow scoring, but because it provided the ultimate test of batsmanship against two great bowlers. In fact, the batting failed, as should be obvious from the scores, but never have I seen the ball beat the bat more than in that match.

The last time any of us had played on the mat was at school and that was on matting over concrete where the ball would be consistently at or above bail height. But here at Karachi it never got above stump height for Fazal and Khan, who must surely rank as two of the greatest bowlers the world has ever seen in these conditions. Fazal was coming in from his slightly slanting run and whipping his fingers over the ball so that it cut from the leg like a fast leg break. At the other end Khan cut his fingers under the ball so it reacted like a fast off-break, and all around were crouching fieldsmen waiting for the inevitable edge. I made four in the first innings and was beaten 20 times. I made 56 in four hours in the second and nine runs came from the middle of the bat, the other 40-odd coming from the edge and somehow finding their way between the grasping fieldsmen. Unfortunately our bowlers just didn't know how to use the same conditions and we fell between two stools of sheer pace, with Miller and Lindwall, or spin, with Johnson and myself. None of us looked like dismissing Pakistan for a reasonable total and we eventually lost quite deservedly by nine wickets.

I never saw Fazal bowl on turf but, I believe, that whilst his skill would have been to a certain extent blunted, he would still have been a very good bowler in any conditions—a suggestion that he proved when touring England in 1954 with the Pakistan side. It was his skill that won for them the final Test match at the Oval that year when Pakistan beat England's side led by Len Hutton.

One of the best equipped players in the world is Pakistan's present captain, Hanif, who has made nearly 4,000 runs in Test matches. He is recognised as a great player, known to some as the "Little Master", and regarded by others as being primarily a defensive player. The latter description is rather unfortunate because, when he cares to be, he is one of the best attacking players in the world today, as well as having a superb defensive technique. He holds the record for the highest individual score in first-class cricket, 499 in 1958–9 against Bahawalpur at Karachi, being run out off the last ball of the day in trying for his 500. His is a great cricket family with Wazir, Raees, Hanif himself, Mushtaq and Sadiq all having performed wonderfully well in Pakistan cricket over the years.

We in Australia saw nothing of Pakistan after the 1956 match until in 1959 we were scheduled to go to play three Tests at Dacca, Lahore and Karachi as part of a 13-week tour of Pakistan and India. On the way my side had to play a centenary match in Brisbane and we took the opportunity of obtaining some jute mats and laying them down on the turf practice pitches, to try and give the players some idea of conditions they might encounter. There was some hope that the matches would be played on turf but when we arrived in Dacca we found that, although the square looked like Lord Witherspoon's front lawn, there was an orange strip in the centre and that we were, after all, to play the First Test on matting.

The practice we had in Brisbane on mat was beneficial but

even more so was the net practice we had at Dacca on arriving, where we were able to use mats all day and every day in the ten days before the Test match began. Experience in 1956 had taught us that sheer speed was of little use on this surface and I felt that in Ken Mackay, who bowled at round about the same pace as Fazal, we might have a match winner on the mat, if not on any turf pitches that we might strike later on. It turned out to be so for "Slasher" produced his best bowling performance ever in taking seven wickets in the match and bowling in all 64–38–58–7—an astonishing performance.

I was often asked on this tour by keen Pakistan officials and players how I thought local cricket could be improved and really there was only one answer—to get rid of the mat and play in conditions as close to those in other countries on turf. Both manager, Sam Loxton, and I passed this advice on to the President of Pakistan, Field-Marshal Mohammed Ayub Khan, when the team was presented to him in Lahore and he promised to look into the matter. When we played the last Test in Karachi former American President Dwight Eisenhower was present and both sides were presented to him, after which he made the remark that he thought this cricket game was supposed to be played on grass rather than mat. The Pakistan President said then "This is the last time a Test match will be played on matting in this country" and he gave orders to that effect—orders that have been strictly carried out, to the benefit of the game in Pakistan.

Hanif, Saeed and Mushtaq have been three of the better batsmen for Pakistan in the years they have been in Test cricket with Fazal the outstanding bowler, together with Mahmood Hussain and Khan, both of whom were pacy and accurate. Imtiaz was a fine all-rounder, catching 78 and stumping 16 whilst keeping in Test matches, and making over 2,000 runs besides, and Waqar, Javed Burki and Alim-ud-din are the only other players to have made a thousand runs in Test matches.

In 1964–5 Pakistan made a short tour of Australia, drawing the only Test match played, and then went on to New Zealand where they drew all three Tests. They have, in fact, a tremendous record of drawn matches in the years they have been in Test cricket, having played 53 Tests, winning 10, losing 16 and drawing 27, but many of the draws were achieved, if that is the word, against India in local "Derbys" where at one stage the two countries met 12 times without reaching a decision. Not really the stuff to set anyone's blood afire, and, whilst the pitches must have had something to do with such a string of no decisions, the attitude of the players and the political implications thereof must also have had a great bearing on the lack of results.

But, in England in 1967, there were very real signs of a number of young players improving sufficiently to lift Pakistan's record in future international cricket. The two I particularly liked were Majid Jehangir and Asif Iqbal, the former playing well in county games whilst Asif, probably destined to captain Pakistan one day, shone in the Tests with both bat and ball. The latter played one of the best post-war Test centuries I have seen in the final Test at the Oval when, after Pakistan had been 65 for eight, he shared in a world record partnership with Intikhab that must have brought renewed hope to his captain and to the rest of the cricket nation. Majid on the same tour established a new English record for the number of sixes hit in an innings, striking 13 in a magnificent innings against Glamorgan at Swansea. He, like Asif, is a medium pace bowler but both of them for young men suffered a surprising amount of muscle trouble that denied them the chance to show their full ability in this direction.

Even in the last match, at the height of his triumph, Asif was troubled by muscle strains and it would be a great pity if his career were to be dogged in years to come in this manner.

From the point of view of potential, I felt in 1967 that Pakistan had the edge on India though in the near future India had the advantage of undertaking a full tour of Australia and New Zealand. On a tour of this kind their young players are allowed full chance to improve their potential and they could develop the nucleus of a fine Test team. But when I saw the six Test matches in England, it did seem to me that Pakistan had more purpose in their play and that they were inclined to be more determined in their approach. They, like India, suffered from a lack of pace bowling but, in fact, were much better off than India having in the side Salim, a promising young medium fast bowler, as well as Asif and Arif, both of whom bowled at medium pace. Salim at Lord's, in the Test match that was drawn, bowled impressively and, until muscle trouble caught up with him, he caused the England batsmen quite a bit of bother.

There were several lessons to be learnt from the twin tour of England by India and Pakistan, the most important of which is that they must develop pace bowlers if they are to succeed in international cricket. This applied more to India but Pakistan will find too that going into a Test match with only medium pacers in the side is a losing proposition. Hanif has developed into a good sound captain and is, as well, a most reliable slip field, and as long as he continues to play Pakistan will have the much-needed foundation on which to build their side.

But one point where I thought they fell down on that tour of England was in the use of Pakistan players resident in England to bolster up the Test side. Four men, Ibadulla, Nasim, Intikhab and Mushtaq, were used in the first two Test matches though they had not come over with the actual side and were not fully attached to it throughout the tour. Nasim and Intikhab were playing League cricket, Ibadulla is a regular with Warwickshire and is a much-travelled cricketer, having played not only in England, but in India, Pakistan and New Zealand. Mushtaq in 1967 had qualified for Northamptonshire so it is problematical whether or not these four players in the future will be of any great value to Pakistan.

They are all fine cricketers and no doubt the Pakistan authorities did not wish to deny them the chance of playing for their country simply because they have chosen to play professional cricket. But I have never yet seen a cricket team play as a team when a number of players are engaged elsewhere and I would respectfully suggest to the Pakistan authorities that in a like situation in the future they should insist that the team, as chosen, should be together throughout the tour. Young players like Purvez played only restricted cricket though, on the occasions I saw them, they looked very promising players for the future.

The potential is there and if the Pakistan authorities and groundsmen can only be persuaded to leave a little grass on their pitches to accustom their batsmen and bowlers to playing on less than shirt front surfaces then I believe the next ten years will see cricket in that country make great strides forward.

8
New Zealand

New Zealand cricket finally came of age in 1967 when, for the first time in the history of international cricket, a Board of Control Australian team was defeated in that country. The defeat coincided with another at the hands of South Africa, with the Springboks beating the first XI and the New Zealanders taking the honours from Les Favell's side. The fact that it wasn't Australia's top team that went down means very little. For many years Australia was so strong and New Zealand so inexperienced that the results of "Test" matches was a matter of course. But in recent times there has been a levelling out of Test standards and nowhere more so than in New Zealand where they have shown a most sensible approach to the encouragement of young players.

There have been some very fine cricketers from New Zealand in years gone past and yet until this victory over Australia the New Zealanders had never won a Test against England, Australia, Pakistan or India though they had taken one Test off the West Indies in 1955–6 and two off South Africa in a great drawn series in 1961–2. One of the great joys of my young cricket life was to see Martin Donnelly bat in a minor match in Sydney and I can well believe the comparisons freely made that he was a player of the same type and very close to the same standard of the great Australian left-hander Arthur Morris. Sadly, because of Australian neglect, Donnelly and other players like him, Bert Sutcliffe, John Reid, Walter Hadlee, have never been seen in Australia on an official tour, and it is a remarkable thing that a New Zealand side visited Australia in 1967, more than 40 years after the first such tour of my country.

Looking back on it, I never cease to be astonished that the first New Zealand cricketer I ever saw was in 1957, 11 years after leaving school and five years after playing in my own first Test match. There must be something wrong with a system that allows this and denies young Australians the chance to watch great batsmen like Sutcliffe and brilliant all-rounders like Reid in action. I don't blame only Australia for this, although I do feel that Australia's authorities have been sadly remiss in their attitude to New Zealand—but equally I feel that New Zealand too easily have adopted the role of poor relations to their Australian big brothers. Cricketers only become good or great through the sternest possible competition and let me put to you the case of Australian cricket if it had been treated in the same way as the New Zealanders.

Let's suppose, for instance, that Australia, as a small country lacking success over the years, had been denied the chance to visit New Zealand, one of the great countries and top dogs in world cricket—and only 1,200 miles from Australia's East Coast. There would have been something of a scream go up, I can assure you, with lots of talk about the system being unfair and New Zealand being interested only in going to and receiving countries that would bring in great revenue. And what of the effect on Australia's brilliant young players like Harvey in the 1947–63 era, Davidson in 1949–63, and what of the Millers and Lindwalls who, instead of touring the world inspired to great deeds by almost perpetual competition, would have been languishing in the Southern Hemisphere playing solely in Sheffield Shield cricket?

It says a lot for New Zealand cricket that they have done as well as they have over the years and I am very hopeful that the fact they have at last broken through and undertook a visit to Australia in 1967 is going to be the forerunner of many more similar visits that will produce great competition and good cricket between Australia and New Zealand. It is quite astonishing that although Bert Sutcliffe scored over 2,600 runs for New Zealand on the 1949 tour of England the only way he could get to Australia was for the team to call there and play three State matches on the way back from a tour of another country.

I will always have a soft spot for New Zealand cricket for a tour of New Zealand was my very first goal in 1949–50 when the Australian first team was in South Africa. I missed that tour through lack of performance but Alan Davidson went and turned in some great efforts with both bat and ball that started him on his international career. I made it in 1957 at the end of the Sheffield Shield season in what was a prelude to the tour of South Africa later the same season. This was the tour under Ian Craig where Australian cricket started on the way back after a disappointing three or four years, in the course of which the only victory was over the West Indies in 1955. Pitches in New Zealand are something along the same lines as those in England though, if anything, and, if possible, they are slower. It was great experience, having returned from India with a shortened run, to spend a short tour in New Zealand concentrating on this aspect of my cricket and knowing that this could be the start of a new and successful era for me in Australian cricket.

Although there have been some sterling performances in New Zealand cricket since the end of the war, fine bowlers like Harry Cave, all-rounders like MacGibbon and Motz, the two players who really stand out in recent years are Sutcliffe and Reid. It was Sutcliffe who, against Adcock in 1953, was struck on the head and laid out trying to hook a bumper. He then came back to play a brilliant innings that is still talked about whenever visitors to South Africa mention the finest batsmen who have appeared in that country. Reid has made his name more in New Zealand and South Africa than any other country and his career reached its peak in 1961–2 in South Africa when he led New Zealand to a drawn series against what was then a very good South African side. Reid himself made nearly 2,000 runs on the tour in five months of batting that put him ahead of even such a great player as Denis Compton.

Recently the New Zealand selectors and administrators have been concentrating on youth in a bid to build up a side that will allow them a higher standing in world cricket ratings. The team that came to England in 1965 to play a short tour was well beaten by the home country and yet there was much delight about the play of some of the younger members of the side. Dick Motz was the most successful bowler, a good strong medium pacer, able to move the ball both ways and one who worried the best of England's batsmen, at a time when they were striving for places in M.C.C.'s side to tour Australia later in the year. Other young players like Collinge, Congdon, Dowling, Sinclair and Taylor caught the eye with promising, if not consistent, performances, and it was only two years later that these players formed the nucleus of the side that gave New Zealand its victory over the Australian team.

Some have said that in the Southern part of the cricket world that evening there was a reddish glow reflecting embarrassment from the faces of some cricket administrators who, over the years, had refused concerted pleas to improve New Zealand's cricket status. That perhaps is taking too harsh a view—it was probably just the New Zealanders themselves painting the town red, and well might they do so. I want to see New Zealand cricket encouraged as much as possible in the future but it needs impetus from New Zealand as well as from Australia to bring this about. The result would be good not only for New Zealand but for Australia as well.

9

Leg Spin Bowling

Nothing is more fascinating to a slow bowler than a new ball in its untouched state, the maker's name in gold and the shine unbroken by either bone hard pitch or a flourishing bat at the other end. It is one of the strange things about bowling that slow bowlers generally picture themselves as being able to use the new ball and, if playing in any lower class of cricket, will move heaven and earth to get hold of it and talk the captain into letting them have first over.

I once opened the bowling for Australia in Adelaide against South Africa in 1952–3—Miller and Lindwall were both injured and I managed to talk Lindsay Hassett into letting me bowl at the other end to Bill Johnston when the second new ball came due. I don't think there were many other takers in the 100 degree temperature and the batsmen, scarcely able to believe their good fortune, struck the new ball so hard that after the first over Lindsay, with his wry sense of humour, was able to stroll up and say "Very sensible of you to get the shine off as quickly as possible so we can use spin again—I think you had better bowl your 'leggies' from now on."

There is, in fact, no more fascinating part of the game than leg spin bowling, with the over-the-wrist spin ensuring that the bowler, no matter how hard he tries, can never be quite as accurate as his counterpart who merely bowls with the fingers. It is an art, and I don't use the phrase to signify that to bowl leg spinners you must be an artist in knowledge or interpretation of cricket, but really to try and convey some appreciation of the amount of time and study that goes into this side of the game.

Leg spinners, and I include the unorthodox left-arm over the wrist spinners in this, must have some sort of extrovert tendencies otherwise they would never want to bowl in this fashion. Instead, they would become medium pace, short of a good length bowlers or off-spinners with a flat, low trajectory denying the batsman any sort of challenge and allowing him little chance for quick-footed movement to take him to the pitch of the ball. The over-the-wrist spinner distributes his bowling gifts like a millionaire, as does the really fast bowler who himself is of variable length, and often direction as well. The stock medium pacer and the flat spinner hoards his talents like a miser, only occasionally producing some little gift and being correspondingly annoyed when it happens.

There were two things that started me on the road to being a leg break bowler—the most important was that my father was himself a very good bowler of this kind and it was a question of imitation as well as the fact that I rarely, in practice sessions as a boy, saw any other type of bowling. The other was that Grimmett was the first top bowler I ever saw and, as with many young cricket watchers, this is the sort of thing that sticks in the mind—the little man wearing a cap and drawing the batsman down the pitch almost as if on an invisible string.

Leg break bowlers, despite the spin they can impart to the balls, are shackled by different conditions just as much as their finger spinning counterparts and over the years I have found that, in general, England provides the least attractive surfaces on which to bowl. It is generally a question of eras for before the war, when O'Reilly, Grimmett and Fleetwood-Smith were in their prime, it was over-the-wrist spin that won so many Test matches for Australia. From 1953 onwards though when I was touring England I found the pitches to be far slower and grassier than I had ever imagined in conversation with pre-war cricketers and I can't say that I really enjoyed bowling on an English pitch, simply because pitches throughout England generally denied an over-the-wrist spinner the same amount of bounce he would get in overseas countries. It wasn't that the ball didn't bounce above stump height, as it might do in Sydney or Adelaide, but generally it didn't get anywhere near stump height, no matter how much it might spin. I much preferred bowling in Australia—spinning the ball only an inch or two but getting it to bounce and being able to use flight and know that when the ball landed it would not be coming off the surface with the pace of a cannon ball bouncing off Plasticine. I was always able to turn the ball in England but, in common with many other over-the-wrist spinners in post-war years, found that the lack of pace was always making the task extremely difficult.

I came to England in 1953 having had two years' experience of Test cricket but only having bowled on grounds from Sydney to Perth against batsmen always prepared to get down the pitch and never averse to having their dismissal go in the scorebook as stumped. When I played my first match at Worcester in 1953 it was on a pitch that only a few weeks before had been flooded and had the consistency of soft putty. At the end of the day I exclaimed to Keith Miller that not a ball had got above bail height all day. "Don't worry about that," he said, "you'll find some slower than this before you finish the tour."

There have been very few successful over-the-wrist spinners in Test cricket in England in the post-war period although two Australians, George Tribe and Bruce Dooland, did remarkably well in county cricket for a number of years. But both these fine bowlers had to change their style radically to counter the slower conditions, in the same way as I myself had to bowl differently after the 1953 tour. Both Dooland and Tribe had fairly high actions—Dooland particularly—when they came to England to play in Lancashire League and both had to lower their arms and bowl more with the fingers than over-the-wrist. This allowed them to get more zip off the pitch whilst in no way diminishing their turn and also seemed to be of benefit to them in the bowling of their top spinner. Dooland shortened his run to an economical six paces and bowled with a more round arm action that allowed him to deliver his very good top spinner with no change in delivery action. But, if they had returned to Australia, I suspect they would have needed to change back again to be fully effective in conditions out there. Lindsay Kline and Johnny Martin are two over-the-wrist spinning left-handers who found English conditions far too slow for their liking and even Gary Sobers will bowl his orthodox spinners rather than be denied bounce and pace with his over-the-wrist variety.

All this means, of course, that the slow bowler must be versatile and be able to change his method, and bowlers from other countries coming to England are often not as badly done by as Englishmen going abroad. The man who has turned the ball square on under-prepared county pitches, for instance, must wonder what has hit him when his orthodox finger spin preserves a straight line for the first three days of the first match of a tour in Perth. The orthodox off-spinner and left-hander trying to turn the ball in Jamaica or Barbados has, I think, a relatively harder task than the bowler who goes to England and is at least able to get something out of the pitches by way of turn, though nothing by way of bounce.

I found leg spinning the most interesting part of cricket, particularly once I became a Test player and was able to pit my wits against players from all other countries of the world every two or three years. There are very few bowlers who do not know a great deal about bowling—that need not be as obvious as it sounds for there are some who, with a tremendous natural ability and no bowling brains, have been extremely successful. There are others who, in private life, might show a complete lack of common sense but, with a ball in their hands and a batsman at the other end, become masters of their craft. The game hasn't changed a great deal in batting, bowling or fielding over the years and since it first started there has always been this constant battle of wits between the batsman and bowler. On balance, the batsman wins because, no matter how many people play the game, it really is a batsman's game and spectators and cricket followers are far more interested in batting than bowling.

Occasionally outstanding bowling performances, with a thought of seeing a great bowler in action, will drag spectators to a game where normally they would have done something else that day, but these instances are few and far between. Far more often spectators will go to or be interested in a match because of the teams playing or because they want to see a particular batsman in action and the bowlers are incidental. If you doubt this, just think back to the last time you made a trip to watch a certain bowler in action and then compare it with the number of occasions where you have gone to a ground because someone was not out overnight or because he was obviously due to bat later that day. The bowler, in fact, is the poor relation of cricket, there specifically for the amusement of the batsman, but, at the same time, he can get plenty of amusement out of the game himself and certainly a great deal of enjoyment.

The young cricketer who sets out to become an over-the-wrist spinner has plenty of heartbreak ahead of him, simply because he is never going to be possessed of the pinpoint accuracy of the rest of the bowling fraternity. There must be exceptions to every rule, and I suppose O'Reilly was one and Grimmett another, but in 99 per cent of cases the over-the-wrist spinner will be expensive when compared to his more straightforward colleague. Lest it be thought that I look with a cynical eye on all but my own brand of delivery, I hasten to say I believe firmly in every type of bowling, so long as it is delivered with attacking intent. I could well have become a medium pacer or even, with my height, something quicker than that. But, looking back on it, I could not have wished to do anything more exciting than bowl over-the-wrist spin.

One of the first requirements is to have a good memory for batsmen and be able to picture them in 1967 as they batted in, say, 1963. Some batsmen change in style, others in method, and, whilst all this must be taken into consideration, it is very important that a bowler of any kind should remember methods of dismissal and methods of attack. There are some great batsmen who will always be difficult to bowl to and there are others who, whilst never being easy, will fall time after time for some particular delivery. But batsmen, particularly good ones, have tremendous ability for improvisation and a general dislike for sitting in the pavilion when they could be out murdering some bowler they consider hardly worthy of their attention. Consequently, any intelligent batsman will try and avoid being caught twice in the same trap.

If I had to pick on one attribute that a leg spin bowler must have—always assuming that he has some ability in the various departments of spin, flight and accuracy—I would mark it down as a photographic memory. With this he is able to form a quick appreciation on any given day of the strengths and weaknesses of particular players in the one side, even to the extent of setting completely different fields for, say, two right-handers batting at the same time.

I would never, for instance, bowl to the same field for Peter May and Colin Cowdrey if both were together, nor could anyone bowling leg breaks to Ken Barrington and Ted Dexter think of using the same field for both. Colin and Peter often batted together in 1954–5, 1958–9 and 1961—Peter was a magnificent player, particularly strong on the on side though by no means weak on the off, and one of the most perfect drivers I have played against. He didn't cut a great deal though occasionally used the stroke and he very rarely used the sweep. A field setting for him would cover the intent to bowl at his off-stump so that he had to play forward all the time, working on the basis that he didn't often dance down the pitch to destroy length and that to bowl at his leg stump would be fatal.

On the other hand, in his early days, Colin was such a correct player that his bat did, in fact, go back completely straight and come forward in the same arc. This often made it difficult for him to play on the on-side and a field setting there would cover the fact that the direction of the bowling would be at about middle and leg so that he couldn't bring into play his tremendous cover driving. In later years he strengthened his on-side play and added a quite effective sweep to his repertoire and I should think that any plans of this nature would have to be revised if bowling at him now.

For May, and depending always on the pitch and circumstances, I would probably have bowled to a slip and a slightly backward point with cover, extra cover and mid-off, together with a short extra cover on the off-side. I generally used a square leg, mid-wicket and mid-on but if he was in good form, as he so often was, I would probably take away the short extra cover and play him at long on. I usually bowled to a leg slip for Colin with no man in the outfield on the on side but very rarely found any point in playing a short cover to him, so good was his driving in that area.

The main thing I found with leg-spin bowling was that the type of delivery itself practically forced the bowler to attack rather than go in with any thoughts of outlasting the batsman's patience at the other end. The medium pace seamer can drop it on the spot over after over and at the end of an hour he may have bowled 10 overs 6 maidens and have no wicket for 10, bowling to a restricting circle of fieldsmen and inviting the batsman to commit suicide. In those 60 deliveries he will have made sure that nothing as serious as a half volley has been delivered and that ball after ball has denied the batsman the chance to drive. The leg spinner, on the other hand, will see the drive as one of his most productive wicket-taking deliveries, floating the ball into the breeze and needing just a fraction more overspin to have the ball drop a little more sharply. The batsman, instead of hitting the shot along the ground, in fact lofts it at catchable height anywhere in the arc from cover to mid-wicket.

For every one of those successful bowling ploys, however, there are 50 that don't come off, but half the enjoyment of bowling this way is in the setting of the plan and in the bid to try and outthink the batsman. In this sense bowling is a little like advertising in that you only hear of the successes and never of the failures. The leg spinner, like all bowlers, is only too willing to admit "that was the top spinner" or "it dropped a little on him just as he was playing the shot", or "he didn't pick the bosie". You never hear though of any bowler saying "Well, I bowled him a slower one and he hit it for four 26 times" or that the trap had been baited and the top spinner produced, only the batsman struck it firmly into the crowd. For some reason over-the-wrist spin, with its emphasis on open-handedness, seems to produce more bowling conversation than any other variety, except perhaps the really fast bowlers who have their own particular methods that endear them to the watching public.

I stared off as a leg-spinner at the age of six in the cement-walled store room at Jugiong. I was O'Reilly, Fleetwood-Smith and Ward as well, who had come into the Australian side to replace Grimmett after the 1935–6 tour of South Africa. I was in those days the complete all-rounder because I was McCormick too, and McCabe and, when it came to batting, I was Fingleton, Bradman and Brown combined. I used to dream of one day playing for Australia but couldn't quite see how it was going to happen because, although I had reached the mature age of six and had been playing Test cricket for some years, we were stuck here in the country nearly 300 miles away from Sydney. I used to pick my own sides because I had a 1937 N.S.W.C.A. Cricket Annual and it contained all the scores of Gubby Allen's M.C.C. team. I had never seen any of these players and I chose my teams on the names, both well-known and resonant. On that score, Worthington and Fagg were always listed in the one side and so was Jim Sims, the Middlesex slow bowler, whose name would roll off the tongue of any aspiring six-year-old. The method was merely to bowl the ball against the wall and play it on the rebound but, coming from only the distance of the wall to oneself, it could still be a reasonably difficult assignment.

When my father moved to Burnside School in Sydney I bowled gentle off-breaks, simply because he had decided that my fingers were too immature to attempt the difficult business of leg spinning at that age. We played our primary school competition on the concrete with a composition ball made of cork and rubber and because it bounced so much it provided plenty of problems for opposing batsmen. Twice we were in the final of this competition, the first time meeting a school called Canley Vale, and we rather fancied ourselves to carry off the trophy. In fact, a big left-hander who, looking back on it, seemed about six feet tall and, in fact, was probably about 5ft. 4ins., hit 160 against us. I can't remember his name but I can remember the fact that he gave us an almighty belting and that his side made over 300.

The following year we were more fortunate and, playing outside Cumberland Oval where I was later destined to play inside for Cumberland Club, we scored enough runs to beat the opposition outright and win the competition for the first time. It is a long while ago but all sorts of things stick in the mind, the most important of which then was that I wasn't allowed to use my own bat in making 50 not out in the second innings. I used to get a bat for Christmas every year and it was always a Sports Master brand—I haven't seen those around for 20 years. When this final was on I had made nearly 400 runs for once out and after being dismissed cheaply in the first innings then agreed to allow one of the other boys to use the bat, so long as I could borrow it when I came in. But when I got in he was going so well that he wouldn't come near me and said that I'd have to use one of the others. A sad moment for an 11-year-old!

I still bowled off-spin for the first two years at High School in 1942 and 1943 and in 1944 I played a season in junior cricket on matting over concrete. In this competition I bowled with the new ball on Saturday afternoons but it had been decided that I was just about ready to start leg spinning in competition cricket, the basic fundamentals of length and direction supposedly having been well learned. By 1945 I was playing lower grade cricket for Cumberland, bowling leg spinners and batting down the list with inconspicuous success. I started my first match in Third Grade making 12 runs and watching from cover while a left-arm bowler called Jim Russell ripped through the opposition so quickly that he was taken straight into First Grade. I managed to get into Second Grade at the end of the season simply because there were lots of players dropping out with football starting, and had one game against Gordon on Cumberland Oval before the season ended.

There was a good top spinning leg spinner called Jack Prowse playing with Gordon at the time, a man who had in years gone past been a fine First Grade cricketer and was still a useful bowler in the lower grades. A square-built cricketer, his top spinners zipped off the pitch at a pace sufficient to make one wonder about the scientific theory that a ball cannot gain pace off the pitch. Jack Hill, who played for Australia, always seemed to make pace off the pitch and, certainly to a 15-year-old Second Grader, this fellow Jack Prowse seemed to do the same. Before I went to the game my father, who was playing First Grade at the time, gave me a word of advice: "As he brings his arm over you play forward and don't move your bat off a straight line," he said.

Jack Prowse gave me a pleasant nod as I walked nervously to the crease this day and then ran up and flipped at me a ball that was quite obviously going to turn sharply from the leg. But dutiful son disregarded the obvious turn and the fact that the ball was short and played forward with an impeccably straight bat. "Ah!" came a voice from the other end. "Who's been talking to you?" "My father said that I had to play straight at you" I piped timorously. "He says you can't turn them." I thought perhaps it was the sun that had turned Mr. Prowse a slight shade of puce but he was kind enough to pat me on the shoulder and say, after I had made a dozen, "Well-played son—give your Dad my regards."

I played a match in Third Grade the following year and made 90 against a side that included Phil Tresidder, now a good journalist friend, and then one game in Second Grade before being promoted to First Grade to play in the same side as my father. It doesn't often happen that father and son play together in First Grade cricket in Sydney and it was a great thrill to walk out alongside him the following week after selection, though the performances were nothing to write home about. But in the second match I managed to get some wickets and then made 98 when Cumberland batted against what was quite a useful bowling attack, being dismissed whilst father was standing at the non-striker's end. I was out stumped to State off-spinner Vince Collins with whom I had been having some trouble and Dad had wandered down from the other end to tell me that just because I was being pinned down there was no need to throw it away. Foolishly I selected the wrong ball to jump down the pitch to next over and was stranded and one of the papers the next day ran a story that nervousness at having my father at the other end had cost me my first century in First Grade cricket.

There was varying success for the remainder of the season, probably more with bat than ball because in those days I was primarily regarded as a batsman, a fact that will no doubt bring a quirk to the lips of many bowlers the world over. It was much the same story in 1947–8 when I made plenty of runs but found wickets rather elusive, at the same time doing well enough to give myself a chance of playing in the State Colts fixture in October 1948. In fact, in this fixture, which was the first one of a representative nature in which I took part, I was only the second leg spinner and was not really needed anyway because of the run getting of the early batsmen and the tremendous fast bowling burst from Alan Walker who made the first moves towards going to South Africa the following year with the Australian side. Brian Flynn was the number one leg spinner who went on to play for the Second XI but whom I eventually beat for a place in the State side, not because I could bowl better but because I could bat better. He was the finest leg spinner I have ever seen in the nets, absolutely unplayable on a good practice pitch, and the dread of my life at the S.C.G. No. 2 was to have to bat against him with the State selectors present. His length never varied, his direction was perfect and he spun the ball sharply and dropped it into whatever breeze was blowing at the time. He later played for Queensland with some success, taking eight wickets in his first innings against New South Wales, but eventually lost rhythm and confidence and ended up bowling off-spinners after a season in Lancashire League.

This Colts side to go to Queensland contained players like Jimmy Burke, who made a hundred and later played for Australia, as well as eight other eventual State representatives and the game was easily won. The injury in Melbourne followed soon after, having already played in one State match against Queensland, and I made what was almost a comeback in 1949–50. I have already written about the effect of the 40 over new ball rule on leg spinners in Australia and it wasn't for a few years that any young leg spinner was able to make any sort of name in cricket in my country. Fortunately though, batting and fielding gave me an added chance to impress and by the time the end of the 1950–1 season had come along I had been given one or two minor chances that augured well for the future.

There is no better way to learn to bowl leg spinners though than to go on tour with an Australian side and I was decidedly lucky that on my first tour in 1953 I had a player like Doug Ring in the side. A great humorist, though sometimes acid of nature and very down to earth, he was also a great helper to a young spin bowler on his first tour overseas. He had been to England in 1948 and had been a fine bowler for Victoria for a number of years and was quite willing to pass on various tips from his bowling storehouse. Very grateful I was to receive them too, and it was this tour that first began to change my approach to leg spin bowling.

Doug spent quite a bit of time in the nets with me on this tour and if I were lucky enough to be sitting at the same table on a train journey from county to county then there was always the chance of sorting out some particular point that had been bothering me—and there were certainly plenty of those about at that stage. There was a fascinating talk on the way to Somerset one night when, producing an apple from a passing waiter's basket, he explained to me exactly how he bowled his top spinner from between the second and third fingers of his bowling hand. The only top spinner I had bowled before this time was what is normally known as an overspinner with the ball coming over the top of the little finger and going straight on in pitching with a little more bounce than usual. In England this was useless because the ball just hit and stopped and obviously what I needed was the delivery that hit and skidded. This was the one Ring expounded to me that night and it was the one that formed the basis for the top spinner I used over the next ten years.

Also on that tour was Jack Hill who looked like a leg spinner but in the main came straight on to the batsman, apparently gaining pace off the pitch and often forcing his opponent to hurry his stroke. Hill was a fine performer in Sheffield Shield cricket in Australia and made two tours overseas, one to England and one to West Indies in 1955 where it was hoped his accurate, quicker deliveries would cause the batsmen a great deal of trouble. Ring retired after the 1953 tour and, with the new ball position as it was in those days, there was really no other opponent on the Australian scene to challenge a batsman-leg spinner for a place in the side.

In 1956 Australia took only the one leg spinner to England although there were two orthodox spinners in Ian Johnson and Wilson, together with part-time bowlers Burke and Rutherford. It was in 1957 in South Africa that over-the-wrist spin began to come back into the reckoning with Kline, Simpson and myself in Ian Craig's side. By 1961 every Sheffield Shield side in Australia had more than its share of leg spinners and over-the-wrist left-handers and Kline had to battle against Johnny Martin for a place in the touring side to England. Eventually Martin had to wait until 1964 for his tour when he was accompanied by other slow bowlers in the captain, Bobby Simpson, Rex Sellers, Norman O'Neill and orthodox off-spinners Veivers and Cowper.

The only leg spinners who become stars overnight—in fact, the only bowlers who become stars overnight and retain that billing—are those of the unorthodox variety. Iverson, flicking the ball off his middle finger as one would flick a ball of paper at a schoolboy friend, came up almost overnight in Australian cricket and so too did Gleeson who, after very little first-class experience, was picked to tour with the 1968 side. But it is a hard road and, in many cases, a painful one for any youngster who wants to devote his life to bowling over-the-wrist spin at either quick-footed batsmen or those who prefer to play it from the crease.

A wicket-keeper like Wally Grout can be very useful to a bowler—he is a great judge of an opposing batsman's weaknesses and would often pinpoint various things for me. Queensland, in fact, has produced two of the greatest wicket-keepers in Australian history in Tallon and Grout; both of them possessed of beautiful "hands" and an earthy wit. Don Tallon had a brother, Bill, who used to stutter a little and is a great story teller, often when the story goes against himself. He was a leg spin bowler, good but not a great, so his team mates say, and he took 21 wickets in Sheffield Shield at an average of 41 apiece—an average that was boosted a little by his encounter one day with Cec Pepper in a New South Wales–Queensland game. Pepper hit him out of the ground a number of times on to the tram lines and into the flowering shrubs and the worried skipper came over with the advice "Spin it Bill, spin it mate." "Spin it?" he replied scornfully. "It's so covered w-w-with tram tickets and l-l-lantana thorns that I can't bloody well grip it, let alone spin it."

It was Tallon who was a member of the side that devised the plan to get rid of Bradman in a match in Adelaide before the war when the "little bloke", as they called him, was right in his prime. As Bill tells: "We decided to p-p-put them into bat so the 'quicks' could have a go at the 'little bloke'—see. Big Jack Ellis gets the opener to edge one and b-b-brother Don does the rest; they're one for naught. 'Little bloke' gets a single at the start for one. Next batsie gets an edge and b-b-brother Don does the rest—they're two for one. 'Little bloke' gets a single at the start of the next over, two for two; and then b-b-brother Don snaps up another one and they're three for two. There I am at mid-on, with the s-s-sun beating down, and 'Braddles' goes for the hook, gets a top edge and I run round and get under it and think, 'f-f-f-for heaven's sake don't miss this one, Billy boy', and I catch—f-f-f-four for four hundred and seventy-one."

Wally Grout was keeping when Ted Dexter made his debut in Sydney in 1958 and asked for, what to Wal, sounded suspiciously like "two laaigs please". Gloved hand to mouth, Wally murmured to the slips "blue-blooded ones of course". He was quite prepared to accept anyone having a shot at him as well, but the game was never quiet when Walter was keeping wicket. A weak throw from Don Seccombe that bounced seven times and ended resting at his feet in a Sheffield Shield match in Brisbane brought a wave and a cheery "Thanks, Frankie". "Frankie . . . why are you calling me Frankie?" asked the perplexed Seccombe, "My name's Don." "No," came the reply over the shoulder, "you're Frankie Sinatra aren't you—the Man with the Golden Arm." A humorist—but what a valuable one both for Queensland and Australia over the years.

I always enjoyed batting and fielding but, unless the situation demanded, I never found the same challenge in those two aspects of the game as there was in leg break bowling. I started off by copying Doug Ring in 1953, having already had two or three bowling actions in my time, none very different from the other but just covering different little things I had seen from watching other better-known bowlers. Ring had a longish run to the crease and so did I but this was by accident rather than design. I had started off when moving into grade cricket trying to develop a full swing of the arm which I did, in fact, possess by the time I got to Test standard. This was restricted in later years after I suffered a shoulder injury and even now it takes me a few overs before I can take my bowling arm in a full circle.

The shortening of the run came in 1956 on the way back to Australia when we played the First Test match in Madras. I shortened it by another yard when that ridiculous front foot law was brought in some years ago forcing the bowlers to keep every part of their front foot behind the popping crease. This was one of the worst rules ever brought in to curb bowlers and originated as an effort to stop the fast bowlers dragging and getting too much advantage from a long follow through, sometimes skidding on their back toe up to three or four feet. The trip to New Zealand in 1957 was the first real occasion where I could try out my shortened run on a tour and it was certainly the first time I had been in a side as the number one spin bowler. It was a prelude to the South African tour to be undertaken later that year and provided me with that most valuable addition to the spin bowler's armoury—a remedy for torn fingers. At one stage on that New Zealand tour I had both corns torn from my first and third fingers where the seam rested and bowling was sheer agony. But I found a chemist in Timaru able to provide a remedy he used for leg ulcers and since then I myself have been able to pass it on to a number of spin bowlers the world over.

It had taken me nine years to get to the stage where I was in South Africa in 1957 the number one spin bowler for Australia and any young cricketer wanting to become a Test bowler in later years would do well to take note of the time lapse between debut and success. I don't think I was any less bright than other spin bowlers over the years but the fact remains that it does take a long time to become experienced enough in first-class cricket to take one's place in a side as a spinner. Fast and medium pace bowling is not quite so difficult for, in general, it is a more direct attack, but with spinning there is no substitute for hard work—and when you have finished then you go out and work hard again.

A successful tour of South Africa was followed by another successful series at home against England and a trip to India and Pakistan that, whilst not materially assisting my health, at least brought success in the bowling field. But in 1961 when I brought the team to England I suffered the setback that was to call a halt to my Test career—or at least play a great part in making me decide to retire in 1964. I was playing at Worcester in the first match of the 1961 tour and late on the first day bowled a wrong'un to Tom Graveney. There was a click in my right shoulder, accompanied by a sudden stab of pain which then didn't return whilst I bowled another two or three overs to conclude proceedings for the day. As soon as I stopped bowling though the shoulder began to stiffen up and by the time I got out to the car I was in some pain and very worried, mainly because I had no idea what had happened.

When we arrived back at the Raven Hotel at Droitwich the pain had become an ache and I could hardly lift my arm to pick up a glass in the attractive bar on the ground floor of the hotel. It didn't worry me a great deal during the night but the next morning I found that if I wanted to go to the golf course shaven then it had to be done left-handed with an electric razor because to lift my other arm above waist height was just about impossible. I told manager, Syd Webb, and assistant manager, Ray Steele, about it and then went off to play golf, working on the theory that all it needed was a bit of exercise to be put right. I got round 18 holes which, as it turned out, was the most stupid thing I could have done, and as soon as I stopped playing the arm once again stiffened up.

I decided that I wouldn't bowl again during the match and would go back to London, although at this stage I had no idea how serious the injury was or, in fact, what treatment would be needed to fix it up. I didn't bowl the next day but on the last morning when Worcestershire were in with a chance to win, and ourselves also with a chance of victory, I decided to bowl an over or two to see how it was and to try and remove Martin Horton who was batting stubbornly at the time. They turned out to be very slow deliveries but one of them spun out of the footmarks and bowled Horton round his legs, whereupon I retired again and and rain washed out play for the day. Manager Syd Webb had made arrangements for me to see a specialist in London and I had steady treatment there for the next few weeks, wearing a sling to keep my arm safe from movement and having several needles that looked to be about a foot long thrust into the point of my shoulder. I was told I needed time and that I had to rest the arm if I wanted it to get right. Time, unfortunately, was something I had nothing of; I was impatient to get on the field again as a bowler rather than a batsman as I had been for the past few weeks. By the time the Sussex match came the arm was much improved but still not quite right though I managed to take five wickets, including that of Ted Dexter, for 80-odd runs and suffered no ill effects afterwards.

It was during this game that there occurred the first incidents that led to the so-called gag being applied to an Australian captain—I was 'phoned by a paper in Australia to ask how my shoulder was and replied that it wasn't too bad and that I thought I'd be fit to play in the Test the following weekend. This appeared in print as "I'll bowl till my arm drops off . . ." which, understandably, caused a flutter in the Australian Board of Control, concerned that the captain of their side should be indulging in such far-fetched clichés.

When we got to Birmingham I came through a fitness test without any trouble and bowled well enough to take three wickets in the first innings of a match where Australia had very much the best of things until Dexter played his grand innings on the last day. It was here that the shoulder went again on the evening before the last day, and I was hardly able to bring my arm over when we got on the field the next morning. Now it was to be rest again and, with the Tests coming thick and fast, it was one of the most galling experiences of my life to be on tour as captain but not be able to take part in the matches.

In the end I was fit for the crucial Fourth Test at Old Trafford simply because a good mate of mine, Brian Corrigan, rang me up on the morning after the Birmingham Test and asked would I come along and see him. He told me that he had no doubt that I needed a very specialised and intensive treatment and that if I wanted to get fit for later Test matches I should go and see a

Dr. Alan Bass at a London hospital. I couldn't really see at the time that Bass would be able to provide any more effective treatment than the next man but I was prepared to give anything a try and had only a couple of weeks before the Lord's Test Match in any case.

Intensive was certainly the word for it and there were all sorts of X-rays and blood tests taken the day I arrived at the hospital, as well as certain forms of electrical treatment that moved muscles and tendons in the arm without me in fact having to move it myself. Then a course of treatment was evolved after I had demonstrated my bowling action to the assembled doctors. From this bowling action, with the arm going through a full arc, a series of exercises were produced, along the lines of treatment given to multiple sclerosis victims, where I moved my arm through different arcs against the pressure of a physiotherapist's hand. This was an entirely different treatment from the rest that had been ordered—in fact, I haven't worked as hard for years—with each treatment something similar to bowling 20 overs in the nets without stopping. The next thing I was ordered to do was go and have a fitness test at the Lord's nets but not to bowl! "Not to bowl," I said. "No," came the reply, "you're not playing in the Test match but we'd like to give you a bit of exercise." This was the day I conveyed to my co-selectors, Neil Harvey and Colin McDonald, the fact that I wouldn't be setting foot on the field, just as masseur Arthur James appeared alongside my left shoulder to tell me Davidson wasn't fit either.

Every morning from the day I first appeared in Dr. Bass's rooms I went through this treatment until in the end the shoulder felt quite normal though a fraction stiff, as it still is. But I was fit for the Third Test at Leeds and, to make sure I got on the field, Alan Bass came up to watch the match and ran me through these exercises before the start of each day's play in the dressing-room. By the time Old Trafford came along the series stood at one all and, without going into the events of the final afternoon of that game, I can say with some certainty that it was Alan Bass who was responsible for me both being on the field and able to bowl 30 overs at that stage of the season.

The shoulder is still not right though I played until the end of the 1964 season in Australia and still play occasionally in minor cricket. I should think I could manage three-day matches without much trouble but Sheffield Shield in Australia and Test matches would be taxing the muscles a little too much, I fear, and it was a wise, though greatly regretted, decision to retire when I did.

In the early days it was off the first joint of the first and third fingers that I used to spin the ball and I used to tear the resulting corns from those joints shortly after the start of the season. But since the shoulder injury I have worn the corn on the knuckle of the first finger and a spot alongside the top of the nail on the inside of the third finger. Why this happens I haven't got the slightest idea, though I would think that subconsciously, with the shoulder trouble, I stopped flinging the ball out of the fingers and rather tended to roll it out so that the stitches move just half an inch up the finger and it tore the skin a little farther up. I have tried all sorts of methods of holding the stitches across the fingers, but to no avail, and can only conclude that the injury, plus the onset of advancing years, have taken away the zip so essential in an over-the-wrist bowler.

There are a number of things essential to any bowler but even more to an over-the-wrist spinner. There are general rules that should be followed though there will always be the unorthodox bowler who can still be very good whilst breaking all of the orthodox laws. First of all, the leg spinner should be side on in his delivery stride and he should look over his left shoulder and inside his left arm, that is with his left arm as high as possible but pointing as well across his body. His left arm should not get down too quickly and should, in fact, still be coming down when his right arm starts a full circle to deliver the ball. This ensures that his left hand is not down alongside his left knee as the ball is let go, for if that position is used the ball must be pushed out front on and will correspondingly lose zip off the pitch.

If I am coaching young players then I try and convey all this in the simplest terms possible, reducing it, in fact, at the beginning to one rule. That is, that the back foot should be put down parallel to the bowling crease. That rule is the most important thing of all because, if that is done, then it is extremely difficult to bowl front on without tearing every muscle or ligament in the right knee. If the back foot is put down, say, at right angles to the bowling crease, then it is correspondingly difficult to bowl side on and you would really need to be a contortionist to do it successfully.

That is the position from which everything else naturally comes. Put your back foot down in the right position and then everything else seems to happen naturally—it is a normal thing from that point on for your body to slip into a side on position and your left arm to go up, and for your left foot to land as close as possible parallel to the batting crease. It will, in fact, be turning because of your body action as you bring your bowling arm through and by the time you have finished delivering the ball it will point to the approximate position of the square leg umpire.

Have a look at all the photographs of the really good bowlers and you will find that, almost without exception, they finish up in this final position as they are letting go of the ball. But for any young player interested in becoming a leg spinner, it must be emphasised that only hard work will get you to the top unless you are something of a freak bowler. Get the fundamentals right and you are part of the way there, work tremendously hard year after year and you are another part there, and then all you need is that most important asset of any bowler—a few slices of luck. But if you decide to become a leg break bowler I can promise you that all the hard work will be well worthwhile for, to me, it is the most wonderful part of a very wonderful game.

10

The Greats

"I would like you," my friend said, "to choose me a side to play against the Rest of the World tomorrow. The only restriction I place on it is that we don't go back past players you yourself have played against." It seemed a fairly easy task for, after all, there are only a certain number of combinations one can come up with and there are only a certain number of great players spanning an era from 1948 to 1968. And, in addition, we'd always fancied ourselves as amateur selectors, given to critical appraisal of the choices the selectors themselves make in Test matches at home and abroad. We decided to do it, as would the selectors, by concentrating on balance and selecting the names with an eye to batting order. If you have ever endeavoured to select a world side you will understand the tangle into which we got ourselves in a short space of time.

The opening batting position at any rate seemed relatively simple. I plumped immediately for Morris, the left-handed Australian who was at his magnificent best from 1946 to 1953, and for Hutton who, I would anticipate, would be in anyone's World XI. However, I then found I had given no thought to Simpson, the prolific Australian run-getter, nor to Conrad Hunte, the West Indian who, in recent times and before his retirement, has made 3,000 runs going in first for the West Indies with no recognised opening partner at any stage of his career. Simpson's qualifications are increased by the fact that I list him as the finest slip field I have ever seen in first-class cricket and that in this department he adds a great number of runs to anything he may pick up with the bat.

There are others, but why go on? It was suddenly quite obvious that in every selection we were going to have a variety of players, most of whom could fit into anyone's World XI. Morris was a gifted cricketer for Australia, probably at the height of his powers in 1948, and I suppose impressions in one's own country tend to colour an appreciation of a player. But I saw him play some magnificent innings over the years when he was leading New South Wales and I would always have him in any World XI of the last 20 years. Hutton was the superb technique player of my time and I watched him in action in 1950–1, 1953 and 1954–5 and never ceased to marvel at the way he was always in position to play every type of bowler. There was only one criticism I could ever find of his batting and that was that he seldom used his feet to slow bowlers, in the sense of coming down the pitch to drive. But, in fact, he played slow bowling as well as anyone in the world and was a superb player against fast and swing bowling, and would certainly go into my side in preference to the other names.

In choosing any World XI there must be some eye to balance but the overriding feature must be to choose a team that would win the match and that is what I have set out to do here. I would have Harvey at number three. He was one of the best players I have seen on all types of pitches and, when I think back to 1956 and consider the innings he played in those Test matches on bad pitches, I marvel that anyone could play as well. He was already an established player in the Australian side when I came into the team. A fine player of fast bowling, magnificent against spin and a great plunderer of mediocre bowling. The latter is one ability to possess but he was also a great player against really good bowling, and at his best when the going was tough. This, to my mind, is always a feature of the really great player. There are plenty of batsmen who are good when circumstances are easy—few of them rise to greatness in difficult conditions. In 1948 Harvey toured England under Bradman and from that moment on he was the number one batsman in the Australian side until he retired. A world class fieldsman in any position—I pulled him from the covers and outfield in 1958 to field at slip, and I am convinced that had he fielded there all his life he would compare with the best ever to hold down that position.

But what of the others? If we play Harvey, what then do we do about May, Dexter, Compton, Kanhai and Barrington, all of whom have been or could have been marvellous Test players at number three over the years. I am afraid we put them on one side. "Now," I said to my friend, "I have something of a problem for you. At number four I have Worrell, Walcott and Weekes. But as I want to bat Graeme Pollock at number five I am afraid I can only get one of the Three W's in and, since I am convinced that Everton Weekes is one of the greatest players the world has seen,

I intend to put him in at four and I can find no room for Worrell and Walcott." The West Indian side in the 'fifties had these three players in the team at the one time and I have no doubt they are all world class. But this has to be a composition of 11 cricketers and if we were to include the trio then there would be no room for some of the other great players, purely on the score of balance. Weekes then goes in at number four.

Pollock, in my mind, is indisputably at number five though, with his genius, he could bat anywhere in the list, and that gives us five batsmen, all of whom do nothing but bat and field. For the purposes of comparison, I would then play two all-rounders at six and seven, and what a ghastly choice to have to make. Because I believe Sobers to be the greatest cricketer of my time, I include him at six. He would be in as fieldsman, medium pace bowler, and double up as orthodox and unorthodox spin bowler. At seven I would play Miller—what a batting order that can have Miller going in that late in the list. He was a wonderful fast bowler, a brilliant batsman and effervescent fieldsman and I think it unlikely that a World XI for the past 20 years could be chosen without him.

So far we have two quick bowlers and five batsmen and to open the attack with Miller I would choose Lindwall who, in partnership with the former, provided one of the great combinations in cricket history. I can't believe there has ever been a greater fast bowler than Lindwall with his late outswing, superb control and tremendous pace. His variations of pace were one of the features of his bowling but then, of course, one has to take into account a variety of other names. What of Hall, Adcock, Tyson, Statham, Trueman, McKenzie and Peter Pollock? Great bowlers all of these and how on earth can anyone choosing a world side leave out any one of them? This might give amateur selectors some idea of the task often faced by selectors of any national side—you can often only get one name into a particular position where several are offering and, in this case, I go for Lindwall.

My friend looked at me and said with a note of triumph, "You have forgotten Davidson." I hadn't, in fact, forgotten him but was treating him in the light of an all-rounder, in the hope that I could get him into the team later in the line-up—but without any great hope of success. He was the same type of player as Sobers and, I believe, more valuable to Australian cricket in his time than Sobers to West Indian cricket, because when Davidson played Australia had a good but not great side. He lines up then

N

against Sobers but I can't include him in front of the West Indian as I think Sobers to be a better man if 11 are to be chosen in the side. I don't want two fast left-arm bowlers in this team and I believe Miller and Lindwall to be the best combination with the new ball. So I will leave Davidson till later.

We now have five batsmen, two fast bowlers, one fast medium left-hander and three places still to fill. One of these must go to a wicket-keeper. I am tempted here to follow Arthur Mailey's line. When he chose a side some years ago to represent Australia in a Test match he omitted a wicket-keeper. When taxed about this he said, "With that side, my friend, you wouldn't need a wicket-keeper." In nominating Sobers to bowl two varieties of spin left-hand, I am not forgetting that we need another spinner in the side. The names that immediately come to mind are Gibbs, Tayfield, Ramadhin, Valentine and Mankad, who was a great spin bowler for India for many years. Others like Lock are there as well and there is Laker who was his partner over many years in English cricket. I would choose Laker. Again, as you can imagine, it is a difficult choice but I think, technically, the great English off-spinner was the best of his craft I have seen. Perhaps the imagination runs riot to great performances but in 1956 on pitches that were difficult no-one could possibly have bowled better. In 1958–9 he bowled magnificently on hard Australian pitches and over the years took almost 200 wickets in 46 Tests in England. At any rate, I nominate Laker to balance with Sobers' left-arm spin and one of my sorrows is that I could never see the pair operating together.

In the wicket-keeping section I saw Evans from England, Langley and Grout from Australia and Alexander from West Indies, as well as Waite and Lindsay from South Africa. Here I go for Grout—"I knew you would," my friend said, "just because he played for Australia." I thought about this for a moment and then replied, "Not quite, there is never a great deal between top wicket-keepers and a lot depends on circumstances in which you see them." Evans, for instance, was the best wicket-keeper over the stumps I have seen from a visual point of view. But I saw him miss chances because he was standing over the stumps to Alec Bedser—I saw him take some great catches as well. I will always remember his keeping in his first Test against Australia in Sydney when he didn't allow a bye in over 600 runs. Grout, in combination with Davidson, and, in keeping to him, missed so little that I can hardly remember a chance going to ground.

My biggest problem here is that I want to have Bedser at number eleven in the side for he is the best medium pace bowler I have ever seen. He came to Australia in 1946, 1950 and 1954, losing his place in the latter series purely because of Hutton's fetish for speed, as distinct from skill, in moving the ball. A successful fetish too but one that cost Bedser many wickets in Test cricket that year. But if I include Bedser at eleven, what of Fazal from Pakistan and, for heaven's sake, what of Davidson? Should I have Davidson in the side because he carried Australia for six years, almost without support from any other fast bowler? Should I have him in because of his marvellous combination with Grout?

In the end I decided to include Bedser, make Davidson 12th man and appoint myself manager of the side, with authority to instruct Grout that he was to stand over the stumps to Bedser who detested seeing a wicket-keeper stand back to him. That left me with:

Morris
Hutton
Harvey
Weekes
Pollock
Sobers
Miller
Lindwall
Laker
Grout
Bedser
12th man Davidson

to make up my World team. I have no intention of trying to select a Rest of the World XI to play against them—I have had enough trouble picking this XI—but just have a look at the discards. Simpson, Hunte, May, Dexter, Compton, Worrell, Walcott, Hall, Adcock, Evans, Gibbs, Tyson, Statham, Trueman, Tayfield, Ramadhin, Valentine, Davidson, Barrington, Kanhai, McKenzie, Peter Pollock, Mankad, Fazal . . . and throw in Reid and Hanif, the Pakistan captain, and you can almost choose three sides to represent the Rest of the World!

* * *

Sadly, we will never see that World side in action. Time is the great destroyer in any sport, and indeed in life itself, and we will never have the chance to see Graeme Pollock batting with Hutton, or the genius of Bedser adding to Sobers' lustre as a cricketer. But what a great moment it would be for any young cricketer if he could be coached by any of these players or even those from whom a Rest of the World side could be chosen. There are certain fundamental things in coaching a young cricketer and all of the players I have listed above were "greats" because they observed these fundamentals. Some of them went on to become unorthodox players but even in their unorthodoxy they remembered the fundamentals of each department of the game.

Often in Australia I am asked to look at young cricketers, with an eye to judging whether or not they will eventually move on to higher honours. Generally speaking, 95 per cent of the youngsters I see have been taught the wrong things to begin with, or they have been allowed lazily to slip into the wrong methods early in their lives. The time for unorthodoxy is not round about the 11, 12 or 13 age group but later on when the player has become a star. I see no reason, for instance, why Morris should not dance down the pitch to a ball outside the off stump and hit it over mid-wicket, as he often used to do against Sheffield Shield bowlers in Australia. No reason why Harvey should not lean slightly away from the ball as he square cuts, simply because it is his own style and he is perfectly balanced anyway when he plays the shot. One of the joys of watching cricket these days is to see Graeme Pollock hitting off the back foot against a good length delivery—not in the text book but the ball goes to the boundary at great speed and the spectator is delighted. So too is the batsman himself.

There was nothing orthodox about Weekes when he was cutting loose against all types of bowling and yet he was always perfectly positioned for the stroke. So too is Sobers, and Miller was one of the most unpredictable cricketers the world has seen in both batting and bowling. Lindwall, Laker and Bedser, as well as Sobers with his bowling, form a mainly orthodox quartet in their method of delivery and it is for this reason that I believe bowlers probably lean more towards the orthodox than batsmen. Lindwall was slightly round arm in delivery but he was also side on, as were Bedser and Sobers, and these three are fine models for any young player about to take up pace bowling. Miller too, if you study his bowling action, was side on, left arm well up and getting great purchase in his delivery stride though, with his flapping hair, he looked more of a character than the others. Laker was nicely side on and observed all the fundamentals of bowling. I lean then more towards the orthodox in bowling than in batting. This is not to say that because a bowler bowls front on he is unlikely to be any good. I have seen many who are good but, in the bowling department, they are the exception rather than the rule. It is the unorthodox batsmen who catch the imagination and, by unorthodox, I don't here mean those who play with a cross bat without regard to the position of the feet. Every player I have listed was invariably in position with good footwork against the ball whether it be swinging, spinning, or cutting off the pitch.

With regard to batting, there are two fundamentals every young player should look to. I don't believe in intensive coaching, best illustrated by the English style of bringing on young cricketers, possibly because I have no real experience of it. I played my cricket in Australia where coaching is always at a minimum and where you are taught rudimentary things about the game and allowed to make your way as best you can. You soon find out in a hard school if you are doing them incorrectly. The two aspects of batting that require coaching are the forward defensive and back defensive strokes, and from these stem almost every other stroke in the book. The forward defensive shot is played with bat close to pad, left foot moving to the line of flight of the ball and the eyes glued on the ball until it meets the bat. On Australian pitches it is not as important that there should be no space between bat and pad but where the ball is moving a lot off the pitch then young batsmen are compelled to make sure there is no gap for the ball to slip through. The other fundamental stroke is the back defensive shot where the back foot goes back and behind the line of the ball and the bat comes down again to leave little space between it and the pad. The left elbow in both these strokes—or non-strokes if you like—is relatively high, making sure that the bottom of the bat is always well behind the handle so that the ball will drop to the ground rather than fly in the air.

These are the only two strokes I believe should be absolutely drummed into a young player. But they are only the starting point of what should become a stroke-filled game of cricket. From these come every variety of drive off either the back or front foot—through the covers, straight down the ground past mid-on or through mid-wicket, and the back foot drive as well. Moving down the pitch to the slow bowler is an extension of the forward defensive stroke. Off the back foot there are the cuts square of and behind the wicket, the back foot glance and the hook and the pull. Master those two fundamental defensive strokes and you are a long way towards mastering the attacking shots.

To my mind, much more essential than incessant coaching is the business of instilling into young players that they must have correct footwork. Too often this entails drumming into them that their feet must be towards the line of flight of the ball—full stop. That in itself is true in that if they are not near the line of the ball they stand more chance of getting out through playing away from their body. But if too much emphasis is placed on having the feet towards the line of the ball it will inevitably become a stilted movement without any real footwork. If the ball is coming down just outside off stump then the feet will go through and, in 80 per cent of cases, a defensive stroke will be the result. But what should be instilled into young players is that when that ball is coming down it is there to be hit. Don't just put your foot there but get your feet there is the best advice I can offer. One foot means defence in most cases, but if you get your feet there then you have a good chance of playing an attacking shot. This particularly applies when you are batting against a slow bowler, in that if you move only one foot and the ball is of good length you are virtually condemned to pushing at it. If dancing footwork has taken you to the pitch of the ball with both feet you have a good chance of playing a punishing stroke and, after all, that is what the game is about. It is a battle between bat and ball and if you are batting your task is to score off every possible delivery. Hit it for four. If you can't hit it for four then take three or two from it and, if it is such a good delivery that you can't score in that way, then push it for a quick single to a vacant spot on the off or on side. Any young batsman who is taught to thrust out his pad and put the bat alongside it leaving no gap is doomed to play minor cricket for the rest of his life. There have been very few successful batsmen who have used the pad as the first line of defence. The good ones get the bat on to the ball and, if the ball proves to be too good for them and gets through, then the pad is there only as a second line of defence.

Look at the names I have listed in that World XI. Morris, Harvey, Pollock, Weekes, Sobers and Miller were possessed of magnificent footwork, with Hutton the only one not likely to come down the pitch to slow bowling. But he was such a batting genius that he devised his own method of playing it and slow bowlers rarely got him out. The others would murder bowling of every type, primarily because they were always in perfect position. As I write this, I have only just noticed that every one of the batsmen I have listed was, or is, a wonderful player off the back foot. Often these days the first movement of a young player will be forward, to play defensively off the front foot but I want to give you a simple test that might stop this automatic step being taken. Stand with bat as you would if facing a medium pace bowler. Imagine him bringing his arm over and you making your automatic movement of one pace with your left foot (if you are a right-hander) to take you to the line of the ball as it is on its way down the pitch. All your weight now is on your front foot and you will immediately sense the difficulty of playing a back foot stroke if the ball happens to be short of a good length. The great players rarely made any movement at all until they had judged the length of the ball but in modern times there has been something of a fetish for playing off the front foot, particularly against medium pace bowling. I don't agree with it and I urge young players to make no movement at all before they have made up their minds about the stroke they intend to play. It hardly seems logic to make up your mind almost before the bowler delivers the ball what you are going to do with it, because half the time the bowler himself doesn't know where it is going, give or take a yard or so. Try then and not make any movement, or, if you feel compelled to be on the move in some minute way, just shuffle your back foot a fraction—but don't get all your weight on to your front foot otherwise it throws you completely off balance.

With regard to bowling, the two essentials for any youngster are length and direction. If he is being coached then more attention should be paid to the orthodox side of his bowling action than to the orthodox side of any batting ability he may have, with the exception of those two fundamentals I mentioned earlier. When I talk of length and direction, I don't for a moment think of negative length and negative direction but rather of the bowler attacking the batsman at every opportunity to try and get him out with every delivery he bowls. No-one, of course, can get wickets as regularly as that but don't, for heaven's sake, fall into the trap of bowling negatively, or even thinking negatively, when you have a ball in your hand. The young bowler who does that will finish up a "nothing" bowler, ploughing the ball in short of a length and getting his wickets only because batsmen eventually get themselves out through frustration. Cricket is a game to be

THE GREATS

Len Hutton began his cricket career before the war, establishing the then world record individual score in the Fifth Test in 1938, and one of the highlights of his career was when he led England to victory at the Oval in 1953 to regain the Ashes. He is pictured here square cutting Bill Johnston mid-way through his innings—he and Arthur Morris would be the openers in my World team. Morris, round the 1948 period, was a marvellous cricketer, very good against pace bowling and a wonderful player of spin. Any batting side would feel the more comfortable for having this pair go in first.

At three I would have Harvey, who next to Sir Donald Bradman has been Australia's finest post-war batsman. His records stand next to The Don and with him he ranks very high in the entertainment field as well as for his fine strokeplay, depicted here as he drives Alec Bedser through the covers. Everton Weekes, the only one of the Three W's I have included, was a brilliant all-round player, very straight in defence, as he shows here, and a brilliant cutter and hooker.

To have Weekes, Graeme Pollock and Sobers following Harvey in the batting order is to emphasise the headaches that would be provided for bowlers if this side ever got on to the field. Graeme Pollock and Sobers, two left-handers in the middle of the order, are both players who can, and often have, murdered opposing attacks. They are shown here in typically aggressive mood.

As is Miller who is pictured sweeping, unsuccessfully, at Jim Laker on a turning pitch. Sobers and Miller, in addition to being brilliant batsmen in this World XI are also vital to our attack and in the cricket they played were true all-rounders in every sense of the word.

Lindwall, pictured having just let go of the ball, gives a perfect illustration of how he used to conform to the present front foot law. If the umpire were having a look at his back foot he may well have called him for transgressing the law. But Lindwall still has something like nine inches to go before he would be called for no-balling under the present law. In our team he takes the new ball and I class him as the greatest fast bowler I have seen.

With Sobers in the side, there is no need for two spinners and the only one I have included is orthodox off spinner Jim Laker, pictured here bowling in a Test match at Nottingham. He was a fine craftsman who proved himself on pitches all over the world and not just on those where he was able to get excessive turn.

Providing he would stand up over the stumps to Bedser, I would have Grout in as wicket-keeper, though I must emphasise that I never saw the best of Tallon from the time I came into Test cricket in 1952. Grout here, with lightning reflexes, has stumped Dexter when the batsman just dragged his toe on to the line. He was a great 'keeper against all types of bowling and you won't find anyone better to take his place in a World XI such as we have chosen here.

The eleventh place goes to the big-hearted Alec Bedser who was a wonderful bowler in all conditions and who carried the England attack on his own shoulders for many years before Tyson, Statham and Trueman came on the scene. There are many pictures of him taking wickets in Test matches but I like this double shot (3 and 4) that indicates to young bowlers how important body action can be.

RIGHT SIDE FACES BATSMAN
BODY THROWN INTO DELIVERY
LEFT LEG FIRMLY BRACED
FOLLOW-THROUGH PIVOT COMPLETED ON LEFT FOOT
3
4

enjoyed and I could never see the enjoyment in this type of bowling.

A number of young bowlers in recent years have come to me with a query of how they can change their action because they are too front on. There does seem a great tendency these days for bowlers to get round front on rather than deliver the ball side on with the bowler looking over his left shoulder with his left arm high. But, if a bowler has a natural style that makes him more successful front on than side on, I would never change him. Not everyone can have the perfect action and, as an example of that, think how few you yourself have seen over the years.

If I were starting a young bowler off, I would explain to him that everything will come right in his action if he starts off from one simple fundamental. That is that his back foot should be parallel to the bowling crease as he puts it down to deliver the ball. You try it for yourself. If you put your back foot down parallel to the bowling crease then it is an automatic thing that your body is very much side on to the batsman in delivery, otherwise there is a tremendous strain on your right knee. Then try it the other way and put your back foot down with the toe facing the batsman and you will find it is almost impossible to bowl side on. There is then a tremendous strain on a number of leg muscles and you finish up putting your left foot down with the toes pointing towards the batsman and bowling front on.

I am constantly hearing all sorts of theories on bowling actions and side on deliveries and yet the above is the simplest method I know. It is also the least complicated. If you start a young bowler off with back foot parallel to the crease, then you have a great beginning for him to continue in the right way in later years. Next time you are watching any bowler operate, have a look at that back foot and you will see for yourself that, except in a very rare case, it governs the eventual method of delivery. It is pictured here and I know of no better advice to young bowlers who wish to enjoy their cricket and bowl with a good action.

The other piece of advice I picked up from a tiny book written by Clarrie Grimmett was that the bowler should always watch the spot on which he wants to land the ball right from the moment he turns to begin his run up. It sounds simple, and fundamental, but in an extraordinary number of cases I find that young cricketers are looking either at the batsman's pads, or his face, or at the stumps, when they are running in to bowl, and consequently their length suffers from this motion. The three bowlers Bedser, Lindwall and Sobers, together with Miller and Laker, all observed these fundamentals when bowling and this is the reason I teach them to young players. You may not eventually get into that World XI but you will enjoy your cricket much more and be far more successful.

11

The Changing Face of Cricket

In the past 20 years cricket administrators have changed the rules of the game to such a degree that the only relation it bears to old time cricket is that a bat, ball and stumps are still used. Not all the changes are big ones—fiddling little ideas have been creeping in in recent years, to the great frustration of the players and those watching objectively from outside. I have long been of the opinion that the modern day game should revert in rules, as far as possible, to the way it was played before the Second War. Basically, cricket is a game between batsman and bowler, with the fieldsmen thrown in for good measure. It is a game at its best when there is a fight on between both sides and it only suffers when hamstrung by defensively minded players and over-zealous administration.

There have been so many different interpretations of the taking of the second new ball since 1946 that I have lost count and find it necessary to carry with me an up-to-date version of the Laws and the increasing multitude of notes attached to them. Various interpretations of the front foot and back foot no ball law have come and gone and still administrators are talking about new ideas on this subject. The throwing law has been changed and rechanged with so many interpretations put forward by each country that the solution is lost in a maze of argument and counter-argument. A bowler one year can polish the ball, the fieldsmen can the next, and then no-one can!

I am sure cricket was nowhere near as complicated as this before the war when the main aim seemed to be to prepare the hardest and most perfect batting pitch imaginable—give the fast bowler his second new ball at 200 runs and let them get on with the game unfettered by regulations and trite little laws. Nowadays the aim is to encumber and to force the cricketers to play the game in the manner in which administrators believe it should be played. But unfortunately you can't force a cricketer to do anything. You can stop him doing some things by regulation but it only acts as a spur to his imagination and he then finds some way around it and administrators start all over again. In some ways it is a funny little game between player and administrator but there is very little about it that is humorous to the onlooker condemned to watch the byplay.

The aspect of the rules that has achieved most prominence in recent years has been the one concerned with throwing. Yet, to me, this in the long term is not as important as the other aspect of no-balling—that of where the bowler shall put his feet to avoid being called for a no ball by the umpire at the bowler's end. Some years ago I proffered the thought that throwing wasn't as important as dragging in the context of international cricket. There have been various throwing incidents since then but none of them have had the effect on the *game* produced by the law requiring a bowler to have his back foot on or behind the popping crease. The solution to the law on throwing lies simply in the adoption of what, for want of a better name, can be termed "Peebles' definition". Ian Peebles, former England Test bowler, suggests that the bowler's arm should be straight from the moment it reaches the horizontal to the instant the ball is released. It is quite simple, quite logical, and uncluttered by the theory that has been produced on the subject. To this should be added the preamble offered by Australian administrators that, providing the umpire is satisfied a bowler is *bowling*, the definition need not be applied. This sensibly avoids the problem of, say, an off-spinner whose arm will not be rigidly straight from the horizontal to the instant of delivery, and if this law were brought in it would quickly remove any suspect bowlers from the game.

Of major importance though, is the fact that in recent years fast bowlers as a group have suffered from the introduction of the front foot law. No-one could ever have been happy at seeing some of the vast drags of fast bowlers in the 'fifties. Some of them were three and four feet past the popping crease when they delivered the ball. To avoid that the administrators went completely the other way and made the bowler put the whole of his foot behind the popping crease. This was always doomed to failure because the umpire could never tell whether the bowler's toe had in fact touched the popping crease. From where he stood the umpire's sight literally pushed the bowler's foot forward so that often, although landing behind the line, he was called for no-balling.

I proved this conclusively to one of our top administrators in Perth one day with a series of photographs taken whilst he was acting as umpire. The administrator called four of the deliveries as no balls and, in fact, with a camera level with his eyes, they were pictured as no balls. But a side on camera level with the popping crease showed that in each instance the bowler had been an inch behind the line. Then the next step was to allow a bowler to put his foot on the line and not to call him so long as some part of his heel had not gone over the popping crease. This has worked in a reasonably satisfactory manner for the umpires who have a distinct guiding line past which they will call the bowler, even if he transgresses by half an inch. But, what a finicky little game it has become when, by dragging an extra half an inch, a bowler can be repeatedly "called" and the game interrupted.

Back in 1961 when there was some controversy about drag, the Australian side played its first match at Worcester. Umpires Buller and Phillipson had that game and, at the fall of a wicket shortly before lunch, they called me over to have a look at the bowlers' footmarks around the popping crease. In those days there was no arbitrary line and there were some marks just behind the crease, some on it and some just over. One or two were well over and there had been one or two no ball calls during the morning. Both umpires said they were quite happy with the fact that, in general, the bowlers had not been transgressing but they had called once or twice when there had been a big advantage taken. This, surely, is the sensible approach, to leave the matter in the umpire's hands and to use the popping crease as a guiding line. No more of this finicky half inch business but say to the umpires, "Use that batting crease to guide you and don't worry about a bowler unless you think he is deliberately taking an advantage."

I am certain this is one of the reasons there is a dearth of fast bowlers in the world at the moment. It has also taken something from the game for there is no better sight than a fast bowler in action against a talented batsman. I am not in favour either of an arbitrary front foot line, such as exists at the moment, or an arbitrary back foot line, as existed when discs were used. But I think this is a matter that can safely be left to the umpires, with those gentlemen to use the popping crease as a guide. The bowler will soon know if he has gone too far—he will be warned at first then called and the mark will be there for him to see. But the bowler himself will be able to concentrate on his bowling without worrying about where his feet are going, and certainly there will be more incentive for young players to take up pace bowling.

There's nothing easy about umpiring in any class of cricket but in first-class cricket the man in white really has a tough job with all the publicity attached to matches these days. Tom Brooks is one ex-first-class player in Australia who has turned to umpiring and, to my mind, he is easily the best of all the younger men in Australia, and might well have a Test match against England next time M.C.C. tour there. He played for New South Wales in the early part of my career and, in one particular match at the S.C.G., was bowling against Mick Raymer, the Queensland left-hander, who was on the deaf side after a wartime accident. Brooks grunted when he bowled and this day Raymer flayed him to all parts of the field on a lively "greentop" pitch where his team mates had no real answer to the bowlers. Asked why he had played such a "blinder" when defence was the order of the day, Mick proffered the explanation that Brooks had been called for no-balling just about every delivery—he went pale when told what had happened.

It was about the same time on the Southern tour that the Queenslanders were quaffing a few beers at the end of a day's play when someone told a tale that brought the house down with laughter. None laughed more heartily than Mick—who then proceeded to tell the same story. That too, quite understandably, brought the house down!

On the question of rules and laws, there are a limited number of changes able to be made to the Laws of cricket, simply because it is basically a simple game between batsman and bowler. The pitch length is never changed and there have been minor changes only in the popping crease and bowling crease, together with the allowable width and height of the stumps. Bat and ball weights and measurements have remained much the same and so has protective gear like pads and gloves. Australia uses the eight ball over, whereas other countries use six, and I doubt very much if there is any great benefit to be derived from a change either way. The main problems have come in changes in the rules which involve a change in technique. The LBW law in 1774 said that if *with design* the striker prevents the ball hitting the wicket with his leg—he will be out LBW. This was changed in 1788 with the design clause omitted, adding that the ball must approach straight. In 1937 the LBW law was altered to read as it stands at this moment. This required a change in technique from batsmen and has appeared at any rate to encourage the bowler who moves the ball into the right-handed batsman, either in the air or off the pitch. It also seemed to encourage captains to use restrictive on side field placings because of the way the bowlers slanted their deliveries, and in 1957 a restriction was placed on the number of on side fieldsmen allowable.

There are all sorts of other bonuses and restrictions brought in concerning points scoring in cricket other than Tests, the size of boundaries, when the new ball could be taken and whether or not it could be either polished or rubbed in the dirt, according to the whim of the captain or bowler. Personally, I can't see that any of them have improved the game—they may not have made it any worse but I can't believe that the Laws, as they stand at the moment, are better than, say, before the war.

One thing I think administrators should give a great deal of attention to in the near future is the question of covering the playing area. In theory anyway, this is a batsman's game because it is kept going by paying spectators who, above all else, want to see batsmen in action, scoring briskly and thrashing the opposition bowler. The pitch therefore should be the best possible, at the same time giving some assistance to the bowlers both at the start of play and towards the end of the match, in order to strike an even balance between the two. There are many who say that pitches should be uncovered and I quite agree that this does provide an interesting spectacle from the point of view of a batsman having to battle hard for his runs when conditions favour the bowler. In 1936–7 when pitches were uncovered in Australia, England caught Australia on two "stickies" in Brisbane and Sydney, bowling them out cheaply on both occasions. They did this mainly with their fast bowlers because the run-ups had been covered and, if we were ever to revert to uncovered pitches, then I believe the run-ups should be left uncovered as well to ensure that fast bowlers flinging the ball down on a length would not derive too much advantage from the conditions. A captain fortunate enough then to catch the opposition on a "sticky" would have to use his spinners with their short and economic run to the crease, rather than his faster men.

I am astonished that in this day and age no one has been able to produce a covering system that will allow water to be kept off either the whole of the playing square or off the square with the exception of the actual pitch being played on. Surely, if we can get a rocket to the moon in 1967 someone can devise in 1968 a roller system with a piece of canvas that would keep water off the required areas and allow the game to start as quickly as possible for the spectators when the rain has ended.

In truth though, my main argument is with the administrators who are constantly looking to some new change in the Laws to provide the fillip they say cricket so badly needs. What cricket needs more than anything is modern day presentation from players and administrators. Just recently in Sydney there was a story that 150 schoolboys were about to attend a golf school for coaching. They were schoolboys who had obviously shown a little promise but it meant that cricket was losing 150 potential players.

Conditions are different in every country so here I speak only of Australia, though I have had first-hand knowledge of cricket in other countries for many years. There has been great diversification of sporting interest in Australia since the war. When the second Services side returned to Australia in 1945, there was tremendous interest in their performances and in the thought that Test cricket was about to start again with the proposed 1946–7 tour of Australia by M.C.C. Around this time I was still at school and, in common with just about every other school in Australia, sport participation was laid down in a fairly rigid manner. In the summer you played cricket, or you could go swimming but this was a bit of a bore for everyone concerned, though it did mean you could get off home at 3.30 rather than five o'clock. In the winter you played football unless you could bring a note from your parents to say there was some reason why you should play tennis or do some form of minor physical exercise outside the thoughts of the sports masters. Cricket and football then were the two main sports in summer and winter. This meant that after the youngster left school they would generally pursue these sports and it was taken for granted by cricket administrators that the game was not only flourishing but it would continue to flourish.

Nowadays in Australia there are many different sports that have taken over both in player and spectator appeal, as well as in publicity from the various media. Baseball, surfing, tennis, golf, all forms of athletics, particularly footrunning and swimming, hockey, bowls, sailing, squash, and three varieties of football,

Rugby League, Rugby Union and Soccer, share the interest and publicity that used to go only to cricket and football. Following the trend towards America in business, so too has there been an upsurge in interest in American style golf, with long waiting lists for Clubs, and every Saturday afternoon many thousands of lawn bowlers turn out to participate in sport rather than to watch it.

Attendances at all sporting fixtures in Australia have gone down in recent years and immediately this happens there is a cry that the particular game is dying. It might be Rugby League or Rugby Union or, in the summer, it might be cricket that has lost the average watching spectator who prefers to do something rather than look at it. There are three big contributing factors in this—one is television and the other two radio and the motor car. Most people in the modern day society own all three and it has to be good entertainment these days to get them to a football or cricket match, or even to the races. In the latter instance, attendances have dropped alarmingly throughout Australia and yet there is more interest in racing now in that country than ever before. People prefer to be doing something else and they know at the same time they can be listening to a race in which they are interested or can even watch it later on television. It is the best of both worlds.

It is the same with cricket where potential spectators don't have to go to the ground to see the match. They can go and play golf and hear the direct broadcast or watch the highlights later that night on T.V.—in England they can watch it most of the day live. The paying spectator, in short, has become selective and where years ago he desperately wanted to go and partake of the excitement first hand, now he has to be wooed because there are so many other distractions.

I don't believe there has been enough wooing in Australia and I think there has certainly been a lack of public relations in our cricket over the years. Spectators will still come and see the top class entertainment when Test matches between strong countries are played but there is much good cricket played outside those games. Indeed, sometimes the Tests will not provide as good or entertaining cricket as a minor match. One of the main reasons attendances have fallen off in cricket in Australia is that it is the only mid-week sport still played. Thirty years ago it was no trouble to take a day off from work to go and watch a Sheffield Shield match. Now your boss would look at you as though you had lost your senses if you made the same request. Sheffield Shield attendances on Mondays and Tuesdays quite often are hardly worth the opening of the gates and this is why I believe that State cricket in Australia in future years will be played on Friday, Saturday and Sunday, each day occupying six and a half or seven hours. There will therefore be two days available to the spectator who wants to go along and watch and is unable to take time off from his job during the week.

Australia has played Test matches on Sundays in India and Pakistan and Sheffield Shield matches have been played on Sundays in Perth and Brisbane in the last few years. Having been mixed up in newspapers for some years, I am in no doubt that cricket publicity falls far short of its real requirements. Very little news is channelled to newspapers and other publicity media by amateur cricket officials. Their professional counterparts in Rugby League are constantly providing news of every possible variety and there is a continual flow of interest in Sydney in this sport. The same applies in the Southern States with regard to Australian Rules and I think that this is one of the main requirements of cricket in Australia in the years to come.

These other games are wonderfully well publicised and cricket should be too. I feel that in this modern era of publicity-conscious spectators there should be a drastic revision of thinking on the part of administrators. I am not suggesting any publicity is good publicity but there should be a determined effort to have the game of cricket constantly in front of the public's eye. Far too often the administrators say "But this is the journalist's job." The journalist himself writes continually during the cricket season because that, in fact, is his job. He writes articles either praising or criticising a day's play, or he finds good or critical words to say about administration of some aspect of the game. But there are many other sports these days that have to take their share of publicity.

When I returned to Australia in 1966 my Sporting Editor, Con Simons, gave me a page of the paper for cricket. The Sydney Sun is a tabloid and, with the advertisements that appeared on this page, it meant that at least once a week cricket was assured of something like 50 paragraphs of publicity—and this on grade matches alone in the Sydney metropolitan area. It was a generous offer and when I spoke to one or two administrators about it they were delighted at the thought that, apart from other publicity during the week, the grade competition would receive this extra publicity.

Accordingly, I wrote to every grade secretary in Sydney asking him to ring me on the Wednesday of each week with any news that either he may wish to get in the paper or that he thought might be of some interest to readers. I had a shrewd idea of what would happen—and it did. There are 16 grade clubs in Sydney—the first week there were 16 'phone calls, the second week we were just in double figures and, from then on, I got one or two calls a week. I had no trouble writing the 50 paragraphs myself each week and, as I mentioned above, many would say this is my job. But it does give an insight into how publicity conscious amateur cricket officials can be in Australia. Had any other sport been given 50 paragraphs of publicity one day a week the writer in charge of the page would have been deluged with 'phone calls every day of the week. The Cricket Associations themselves spend most of their monthly meetings talking in committee with the Press barred. No-one believes that everything should be open to Press and public but the sporting public is vitally interested in all aspects of whichever sport they follow—and they like to read about it and hear about it through some publicity medium.

There is a far more liberal attitude in Australia these days than when I came into the game but it is one that could be improved even more. So too I believe could be the attitude to what, for want of a better name, could be called "other cricket". "Real" cricket has been going on for years but in recent times there has been an influx of different types of competition. Single wicket cricket and one day knock-out cricket have come to stay, particularly the latter which has great spectator appeal with the games being concluded in one day. Single wicket matches are rather more of a "fad" but provide the chance to produce something a little different in entertainment for the spectator. With so many other things to do and watch now, anything that is different will cach the imagination. One day knock-out matches were played in Australia during the war years when there was never any certainty that players in the Services would be available for a second day. It was popular and was appreciated by players and public. It then went out of vogue though it has been played for a long time in England in club cricket and Lancashire League.

Then in 1963 there was a significant introduction to the English cricket competition when the Gillette Cup was organised for competition between the counties on a one day restricted over basis. This competition now has grown to the stage where it is an all ticket final at Lord's and there is great interest and competition between the counties to win the trophy and the honour. Never to be confused with real cricket, it is packed with entertainment for spectators and, on a club basis, is a very real step forward in boosting the game and its spectator appeal in England.

In Australia former Test batsman Jim Burke organised such a competition in the 1967–8 season with Rothmans in Sydney, and other States did the same thing with a variety of sponsorship. No one goes to watch grade cricket in Sydney, or in any other State for that matter, with the exception of the few who have nothing to do on a Saturday afternoon, together with relatives and friends of the players. I am all in favour of this for I firmly believe people should be doing something rather than watching a minor variety of cricket. But it was interesting to note that attendances on the Sundays at these Rothmans/Burke organised matches were far in excess of anything Sydney grade cricket had produced for many years.

There are two aspects of this competition that invited attention from administrators. Firstly that a result was being obtained in one day and spectators did not have to wait until the following week to see the outcome of the match. The second was that they were played on Sundays where spectators had more leisure time to go along, and I know many people who travelled from one side of the metropolitan area to the other to see these games. Administrators were less interested in the fact that they were concluded in one day than they were in the Sunday aspect, a point that has been keenly watched and talked about in Australian cricket circles for quite some time. It needed someone to put on a competition on Sundays to let the administrators see what public reaction would be but those in charge were themselvesloth to make the first move lest criticism be hurled at them for playing sport in Church times.

The game at the moment in Australia needs first of all good players, and there are plenty of those about in all the top grades of cricket. The players always dictate just how much spectator appeal there is in cricket and on them depends the final resting point of the game itself. It needs good administration, with an eye to public appeal and publicity, and the best instance I can remember of producing spectators at minor cricket came in a Sydney grade match of a few years ago when Alan Davidson and I were captaining opposing teams. With a big story every day in each paper, we had the largest attendances at a two-day Sydney grade match since 1937, and fortunately the cricket played was exciting enough to have spectators and readers talking about it for weeks after.

I would like to see cricket diversify by having administrators produce different types of competition, such as the single wicket and knock-out varieties, and here again a golden opportunity was lost in Australia a couple of years ago. West Indies, as the world champions, were playing in India at a time when Australia was being beaten by South Africa. There was no doubt in the minds of anyone who had watched both the West Indies and South Africa in recent years that they had the best two teams in the world, as well as the players with outstanding spectator appeal. There was talk of staging a match, or matches, between the West Indies and South Africa but the talk came to nothing because, we were told, "of difficulties in organisation". But what a tremendous opportunity for anyone with an ounce of entrepreneur blood in his veins. West Indies could have played South Africa in Australia in March 1967 or in October 1967. Both dates were free to both countries and in a month a three-match Test series could have been played, two matches in Melbourne and one in Sydney. The West Indies could have arrived in Brisbane, playing a match against Queensland and then New South Wales, before going to Melbourne for the First Test. South Africa could have arrived in Perth, playing a match against each of Western Australia and South Australia before arriving in Melbourne for the Test. The three Tests would have taken three weeks and would have packed the grounds billed as matches to decide the world champions of that moment. Not a thing was done and there were vague murmurs that it would have taken too much organisation.

South Africans and West Indians play in Rest of the World matches in England at the end of each season and encounter few problems either on or off the field. Indians and Pakistanis played in these same games when the two countries were at war, so the plea of administrative difficulties hardly held water. This is the type of promotion needed in cricket these days for, whilst the basic appeal is always there for tours and Test series between traditional cricket enemies, there is a modern day need for something different to keep the spectator's appetite razor keen.

Cricket has been going a long, long time now and it will outlast me and its present day followers. But it does need to keep up with the times rather than live on deeds produced in the eras when the motor car was looked on as something of a novelty.

12

The Captain

Over the years Australia has had remarkably few captains in international cricket with Bill Woodfull starting in 1930 and Bradman taking over in 1936–7 and leading his country up to the time the Second War began. Vic Richardson took the Australian side to South Africa when Bradman withdrew because of illness and then after the war the latter captained Australia until his retirement in 1948. Lindsay Hassett took over at that point and was followed by Ian Johnson and then Ian Craig for a short time, after which I led the side until 1964. At the time of writing, Bob Simpson has just retired from Australian cricket after a three year period of captaincy in which he has retained the Ashes against England in two series and has led Australia in beaten rubbers against West Indies and South Africa. The heir to the captaincy throne was William Morris Lawry, the 6ft. 2in. opening batsman from Northcote, Melbourne, who has partnered Simpson in many of their record breaking opening stands since 1961.

I first saw Lawry in 1956, oddly enough in a tied match, the first such game in which I ever took part. He opened the innings this day with Colin McDonald and his performances hardly set the Yarra afire, for Davidson picked them up for 1 in the first innings of that game and he was LBW to Alan Wyatt in the second innings for 7. He wouldn't have made any impression on me at all except that Colin McDonald told me later he thought Lawry, who was out of form at this time, was a future Australian opening bat. The season before Lawry had played in one match and made only 3 and in this current 1956–7 season he made just 248 runs at an average of 20 for Victoria and the only batsmen below him in the Sheffield Shield averages were bowlers. McDonald said that Lawry was one of the straightest players he had seen and was possessed of a good temperament and, in years to come, he would make his mark in the game.

It was in 1960–1 that Lawry gained his chance when, at a moment where three or four openers were vying for a place in the Australian side to tour England, he made 266 for Victoria against New South Wales in Sydney. He had been dropped at 12 in that game and, despite his double century, his choice was something of a surprise in the touring side. His first-class form in Australia had been such that he was dropped from the Victorian side in 1957–8 and in part of 1958–9 but thereafter his studious concentration and wide variety, though not always seen, and range of stroke-play has ensured him a prominent place in Sheffield Shield and Australian teams.

He was a sensational success in England in 1961, beginning with the match against Surrey where he played so brilliantly that his Test place on that tour was assured. It was a pretty young side, and in many ways an untried one, and the fact that Lawry made over 2,000 runs in first-class games and over 400 in Tests had a great deal to do with the eventual success of the team. All of his innings—Test centuries at Lord's and Old Trafford—were magnificent efforts. The one at Lord's was played on a pitch that gave fast bowlers every possible assistance and both that and the Manchester knock rank with the greatest Test innings I have seen. With Simpson he has provided one of the greatest opening partnerships Australia cricket has had, and though he himself in recent years has a variable Test record he is still one of the most feared batsmen in the world.

Lawry was born in Melbourne in 1937 and tells the story himself of learning to play cricket by having the ball bowled at him in the little side lane alongside his house. When he was 12 he was playing in minor grade cricket in Melbourne and I would think that even then he was providing plenty of problems for bowlers. Statistically he had played 40 Test matches before the start of the last Australian season against India and had scored over 3,000 runs in those games. Personally, I believe the captaincy will be the making of him, which may sound a rather strange statement to make about a player already established in the history of Test cricket. But then I saw the very best of him in 1961, when on his first tour overseas he played some storming innings and produced shots that before this tour he himself may not have known he possessed. For a time after that tour he became a steady player, unimaginative at times, and more concerned with the stockpiling of runs than the manner in which they would be made. But this I put down largely to the fact that he had been made captain of Victoria at a time when Victorian cricket was at a low ebb. Lawry felt his job in a team of unknowns was to score heavily to try and give his unfashionable bowlers the chance to bowl out the opposition and therefore improve Victoria's standing in the Shield table. Even in 1964 in England he was unrecognisable as the dashing player of 1961, a fact I found extremely sad, knowing the tremendous ability he could apply to his batting.

At this moment though Lawry is the ideal man to captain Australia on a tour of England. Purely on captaincy, he is the best available in Australia, a shrewd tactician and a good judge of players' capabilities. He is an outstanding batsman and, as well, has the complete confidence of every player in every side in which he plays. It will surprise some and astound others to learn that beneath his dour and often unsmiling exterior there lurks an impish sense of humour that endears him to team mates. No one laughs better at himself than the angular Victorian and there will be no lack of team spirit on the tour where Australia is defending the Ashes and, at the same time, trying to win its first Test series against a major country since 1964.

He is known in Australian cricket circles as "Phanto", supposedly a shortening of Phantom following the discovery of the pleasure he derived as a youngster browsing through comic books of the same name. Another story has it that one of his favourite racing pigeons was called Phantom but the name bears little relation to his performances on the cricket field. Sad as I am to see Simpson retire from the game, I am delighted to see Lawry take over the leadership. He is just the man Australia needs at the moment to pull together a new young side, to work them hard and have them in the frame of mind that, if they fail, it won't be for the want of team work and will to win.

I didn't know him very well early in 1961 and on board ship on the way over he was a very quiet member of the team. He and Frank Misson turned out to be the practical jokers of the side and all the young players came under the influence of Ken Mackay who was the oldest member of the team, and one of the quietest himself—he made sure they were well looked after with picture shows, Chinese food, television and early nights.

He has never admitted it, but I have long suspected him as a prime mover in 1958 of the nailing of the Australian captain's shoes to the Sydney dressing-room floor, at a time when I was to appear at a Government reception. Rumour had it in 1961 that, when Australian manager Syd Webb found some solid silver spoons in his pocket walking across the drawbridge of a stately castle and had to return them red-faced, Lawry or Misson had a hand in it.

But I will never forget him for his effort in Brisbane in 1963 after Ian Meckiff had been called for throwing. I hadn't bowled Meckiff from Lou Rowan's end after he had been called by umpire Egar in the early part of the match and feeling ran high in Australia over the whole question. Reports appeared in the newspapers that police protection was being offered to the umpires and I had wryly thought that no one was offering any to the captain. Worse still, play was washed out on the Monday and, seated in the luncheon room next to the dressing-rooms, I was musing on life in general when suddenly the team masseur appeared before me. He was dressed in masseur's clothes with plastic raincoat on top and a hat pulled down over his eyes, and was carrying a copy of the pink Melbourne Sporting Globe over one hand. The paper asked in screaming type why I hadn't bowled Meckiff from the other end and also in big type carried the story of police protection being needed.

Jock, the masseur, when I looked at him had the whites of his eyes showing and he said, "Why didn't you bowl him from the other end?" "Go away" I said, "I have got enough problems . . ." He whipped the paper away to show he had a gun in his right hand and said "You should have bowled him from the other end." All those old stories about your life flashing in front of your eyes are quite true, I can assure you, and he then pulled the trigger, producing a flash from the barrel of the gun. It took me two seconds to realise I hadn't been hit with anything and a wave of relief swept over me until I caught sight of this figure rolling around on the floor outside the luncheon room. It was Lawry, completely overcome by the success of one of the best planned practical jokes of a cricket lifetime.

He can take a joke as well as give one, a fact that makes him one of the outstanding team men with whom I have ever toured. I put the 1961 tour down as the most pleasant I have undertaken and there were a variety of reasons for this. Not least of these was Lawry's presence in the side, both as player and team man, and the team spirit he and others like Misson, Mackay and their tight knit group were able to foster for Neil Harvey and myself. I shall be very surprised if, when Lawry decides to retire from

Australian cricket, he is not widely regarded as one of the best captains and leaders in every sense of the word Australia has had in a long, long time.

It will, though, be many years before Lawry retires from Test and first-class cricket and I doubt if he is liable to move out of the game at an early age, as I did and as did Simpson. I retired at 34 but Simpson's retirement in 1968 at 31 was even more of a shock. I said before 1961 that that would be my last tour and I would not again take an Australian side overseas. This meant, the way the international programme was framed, that I would retire in 1964 before the tour of England and the Australian selectors had three years' notice to make their plans. But although there had been some rumours of Simpson's retirement, nothing specific had been said, and when he retired at the height of his powers it left a great gap in Australian cricket. His last four innings before his retirement announcement had produced a double century and three single centuries. He was the best batsman in Australia, the best slip fieldsman in the world and a more than useful change bowler in the Australian side. Without him Australia, in their losing series against West Indies and South Africa, would have been beaten in even more conclusive fashion.

In 1964 he scored his first Test century and made it a triple century for good measure. It is, I suppose, the era of early retirements in Australian cricket where nowadays more attention has to be paid to one's future in business than in cricket. Simpson will find it very difficult to retire from international cricket, as I can testify, having gone through the same thing myself. But his will be an even more difficult period for he is fully fit and quite capable of playing Test cricket for many years to come whereas, with my shoulder trouble and constantly recurring pain, I probably had no more than 12 months in the game when I eventually called it a day.

Simpson's loss is Lawry's gain but Simpson himself will always have a great niche in Australian cricket. Had Simpson continued playing I believe he would have led Australia back to the top of world cricket where, at this moment, they stand below West Indies and South Africa in terms of results and outstanding cricketers. Lawry then, with this ahead of him, has come a long way since the days where he struck that ball firmly into the rose bushes at the side of his Northcote home. He will need all his skill and cricket knowledge to combat opposition skippers like Gary Sobers and Colin Cowdrey and he will know his days of dark despair as well as those where everyone will want to pat him on the back for some supposedly marvellous tactical ploy he has produced.

On those congratulatory occasions the ploy will have been successful but he'll find there are few merry little quips around on the days when he drops what is commonly known as a "clanger" in the centre. Not least of the necessities of life for a captain is the retention of a sense of humour and once that starts to slide the poor unfortunate is on the way out. I found in 1961 that around the middle of the tour when I was in grave trouble with my shoulder and there were stories in the Press about my being "gagged" by the Manager of the side, that my sense of humour disappeared completely. A good mate of mine said to me around this crisis time "Come on, cheer up," and all I could muster in reply was "What the hell have I got to laugh about?" Things at that moment were desperate for I couldn't bowl, could only just shave and a life's ambition of captaining Australia at Lord's was fast disappearing. In fact, it finally completely disappeared and Neil Harvey captained Australia in that game, the only time he led his country—and what a waste of good captaincy material it was over the years to have him without leadership responsibility. As it turned out, the side was helped by the fact that I wasn't playing, for it gave McKenzie the chance to nip in with five wickets in his Test debut and start on the great career that now sees him a full-time cricketer commuting between England and Australia.

Lawry is something of an anonymous character to many cricket followers and yet I believe that by the time he has finished he will have carved his own niche in Australian cricket. Certainly on the England tour in 1968 he began the right way by inspiring his team to an against the odds victory at Old Trafford over a side that had recently beaten the West Indies in the Caribbean. The Australian team had no right to win this game for they had played in moderate fashion up to the First Test and I am certain Lawry himself would have been content with a draw. But the real test of captaincy is the ability to inspire a team and, in this case, I firmly believe it was Lawry's inspiration, as well as the underlying ability of the young players, that so shocked England.

Back in 1958–9 when I had my own first experience of captaincy, we were up against an England side that, before the start of the tour, had been labelled by most as one of the greatest teams ever to leave British shores. Australia in that series were very much the underdogs, in the same way as Lawry's side were very much the underdogs in 1968. We had a long team meeting before the First Test in Brisbane, trying to pinpoint the various weaknesses and strengths of the M.C.C. team, and, with a little good fortune and some good cricket, we won the First Test and then never looked back.

I don't know quite how Lawry approaches the matter, but my attitude as captain was always that I wanted to be one of the team though retaining an overriding authority that allowed me to make the decisions where necessary. I was always available to any of the team who might have suggestions on how to contain or dismiss any player, or how to go about attacking any bowler or destroy a particular field placing. Sometimes though, their ideas would conflict with my own and it would be necessary to make a quick and final decision which would not always coincide with the ideas put forward by the others. I believe in consulting the rest of the team's senior players because they would not be representing their country unless they were astute in the tactics of the game.

When I started captaining the side, my only leadership experience had been for my school side and for my club side, with just the odd game thrown in for New South Wales. But what a tremendous experience it is suddenly to be thrust into the captaincy of a country. I found it a great challenge and I am sure Lawry does too, and the reason I go back to him is that I don't really believe in living in the past but am more concerned with what happens in the future.

In the context of cricket, the good and bad things I did on the field as captain are quite important though, in the light of present day happenings, they are relatively unimportant. They are part of the history of the game, as are the runs made by the Harveys and the O'Neills of the game, but the important thing is how each successive captain approaches his task. I heard Lawry at the M.C.C. Dinner in 1968 stress the fact that this was one of the most important cricket tours of all time and that in 1961 he wouldn't have believed he could have thought the manner of its playing would be as important as the final result. That is roughly along the same lines as Sir Donald Bradman's remark to me after the tied Test in Brisbane when I said "I would rather have won than played a tie." He said that "in a few years' time I'd have mellowed a bit and would appreciate that this was one of the great happenings in the history of the game".

Australia has West Indies as visitors in the coming season and every cricket follower in the country will be hoping for a wonderful series, chock full of exciting cricket, and I, for one, will watch it with tremendous interest. I treat myself as being extremely fortunate to have played as captain in those exciting games of 1960–1 and many of those West Indians who took part in that series will be back to take on the younger Australians. Again drawing a comparative line with Lawry and myself, his position when the West Indies arrive will be rather similar to mine in that he will have had a full tour overseas to gather the nucleus of a team to take on this great side. When they arrived in 1960–1 they did so with the stated intention, through their captain Frank Worrell, of wanting to play good cricket, irrespective of the result.

I'll be interested to see how Lawry approaches this series and what support he is given by the Australian selectors. You will remember that Sir Donald Bradman came to our team meeting in 1960 to stress that the series, then about to start, could have a tremendous influence on Australian cricket in the future. This gave the team, and certainly myself, the necessary impetus to go out and strive to win the matches, even if in danger of being beaten, simply because we knew the selectors would back this sort of move. It only needed either captain to hesitate for a moment in Brisbane and the game would have been a draw rather than a tie, though the latter result was, of course, incredibly lucky.

One of the great pleasures of captaincy, though it may not seem so at the time, is that it runs so much true to life in that one day all will seem dark and dismal and a week later the luck of the game, and perhaps a successful move on the field, means that the skipper is being féted as a hero. Back in 1958–9, the fortnight before the First Test led Australians to believe the Ashes were as good as being retained by England. In the game itself there was some of the slowest play ever and then O'Neill, at his brilliant best, lifted the clouds with a glorious 70 on the last day. This was enough to boost the hopes and confidence of any aspiring captain and I suppose it will be the same for many years to come.

When the West Indies come to Australia, there will be Sunday play in Test matches for the first time and there may be new tactics needed if the games are to be played on three successive days at the start of the match, rather than on the Friday and Saturday with then a break. Looking at it from afar, this could mean spin bowling will play an even greater part in captaincy tactics but, irrespective of that minor sidelight, much of the success of that coming series, and the one in South Africa, will depend on the captains.

Generally speaking, that is the case in most classes of cricket and, certainly with so much of the spotlight on Test matches these days, it applies to those top bracket games which the spectators follow with such avid interest. Many people over the years have stressed what a fine job Australia's cricketers have done in holding and beating England, in view of the fact that there are fifty million people in the one country and thirteen million in the other. But, in fact, I believe I, and other Australian captains, have had an easier task than appears on the surface for the population figures are very misleading. When I was appointed captain of the Australian team, it had been chosen in the end from something like 100,000 cricketers. They all turn out every Saturday in grade and top grade junior matches and they have the ability and the chance to push their way forward and eventually to move into First Grade where they will come under the eyes of State selectors. Those State selectors, during the season, will get round to see about 200 players in every State, which is around 1,000 in all, and they have even been known to go and watch second graders in action to see if there is any chance of finding a place for them in State Colts teams.

This is in complete contrast to the English system where eventually the England captain has ten players under him, chosen from only around 200 who play in the County Championship. It is misleading then to imagine an Australian captain, such as myself, leading a side chosen only from the 55 players appearing in first-class cricket each year and, personally, I am all in favour of this Australian system that allows club players to be produced in a State squad and even players below the top standard looked at, to see just what they possess as potential. It is one of the beauties of Australian cricket that any youngster playing in the Outback can, if he has the skill, force his way into club cricket, then the State Colts team, Second XI, the State side and, if he is good enough, the Australian team.

It is also one of the joys of the game out there that any youngster doing as Lawry did—striking the ball into the rose bushes at the side of his Northcote home—or, doing as I did at Jugiong way back in 1936—throwing a ball against a storeroom wall—can rise to captain his country and tour the Commonwealth and other cricket countries.